The American
Warfare State

CHICAGO SERIES ON INTERNATIONAL AND DOMESTIC INSTITUTIONS
Edited by William G. Howell and Jon Pevehouse

ALSO IN THE SERIES:

The Wartime President: Executive Influence and the Nationalizing Politics of Threat
  by William G. Howell (2013)

The Judicial Power of the Purse: How Courts Fund National Defense in Times of Crisis
  by Nancy C. Staudt (2011)

Securing Approval: Domestic Politics and Multilateral Authorization for War
  by Terrence L. Chapman (2011)

After the Rubicon: Congress, Presidents and the Politics of Waging War
  by Douglas L. Kriner (2010)

CHICAGO STUDIES IN AMERICAN POLITICS
Edited by Benjamin I. Page, Susan Herbst, Lawrence R. Jacobs, and Adam J. Berinsky

ALSO IN THE SERIES:

How the States Shaped the Nation: Electoral Institutions and Voter Turnout, 1920–2000
  by Melanie Jean Springer

Changing Minds or Changing Channels? Partisan News in an Age of Choice
  by Kevin Arceneaux and Martin Johnson

*Trading Democracy for Justice: Criminal Convictions and the Decline of
  Neighborhood Political Participation*
  by Traci Burch

White-Collar Government: The Hidden Role of Class in Economic Policy Making
  by Nicholas Carnes

How Partisan Media Polarize America
  by Matthew Levendusky

The Politics of Belonging: Race, Public Opinion, and Immigration
  by Natalie Masuoka and Jane Junn

Political Tone: How Leaders Talk and Why
  by Roderick P. Hart, Jay P. Childers, and Colene J. Lind

The Timeline of Presidential Elections: How Campaigns Do (and Do Not) Matter
  by Robert S. Erikson and Christopher Wlezien

Learning While Governing: Expertise and Accountability in the Executive Branch
  by Sean Gailmard and John W. Patty

Electing Judges: The Surprising Effects of Campaigning on Judicial Legitimacy
  by James L. Gibson

Follow the Leader?: How Voters Respond to Politicians' Policies and Performance
  by Gabriel S. Lenz

The Social Citizen: Peer Networks and Political Behavior
  by Betsy Sinclair

Additional series titles follow index

The American Warfare State

THE DOMESTIC POLITICS
OF MILITARY SPENDING

REBECCA U. THORPE

THE
UNIVERSITY OF
CHICAGO PRESS
Chicago and
London

REBECCA U. THORPE *is assistant professor of political science at the University of Washington.*

The University of Chicago Press, Chicago 60637

The University of Chicago Press, Ltd., London

© 2014 by The University of Chicago

All rights reserved. Published 2014.

Printed in the United States of America

23 22 21 20 19 18 17 16 15 14   1 2 3 4 5

ISBN-13: 978-0-226-12391-2 (cloth)

ISBN-13: 978-0-226-12407-0 (paper)

ISBN-13: 978-0-226-12410-0 (e-book)

DOI: 10.7208/chicago/9780226124100.001.0001

Library of Congress Cataloging-in-Publication Data

Thorpe, Rebecca U., author.

   The American warfare state : the domestic politics of military spending / Rebecca U. Thorpe.

      pages   cm

      (Chicago series on international and domestic institutions)

   ISBN 978-0-226-12391-2 (cloth : alk. paper)

   ISBN 978-0-226-12407-0 (pbk. : alk. paper)

   ISBN 978-0-226-12410-0 (e-book)

   1. United States—Armed Forces—Appropriations and expenditures. 2. Civil-military relations—United States. I. Title. II. Series: Chicago series on international and domestic institutions.

UA23.T48 2014

322'.50973—dc23

2013043064

Contents

Tables and Figures

Preface and Acknowledgments

This project began as an investigation of the military-industrial complex. I wanted to know whether local economic reliance on weapons industries encourages more military spending in Congress than national security alone. I was puzzled to find that most statistical studies challenge this assumption—despite an abundance of anecdotal accounts illustrating powerful economic interests in defense spending shared among legislators, voters, and defense industries. As I dug deeper, I discovered various data limitations and questionable theoretical assumptions, which I address in the following pages.

After identifying the locations of major weapons suppliers that emerged during and after World War II, tracking the flow of defense dollars and projects in the postwar era, and examining interbranch conflict in wars throughout American political development, I began to draw a larger conclusion about how a nation so resistant to centralized military force became the largest military economy in the world. Scholars seemed to be missing a key aspect of why legislators exercised strict budgetary control over the military prior to World War II, but consistently promoted large defense budgets and ceded military authority to the president during subsequent decades. Previous research offers numerous explanations, including a heightened national security environment, congressional weakness, executive ambition, flexible constitutional interpretations, legislators' "hawkish" ideologies, and partisan alliances. While I draw on the various institutional imbalances that other scholars have documented, my research also uncovered additional dynamics that have received far less attention. Specifically, I found that large defense budgets became a crucial component of the nation's economic and foreign policy apparatus after World War II, while the costs of war were shifted onto politically marginalized and nonvoting populations. In this new context, legislators do not simply acquiesce to the president's military agenda out of weakness or deference. In addition, many members also gain politically by supplying the defense resources that allow presidents to implement their national security policies independently.

I hope that *The American Warfare State* changes how scholars think about political development and domestic state-building in several ways: First, I argue that that political authority tends to centralize when legislators' interests overlap with the president's goals—despite a constitutional framework designed to limit power. Second, I hope that readers conclude that the failure of institutional mechanisms to reliably limit power and promote accountability is a valuable area for study, which this book only begins to broach. Finally, I also encourage readers to think critically about the tendency of representatives and voters to optimize their own short-term interests, while imposing devastating costs elsewhere.

I benefited from a great deal of support in the years that it took to complete the project. The Political Science Department at the University of Washington provided a productive scholarly environment that facilitated the completion of the book. I owe thanks to all of my colleagues in the American politics and international security fields. In particular, Beth Kier, George Lovell, Peter May, Mark Smith, Chip Turner, and John Wilkerson provided substantive feedback on chapter drafts and offered valuable suggestions that helped sharpen the overall book. I am also grateful for helpful comments from graduate students, especially Adam Forman, Ashley Jochim, Barry Pump, and Allison Rank. In addition, the undergraduate students in the 2011–12 Political Science Honors program helped me think about institutional failure in new ways that continue to enrich my research endeavors.

I am fortunate to have received the opportunity to present the entire manuscript at a book conference sponsored by the Center for American Politics and Public Policy at UW. The conference provided an exceptional venue for in-depth discussion of the project. The critical commentary that I received from conference participants came at a crucial time and helped me reconceptualize the book in important ways.

I am grateful to the Brookings Institution for research support. I was a Research Fellow in Governance Studies in the 2008–9 academic year, which gave me unimpeded time, financial support, and an intellectual community in which to conduct my research. Sarah Binder, EJ Dionne, Bill Galston, Tom Mann, and Darrell West helped make my time at Brookings stimulating and productive.

My understanding of the US political system was also shaped by my experiences as an APSA Congressional Fellow. I owe thanks to the director of the fellowship program, Jeff Biggs, and the office of Congressman Jim Oberstar for the opportunity to gain direct access to the legislative process and the many insights that this afforded me.

A number of other scholars and interlocutors helped improve the manuscript. Jack Gansler, Mark Graber, Wayne McIntosh, and Irwin Morris read earlier materials and offered helpful suggestions. Linda Fowler, Christian Grose, Wendy Schiller, and Scot Schraufnagel gave me useful feedback when I presented parts of the manuscript at conferences. Mike Hanmer and

Geoff Layman provided methodological advice. I am very grateful to Jim Gimpel and Stephan Gmur for time-intensive assistance with Geographic Information System (GIS) software. I am also indebted to Alexi Maschas and Evan Vetere for ongoing support with computational methods, including extracting and parsing much of the data employed in chapters 4 and 6. Finally, the project was continually informed by lively discussions with Mike Evans and John McTague.

Two scholars deserve special thanks. Frances Lee read multiple versions of the manuscript and offered invaluable insights at every stage of the project's development. Her incisive feedback, friendship, and encouragement benefit my work more than she will ever know. As the book came together, Will Howell read three iterations of the full manuscript. He generously gave his time and provided crucial guidance on each individual chapter and the broader framework. His vision and support improved the book in innumerable ways.

I appreciate the strong commitment to the project that I received from my editor, John Tryneski, at the University of Chicago Press. John believed in and supported my vision for this project. He administered a highly constructive review process, and his guidance, patience, and support helped facilitate productive revisions. I also thank Rodney Powell and others at the Press for their ongoing assistance during the publication process.

While most of the manuscript has not previously appeared in print, an earlier version of chapter 6 appears as "The Role of Economic Reliance in Defense Procurement Contracting," *American Politics Research* 38 (2010): 636–75.

I am grateful to my parents, Gregory and Lynn Thorpe, from whom I received unwavering support for and interest in all my political and academic endeavors. I dedicate this book to my father, in loving memory. He read and commented on multiple iterations of earlier chapter drafts and would have loved to see the work come to its completion.

Finally, I cannot adequately thank my partner, Alexi Maschas. He not only provided technical support writing programs to automate data extraction and copyediting drafts, but also gave me critical feedback at every stage of the project. He read multiple versions of every chapter, engaged in endless discussions about the book, and offered encouragement when I needed it most. Our conversations were the initial inspiration for the project and a consistent influence on its development. Although he must have tired of the book at times, he contributed more than he could ever imagine.

THEORETICAL AND HISTORICAL OVERVIEW

INTRODUCTION: PERPETUATING THE US MILITARY ECONOMY

Of all the enemies to public liberty, war is, perhaps, the most to be dreaded, because it comprises and develops the germ of every other. War is the parent of armies; from these proceed debts and taxes; and armies, and debts, and taxes are the known instruments for bringing the many under the domination of the few. In war, too, the discretionary power of the executive is extended; its influence in dealing out offices, honors and emoluments is multiplied; and all the means of seducing the minds are added to those of subduing the force of the people. . . . No nation could preserve its freedom in the midst of continual warfare.—James Madison, "Political Observations," April 20, 1795

[Our country] will avoid the necessity of those overgrown military establishments which, under any form of government, are inauspicious to liberty, and which are to be regarded as particularly hostile to republican liberty. —George Washington, 1796 Farewell Address

One hundred fifty years after George Washington and James Madison warned of overgrown military establishments and perpetual warfare, the United States faced the ascent of Nazi Germany and Japan's attack at Pearl Harbor, followed by the rise of the Soviet empire. To confront these perils, the nation embraced full-scale military mobilization. Yet, after each specific threat ebbed and receded, policymakers advanced new rationales to maintain military readiness. For the first time in the nation's history, congresses consistently supported large defense budgets, despite US withdrawal from specific wars, growing national debt obligations, and periods of severe fiscal crisis. While a "sequestration" was designed to reduce defense spending by about $1 trillion over a decade (compared to what was expected), the proposed cuts would preserve more than $500 billion in annual military funding even if they are fully implemented—roughly the same amount that Congress spent on the military after the attacks of September 11, 2001, and at the height of the Cold War. Despite pervasive concerns about deficits and unnecessary wars, Congress continued to provide as much as $700 billion for the military each year (with a pending $500-billion floor)—more, in adjusted dollars, than any time since World War II and as much as the rest of the world combined.

These patterns of defense spending are not only historically unparalleled; they are also historical accidents. At the time of the constitutional founding, James Madison and his Federalist allies designed political institutions to guard against a permanent military establishment. The founders feared that large, peacetime armies would burden the citizenry with excessive taxation, military service requirements, and lost productivity while empowering the president to commit the nation to war for arbitrary or self-serving reasons. The Constitution's opponents feared worse, given the familiar tendency of British kings to use armies as a means of political oppression. To prevent these outcomes, the framers created a regime of limited powers that divides military authority among separate governing departments. Most critically, the framers gave the power to raise armies, fund them, and declare war with Congress. Since members of Congress would be responsive to local voters, who would serve in the armed forces and pay a heavier tax burden, they assumed that the legislature could check any expansionist inclinations a president might hold. For most of the nation's history, Congress heeded these expectations by mobilizing the military in preparation for specific wars and withdrawing military spending after the war was over. However, the rise of a permanent military industry during and after World War II disrupted these historical patterns.

The fundamental puzzle that this research will address is why a nation founded on a severe distrust of standing armies and centralized power developed and maintained the most powerful military in history. I argue that the shift occurred not only as a response to national security concerns, but also because World War II military mobilization extended benefits widely, while federal policies systematically shifted the immediate costs of war and war spending onto discrete political minorities and foreign populations. New evidence suggests that the economic importance of the military industry for core geographic constituencies encourages members of Congress to press for ongoing defense spending regardless of their national security goals. These members enjoy strong political support and encounter little sustained opposition, because US power projection promotes widely shared political and economic interests without directly imposing on most Americans' lives or livelihoods. As a consequence, legislators' heightened interests in defense spending furnish presidents with the resources necessary to exercise military force independently. A permanent military industry and an increasingly independent executive developed and persist less by coordinated design, executive fiat, or legislative withdrawal than as a byproduct of various institutional actors seeking their own independent goals.

Taking stock of the nation's economic transformations, in 1961 President Eisenhower warned of a military-industrial complex. He acknowledged the need for a weapons industry for victory in World War II and to counter Soviet influence, but feared that the allure of economic profit and military supremacy would promote excessive defense spending, which could threaten American democracy and mortgage the assets of future generations. Scholars widely disagree about whether Eisenhower's message was extraordinarily prescient or ultimately overstated. However, while debates about the motivations driving defense budgets rage, they eclipse related questions about how a permanent defense establishment deviates from the designs of the constitutional framers, alters congressional incentives, and expands the scope of executive military powers. In this book, I attempt to reconcile earlier disputes and address these omissions.

While the military-industrial complex promotes the excessive levels of military spending that Eisenhower feared, his reasoning was not sufficiently nuanced to explain congressional defense spending systematically. Although many case studies have documented legislators' aggressive support for weapons programs built in their states and districts, most quantitative research suggests that the economic benefits that flow from defense activity do not influence members' support for military spending systematically, or in more than a handful of cases. However, by accounting for local economic *reliance* on the military industry, I show powerful interests in continued defense spending among a critical subset of Congress members that previous scholars have missed.

Earlier studies may have understated political influences in defense spending for several reasons. Previous studies generally assume that defense funds are equally important across states and districts with the infrastructure to receive them. Unlike previous work, I argue that districts with less diverse economies are disproportionately reliant on the defense dollars they receive. More economically homogenous areas depend on existing defense infrastructure more than industrially diverse areas with an equal defense-sector presence. Representatives' political motivations are not shaped merely by the presence of defense facilities, but are also influenced by the centrality of the defense industry to the overall local economy.

Previous research is also limited by a lack of available information on the industries that bid for weapons contracts, such as Lockheed Martin, Boeing, or Raytheon. The weapons industry generates hundreds of billions of dollars in revenue annually and employs millions of Americans.[1] Accounting for privately owned companies engaged in weapons development paints a more complete picture of the overall defense economy than military bases, airfields, and naval yards alone. Political scientists have largely neglected defense industries because data on private corporations are not readily available, and most employment information related to defense contracting is classified. I compiled an original dataset identifying the locations of leading defense industries across states and congressional districts to overcome this obstacle.

Earlier researchers also lacked access to reliable data on subcontracting. While prime contracts typically go to areas with defense industry headquarters, defense contractors enjoy wide discretion in distributing assignments and selecting suppliers for parts or technical services for weapons programs. In fact, researchers have speculated that subcontracts are deliberately dispersed as widely as possible in order to attract political support for weapons programs.[2] To examine this theory systematically, I used the Federal Procurement Data System and Geographic Information System software to track defense contracts to the secondary level of distribution, where most defense funds eventually go.

The data suggest that the military industry is at least as integral to the economic landscape in the early twenty-first century as when Eisenhower delivered his warning. Military spending is higher than it was at the height of the Cold War, despite the absence of any comparable enemy investment. While the geographic scope of the national military mobilization in World War II was already extensive, defense dollars are also more widely dispersed. Defense contracts and subcontracts not only flow to every state and a preponderance of congressional districts, but also have systematically spread into more rural and semirural areas where defense jobs account for disproportionate levels of local jobs and revenue. Excessive economic vulnerabilities in areas with a large proportion of defense facilities relative to other industries encourage legislators to press for continued military spending and prioritize defense-sector growth.

Legislators' interests in perpetuating the military economy not only promote inefficient and unnecessary spending, but also undermine Congress's budgetary control over the military. Just as congresses have provided ongoing defense resources available for mobilization at any time, the use of military force abroad has also become more frequent and less controversial. Since President Truman sold the 1950 Korean War as a "police action," using a semantic maneuver to explain the absence of a congressional declaration of war, presidents have directed hundreds of bombings, air strikes, and troop commitments and overseen scores of covert operations without congressional authorization or public debate. Although legislators periodically voice opposition when a war becomes unpopular, Congress provides an uninterrupted source of funding.

Most contemporary observers agree that the balance of war power has shifted decisively in favor of the executive branch.[3] Yet, existing accounts do not fully appreciate why the Constitution's structural safeguards failed to prevent the consolidation of power or minimize war. While scholars offer different interpretations conveying varying degrees of alarm, they often focus on a brief time period—typically looking no further back than fifty or sixty years—as they seek to identify key changes that disrupted the once-stable system of institutional checks and balances governing US military affairs and facilitated the rise of an "imperial" president.[4] The various explanations—a heightened security environment, legislative atrophy, executive initiative, changes in political culture, expansive constitutional interpretations of executive power—either fail to apply consistently throughout the post–World War II era or fail to account for historical variations during earlier periods of development.

While crises and threats to national security certainly motivate heightened defense spending and contribute to the growth of executive power, these explanations paint only a partial picture. Of course, the Soviet threat that fueled the Cold War and the attacks of September 11, 2001, that gave rise to a "war on terrorism" each dramatically altered the course of US foreign policy and military readiness. However, these national security threats cannot explain why Congress failed to eliminate a single weapon-production line after the fall of the Soviet Union, despite testimony from secretaries of Defense, Joint Chiefs of Staff, and presidents that many of these weapons programs were no longer necessary.[5] Nor can they explain why the State Department's entire budget includes only 7 percent of the level of funding in the Department of Defense (DoD) budget, regardless of the ongoing need for international diplomacy and for reconstruction and stabilization assistance after periods of military conflict.[6]

At the same time, a heightened security environment alone cannot fully account for the growth of executive military powers. For example, national security crises fail to explain the leeway granted to presidents during periods of reduced threat, such as when President George H. W. Bush deployed troops in Somalia and President Clinton directed air strikes and committed ground troops in Haiti, Bosnia, and Kosovo without permission from Congress. Furthermore, while scholars and popular media have documented patterns of legislative weakness in military affairs in recent years, they cannot explain why eighteenth- and nineteenth-century congresses were so much less compliant and presidents so much more deferential. Although the United States was never a pacifist nation, presidents routinely sought congressional cooperation for major military operations throughout the eighteenth and nineteenth centuries.

The rise of a permanent military industry helps explain the earlier pattern and the subsequent shift. For most of the nation's history, Congress exercised tight budgetary control over the defense resources at the president's disposal, which limited the president's ability to act independently in military affairs. However, by maintaining large defense budgets and refusing to restrict funding in order to limit ongoing military operations, Congress equips the president with ample resources to carry out his military policies. To gauge the level of budgetary discretion that Congress has historically provided for the military, figure 1.1 displays annual military appropriations from 1789 to 2010, with total federal spending included for a baseline comparison. These amounts are adjusted for inflation and are expressed in constant 2006 dollars.

Clearly, the unprecedented size and upward trajectory of the military budget since World War II reveals a striking contrast from previous eras. In fact, the increase in scale is so dramatic that the figure eclipses variations in military spending in earlier periods of development. To uncover some of this historical variation, figures 1.2–1.3 exhibit military and federal spending from 1789 to 1899 and from 1900 to 2010, respectively (in constant 2006 dollars).

Reduced to scale, it is immediately evident that for most of American history Congress mobilized forces during preparations for specific wars but sharply cut military spending following the termination of hostilities. Military spending exhibits relative peaks followed by prolonged troughs in the nineteenth century, even though the Civil War contributed to massive increases in overall federal spending. Although obscured in figure 1.2, the combined budgets of the War and Navy departments peaked at over $300 million during the War of 1812 (1812–16) and hit $400 million in the Second Seminole War (1835–42), but fell by more than half those respective amounts at the end of each conflict. The Mexican War (1846–48) had a similar effect, propelling military spending to $1.1 billion in 1847, followed by a sharp

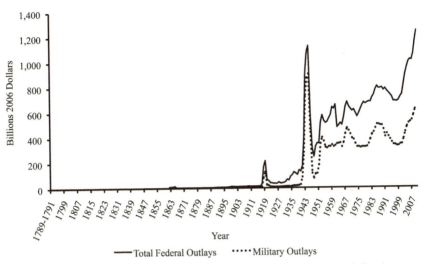

Figure I.I. *Military and federal spending, 1789–2010 (in billions 2006 dollars).*
OMB does not distinguish discretionary and mandatory outlays until FY1962. The figures include total federal outlays until 1962 and discretionary outlays thereafter.
Sources: US Bureau of Census, *Historical Statistics of the United States, 1789 – 1945*, "US Treasury Expenditures, 1789–1945," US Government Printing Office, Washington, DC, 1949, pp. 299–300; Office of Management and Budget, *Historical Tables: Budget of the United States Government*, "Composition of Outlays: 1940–2016" (table 6.1), and "Outlays for Discretionary Programs: 1962–2016" (table 8.7), US Government Printing Office, Washington, DC (http://www.whitehouse.gov/omb/budget/Historicals). Inflation conversion factors are the average of OMB and CBO inflation estimates for each year compiled by Sahr (2009).

drop below $450 million by 1850, until the Third Seminole War (1855–58) pushed spending above a $600-million baseline. The spending during the Civil War (1861–65), however, dwarfs all previous comparisons. Military outlays skyrocketed to over $14 billion before plummeting fourteenfold after the conflict. Spending spiked again during the Spanish-American War (1898), and continued to climb as congresses took advantage of domestic steel markets and invested in naval supplies. Funding increased twentyfold in World War I (1917–18) and plummeted during the 1920s.

Although the United States regularly engaged in armed conflicts, the budgetary figures demonstrate that Congress did not fund a permanent military establishment in these earlier periods. In addition to the strong antipathy to standing armies following the republic's separation from the British monarchy, legislators' responsiveness to local voters led Congress to reduce military expenditures as soon as possible. As many framers had anticipated, military mobilization imposed heavy costs on the public. Lost productivity, military service requirements, and higher tax burdens made it difficult for

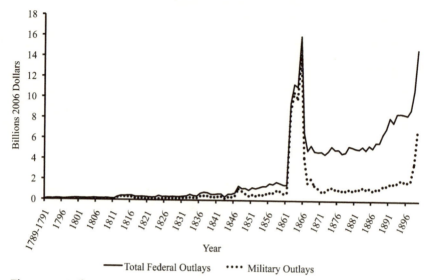

Figure 1.2. *Military and federal spending, 1789–1899 (in billions of 2006 dollars).*
Information drawn from fig. 1.1.

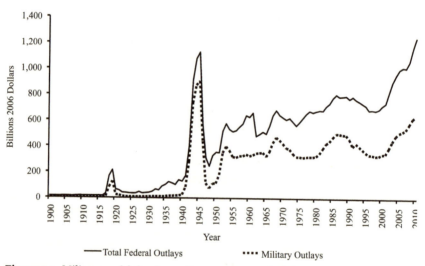

Figure 1.3. *Military and federal spending, 1900–2010 (in billions of 2006 dollars).*
Information drawn from fig. 1.1.

locally elected politicians to authorize military resources in peacetime. In 1939, just prior to US entrance in World War II, the nation possessed a few army bases and naval yards and a handful of private contractors that built airplanes with as few as four employees—nothing even approximating a weapons industry.[7] The absence of a domestic arms industry forced policy-makers to either rely on foreign sources of military equipment or encourage domestic manufacturers to convert their business for wartime production. The loss of taxpayer dollars overseas and disruption of peacetime life made perpetual military buildup politically untenable. At the same time, patterns of military draw-downs following armed conflicts limited the president's ability to direct military actions without permission from Congress.

Unlike earlier periods, the rise of a permanent military industry in World War II created new opportunities for presidents to expand their power. As shown in figure 1.3, post–World War II defense spending fell to its lowest point on record—around $100 billion, or the rough equivalent of the massive spending increase in World War I—during the brief military demobilization after World War II. Since the Korean War (1950–53), defense outlays have not fallen below the $300 billion baseline, despite extended periods without major shooting wars and the decade of reduced conflict after the fall of the Soviet Union. In fact, Congress appropriated more for defense during the Clinton era in the 1990s than President Nixon had at his disposal when he faced the Soviets in the 1970s. This baseline of spending gives presidents access to large reserves of military arms, personnel, and equipment, which they can employ at their discretion. As a result, presidents no longer need to plead their case to the legislature to obtain funding, weapons, and armies prior to military hostilities.

This book will argue that World War II military mobilization created new political interests that the Constitution's framers did not anticipate. New research presented here will show that the scale, scope, and political geography of the World War II effort gave rise to large military industries located in rural and semirural areas that lack diverse economies. A critical subset of Congress members representing these communities have powerful political incentives to press for ongoing military expenditures regardless of actual or perceived national security threats. These members face weak resistance because military spending benefits numerous geographic constituencies, while policy has shifted most of the costs of military spending and war onto political minorities who volunteer to fight, foreign populations where US wars take place, and, ultimately, future generations of taxpayers. The underlying incentives driving congressional decision-making have reshaped the balance of war powers between Congress and the president. This shift in congressional interests rewards key members of Congress who expand the pool of defense resources while increasing the president's ability to exercise force independently. This arrangement also weakens Congress's capacity to check the president's war powers.

A CASE OF INSTITUTIONAL FAILURE: OVERLAPPING INTERESTS AND CONCENTRATED POWER

This is a book about an institutional failure, which occurs when a political institution fails to achieve a goal or operate in the manner that it was originally intended to. Leading constitutional framers designed political institutions to prevent the consolidation of unchecked power and minimize unnecessary wars. Yet, contemporary congresses have unleashed historically unparalleled defense resources that presidents jealously guard and use to achieve their ends militarily. Rather than impeding war and dispersing power, separate, mutually reinforcing interests concentrate power to exercise force in the executive branch.

Institutional failure does not suggest systemic collapse or signal imminent regime replacement. Happily, political pressures and opportunity costs have limited military expansion to its existing size and configuration and prevented the rise of a garrison state.[8] In isolation, however, this extreme point of contrast with an authoritarian alternative conceals new political pressures that encourage rather than impede defense-sector expansion and concentrate instead of limit executive power, while still adhering to democratic norms and upholding political stability. To understand these transformations and their consequences for a constitutional regime of limited powers requires comparison with earlier periods of history.

The constitutional framers began with a basic premise widely popularized by Niccolò Machiavelli and Thomas Hobbes: governing officials desire power. Borrowing from John Locke and Montesquieu, the framers sought to convert private vice into a public good: create separate governing institutions so that each department would jealously defend its own prerogatives and prevent other branches from impinging on delegated authority.[9]

Leading framers promoted legislative control over war spending as a cornerstone of the separation of powers system and argued for budgetary control as a critical protection against tyranny. James Madison's insight that uniting legislative and executive powers in a single office was the genesis of tyrannical government led him to favor a political system of separate and distinct powers in which "the legislative department alone has access to the pockets of the people." The power of purse, he argued, constitutes the "most complete and effectual weapon with which any constitution can arm immediate representatives of the people."[10]

The framers decisively rejected a government in which a single branch could both direct war and fund it. Familiar with efforts by English kings to rely on extraparliamentary sources of revenue for their military expeditions, the US Constitution's framers deliberately vested the power of the purse in Congress.[11] Alexander Hamilton famously contrasted the king of England's power, which "extends to the declaring of war and the raising and regulating of fleets and armies," with the Constitution, which expressly grants these powers to Congress.[12] As Federalists pointed out to the opponents of the proposed Constitution, the legislature must willingly raise troops and appropriate resources before the president can act. Further, Congress's decisions on military spending and armed engagements would always be subject to the judgment of voters who would pay the financial costs of wars and risk their lives in battle. Although the Constitution imposes no limits on Congress's power to declare war and raise armies, representatives' ties to their voters would serve as powerful restraints. Given the president's "supreme command and direction of the military and naval forces," Congress's sole control over the decision to fund wars was construed as a crucial element of the separation-of-powers structure.

Presidents have historically pushed the bounds of their authority in military and foreign affairs, just as the framers expected. Institutional structures encourage presidents to act imperialistically—that is, to promote the authority of their own institution.[13] Whether viewed as "energy" or a "history of aggrandizement," presidents are perched at the top of an executive hierarchy and driven to advance their capacity for leadership.[14]

In contrast, Congress's more democratic structure encourages individual members to respond to a more tangible drive than policy ambition: their own political self-preservation. Members pursue strategies that curry favor with local constituents and fellow partisans, even at the expense of Congress's institutional standing or balance of power in relation to the executive.[15] Congress is a large, deliberative body made up of hundreds of members with varied and competing interests. Further, Congress can only make decisions collectively, and when it does, "congressional penchant for blunt, simple action" often renders legislative outcomes insufficiently precise in light of complex problems and changing circumstances.[16] Individual members' preoccupations with maintaining broad appeal to voters, the institutional demand for compromise, and the need to push legislation through both an upper and lower chamber tend to weaken members' ability to promote their institutional authority.[17]

While the framers expected that presidents would seek to expand their power and the prerogative of their office, they argued that executive dependence on Congress to mobilize the military would serve as a critical check on the president's authority. For most of the nation's history, Congress limited the size of the military during peacetime, which constrained presidents' freedom of action. However, the total military mobilization of World War II created new economic and institutional realities that have transformed the network of political incentives and representational relationships that the Constitution's framers envisioned. After World War II, presidents continued to seek the authority to implement their national security agenda as they saw fit. However, rather than scaling back military spending at the end of specific wars, Congress has continued to provide a persistent baseline of funding. When legislators continually maintain levels of defense spending, they free the president to set the national security agenda and exercise his powers as commander-in-chief. From a separation of powers standpoint, these institutional structures weaken the regime of checks and balances to the extent that legislators' self-preservationist impulses promote the president's imperialistic goals. The upshot is a far cry from the framers' reliance on "ambition . . . made to counteract ambition."[18] In this new context, institutional ambitions of members of Congress work in concert with the institutional ambitions of presidents to greatly expand executive authority. Legislators' interests in continued defense spending weaken their most important check on the president's military powers.

WORLD WAR II MILITARY MOBILIZATION AND THE TRANSFORMATION OF INSTITUTIONAL POLITICS

The convergence of a severe economic depression and a potent national security threat made the World War II military buildup different from previous mobilizations in US history. First, the Great Depression of the 1930s and early 1940s created economic conditions that allowed for total military mobilization. Unlike World War I, which the nation entered during a period of economic growth and high employment, the idle manpower and dormant industrial resources of the 1930s and 1940s facilitated the nation's transformation to a full-scale military economy. Second, unlike earlier administrations, President Franklin Roosevelt prioritized deficit spending and launched a series of policies that minimized the risks of capital investment in the conversion of infrastructure on behalf of the war effort. In doing so, the president not only powered the nation's war machine in a time of conflict, but also advanced the underlying goals of New Deal programs, helping lift the nation out of the Great Depression. Increased federal spending, subsidized wages, and guaranteed cost-plus earnings mobilized industry for large-scale military production, while also providing a potent economic stimulus. The political consequences were self-reinforcing. Widespread economic benefits and employment opportunities muted opposition to increased government involvement in the wartime economy.

World War II is the first occasion in US history in which Congress did not completely demobilize its armed forces at the end of the war. Instead, despite a large retrenchment in 1945, Congress maintained historically unprecedented levels of military outlays. As new research presented here will show, many locations retained defense infrastructure established during the war. Those that did not suffered population loss as residents relocated in search of new employment opportunities. As members of Congress were quick to learn, the closure of a major defense facility was particularly debilitating in rural areas that lacked diverse, industrialized economies. In 1950 President Truman committed troops in Korea, both launching the United States' formal military agenda of containing the spread of Communism and spurring increased levels of defense spending. The defense budget increased more than 300 percent during the Korean War, contributing to a nearly 100 percent increase in overall federal spending. The war pushed total defense industry employment—not including uniformed military personnel and DoD civilian employees—to over 4 million private-sector jobs at the very minimum, and much more if an expansive definition of "defense-related" jobs is applied.[19]

By the time that President Eisenhower took office in 1953, the defense industry had become an integral part of the political and economic landscape. Weapons production and research and development (R&D) were not only more stable components of the federal budget, but also affected large segments of the population. As figure 1.4 illustrates, the distribution of defense contracts extended across every state and a majority of counties during the Cold War buildup, five years after Eisenhower delivered his address and as President Johnson escalated the war in Vietnam.[20]

As the figure shows, military contracts clustered in World War II contracting sites on the East and West coasts, Great Lakes region, and several locations in the South. At the same time, in every decade since World War II, defense dollars have also spread out from major metropolitan locations in the Northeast, Midwest, and Pacific coast into areas with less developed economic infrastructure, including the formerly agrarian South and Southwest and more sparsely populated localities outside of central cities—even while the bulk of defense dollars remain heavily concentrated. Even after

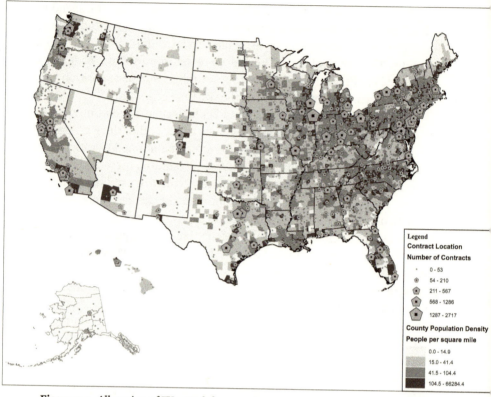

Figure 1.4. *Allocation of FY1966 defense contracts.*

The figure shows the number of DoD contracts allocated per city or town and county-level population density compiled by the author and displayed using Geographic Information System (GIS) software. *Source*: US Department of Defense, Statistical Information and Analysis Division, "Procurement Reports and Data Files for Download: Historical Data, 1966–2006," US Department of Defense, Washington, DC (http://siadapp.dmdc.osd.mil/procurement/Procurement.html).

the fall of the Soviet Union, defense contracting continued to extend well beyond 1970s levels, despite modest reductions in weapons spending and the reduced threat environment of the 1990s.

In the twenty-first century, the "war on terror" spurred enormous demand for additional defense spending. In the first two decades of the twenty-first century, the United States spent nearly as much on the military as every other country in the world combined, despite the absence of any conceivable military rival.[21] As shown in figure 1.5, defense activity not only expanded geographically, but also spread into more thinly populated areas, including desert, mountain, and plains regions. This proliferation of defense contracts increases the number of economic beneficia-

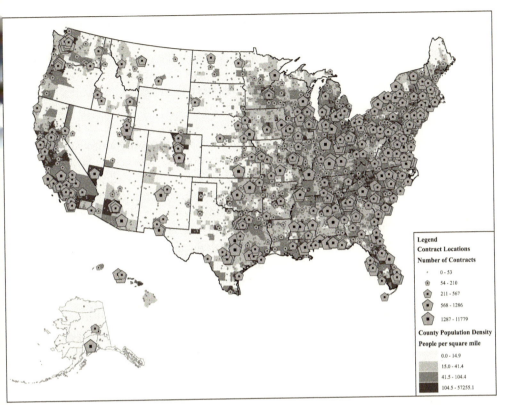

Figure 1.5. *Allocation of FY2006 defense contracts.*
The figure shows the number of DoD contracts allocated per city or town and county-level population density compiled by the author and displayed using Geographic Information System (GIS) software.
Source: US Department of Defense, Statistical Information and Analysis Division, "Procurement Reports and Data Files for Download: Historical Data, 1966–2006," US Department of Defense, Washington, DC (http://siadapp.dmdc.osd.mil/procurement/Procurement.html).

ries, while generating and intensifying local dependencies on the defense sector.

The scale and scope of defense production has created an environment in which members of Congress perceive more benefits in perpetuating and expanding defense production than in reducing costs by demobilizing as had occurred after previous wars. This does not simply mean that members of Congress from areas with defense industries will seek more military spending. As stated earlier, districts with less diverse economies are disproportionately reliant on the defense dollars that they receive.

In broader terms, disproportionate economic reliance suggests that representational strategies differ across rural and urban settings. A defense firm located in a more sparsely populated rural area will typically employ a larger proportion of local residents and contribute more to the local economy than a defense company situated in a densely populated urban area with a more diverse, vibrant economic base. At the same time, more thinly populated congressional districts encompass a larger geographic area than districts within densely populated cities. As a result, companies in rural or semirural areas often draw their workforce from a single district, where one representative can claim credit for jobs and revenue (and anticipate that she will incur blame if a major plant shuts down). Conversely, businesses located in cities often draw employees from across multiple districts, weakening opportunities for credit-claiming. While local employment is a critical concern for any member of Congress seeking reelection, the political importance of a single industry registers differently across distinct local contexts.

Previous scholarship on the politics of defense spending has not considered how disproportionate economic reliance influences legislative priorities. As a result, these studies yield contradictory findings. On one hand, Eisenhower's message planted the seeds of the now-familiar story that economic benefits motivate far more defense spending in Congress than what is necessary for national security alone.[22] Drawing on the concept of an iron triangle, scholars have documented specific cases in which members of Congress work to ensure continued weapons programs that benefit their voters, while defense contractors channel dollars and projects to these members' districts and defense industry managers contribute to their campaign coffers.[23] Shared political interests among these actors also have helped prolong the lifespan of disproportionately expensive weapons systems that presidents and secretaries of Defense tried to terminate, such as the B-1 stealth bomber and the SSN-Seawolf submarine.[24]

The unique characteristics of the military economy exacerbate these structural alliances. Unlike standard US markets, the government is the sole legal purchaser of most military equipment. As a result, the government determines the prices, insures against losses, and subsidizes volume.[25] The limited number of major suppliers and lack of traditional market competition invite companies to manipulate economic conditions in order to enhance revenue—a behavior that economists refer to as rent-seeking. As one study concludes, these problems have culminated in an "overreaching military-industrial complex at least equal to the one that Eisenhower warned against."[26]

On the other hand, however, decades of quantitative studies accounting for the behavior of all members of Congress suggest these are rare exceptions to legislative behavior, and not the rule.[27] Statistical research suggests that members and senators representing areas that stand to benefit from defense spending—locations with military bases, airfields, and naval yards or with the highest levels of prime defense-contract dollars—are no more likely than other members and senators to support nuclear weapons development, space-based missiles, or more aggressive foreign policy.[28] Related scholarship focusing on defense contract distributions suggests that constituencies do not gain considerable benefits from representation on defense committees or other institutional advantages.[29] Most systematic research indicates that legislators' general tendency to seek federal benefits for their constituencies do not apply to defense dollars, despite the vast sums of money involved in major weapons contracts.

However, while the conventional wisdom that members of Congress will protect their local economic interests is correct, these understandings are not nuanced enough to explain congressional preferences for defense programs systematically. To overcome previous theoretical and empirical limitations, I developed a comprehensive database of nationwide locations of leading US defense industries and measured the concentration of the local defense economy relative to other industries. I also tracked defense contracts to the place where most of the work is performed, where the preponderance of defense dollars eventually go. New evidence suggests that legislators representing disproportionately reliant areas take a special interest in defense industry growth and aggressively seek out opportunities to expand their institutional influence over such decisions. Institutionally entrenched interests in military expenditures add to the chorus of demands for increased defense spending that are driven by national security goals. However, while geopolitical realities change and national security threats subside, economic vulnerability and electoral strategies consistently encourage a critical subset of Congress members to fund military technologies regardless of whether they are needed for national security.

As defense spending transformed the nation's economic landscape, policymakers championed a number of initiatives that reduced the public costs of military spending and war. Greater reliance on deficit spending has circumvented the traditional need to rely on the current tax base to maintain existing weapons platforms or commit troops abroad. Instead, policymakers push financial costs onto future generations of taxpayers. The elimination of the military draft and reliance on an all-volunteer force, as well as the increasing use of private military and security contractors, also contribute to lower troop counts and fewer US military casualties. While the ability to exercise force abroad at reduced costs to citizens provides obvious military benefits, these new arrangements also influence political debates over whether or not to employ military force in the first place. Instead, critical constituencies profit from ongoing defense spending at diminished perceptions of public expense. These dynamics make it easier for policymakers to maintain a military establishment and use force abroad with less fear of electoral reprisal.

This new representational relationship no longer imposes the kind of restraints that the framers expected. Instead of encouraging members to reduce military spending, political incentives in the post–World War II environment tend to militate against spending cuts and favor continued defense-sector growth. An institutional structure premised on competing interests has generated a system geared toward policies that maximize the mutual, short-term benefits of voters, officeholders, and defense industries, while imposing costs elsewhere. Important political constituencies benefit from and rely on defense jobs and revenue, while diminishing proportions of voters fight in the nation's wars or pay higher taxes to fund military operations. This arrangement empowers presidents who gain access to a stream of military resources that they can use to project force abroad, while anticipating a continued source of funding from Congress.

INADVERTENT STATE-BUILDING AND EXPANSIVE EXECUTIVE WAR POWER

Congress's control over spending is the traditional hedge against the president's authority over the military. However, since the end of World War II, Congress has completed a gradual shift from its early nineteenth-century frugality to a blank-check mentality. From President Truman's undeclared war in Korea in 1950 to President Obama's unauthorized air strikes in Libya in 2011, Congress has endorsed, condoned, or otherwise funded nearly every military excursion involving US forces—despite hundreds of unauthorized military actions, divided government, polarized parties, and popular opposition to prolonged military engagements. Congress's refusal to limit war funding has downgraded the standard for legislative approval of wars from a matter of absolute necessity to one of mere expediency.[30]

American state-building enterprises that are explicitly designed to increase federal power are usually characterized as incremental processes rife with institutional conflict and ongoing power struggles.[31] In contrast, the development and expansion of the military establishment fueled unusual levels of institutional cooperation and weak opposition.[32] Military growth has fueled overwhelming consensus by extending benefits widely, while shifting most of the costs onto political minorities and noncitizens. In this climate, legislators are not simply more deferential to the president's military policies; rather, many members have vested interests in furnishing the resources that allow presidents to act, while there is rarely strong incentive for individual members to mount sustained opposition. A permanent war economy and an increasingly independent executive developed democratically and with little coherent resistance, as various institutional actors pursued their own independent goals.

Congress's inability to exercise its spending power has fueled a rich tradition of scholarship mourning a "broken" legislative branch and the breakdown of checks and balances, culminating in the "decline of the American republic."[33] The congressional acquiescence narrative rests on a widely shared assumption that Congress refuses to use the purse to challenge executive war powers because members lack technical knowledge and fear being branded as disloyal to the president, the troops, or the nation.

National security and the safety of American troops are serious and legitimate concerns for all members of Congress. However, these goals do not lead all legislators to uniformly defer to executive military policy. Instead, members' national security goals are also filtered through partisan and constituency lenses that shape their loyalties, expectations, and commitments. For example, new research shows that legislative majorities facing a president of the opposing party regularly challenge executive military policies.[34] Even though Congress has not successfully used its spending power to compel a president to end a military engagement in the post–World War II era, legislative majorities can use their agenda power to issue floor statements against a war, hold critical committee hearings, conduct investigations, and stir up negative media attention surrounding the administration's military actions. Presidents anticipate these political costs when they decide whether to initiate force and determine the duration of the mission.[35]

However, while a hostile majority party will go to great lengths to sabotage a president's military agenda, these members almost never unite on critical votes to curtail ongoing military operations. From the unpopular war in Vietnam to Bill Clinton's independent military commitments in Bosnia and Kosovo and George W. Bush's troop surge in Iraq, congressional majorities hardly ever use their spending power to challenge an administration of the opposing political party or terminate an unpopular mission. Partisan explanations alone fail to clarify why some members derail attempts of their own partisan allies to withdraw war funding and end a military conflict.

In addition to partisan loyalties, local economic reliance addresses a vital part of the puzzle. Congress's inability to limit war funding is not simply a result of institutional weakness or the partisan composition of Congress in relation to the president, but is also a consequence of a larger structural imbalance. Withdrawing levels of military funding sufficient to prevent an armed conflict or terminate a war is politically difficult for members of Congress representing areas that rely on the military funding that large defense budgets and major wars generate. Just as local defense dependence encourages legislators to prioritize defense interests and press for increased military spending, these members are also more predisposed to support war and war funding than their partisan allies. Local dependence on military production exacerbates the political obstacles that legislative coalitions seeking to end a war must surmount.

While legislators have relinquished their budgetary control in favor of ongoing defense spending, executives have worked to structure military bureaucracies and intelligence agencies to more effectively control the resources that Congress appropriates. Presidents have insulated national security resources and intelligence information within executive agencies, directed covert military activities, and created new executive departments to carry out their policies. The hierarchical structure of the executive branch has allowed presidents to capitalize on the stream of resources that Congress has provided. Presidents also pursue strategies that expand their ability to operate in secrecy and draw on private companies performing traditional military and civilian functions. These tactics exacerbate information deficits in Congress and reduce effective legislative oversight. Like Homer's Odysseus, who bound and freed himself in a futile effort to hear the sirens and resist their song, Congress's interests in continued defense spending also undermines its periodic efforts to reassert authority over military affairs.

In earlier periods, voters were called upon to sacrifice when war could not be avoided, and elected officials routinely sought to restore peace and reduce defense spending as swiftly as possible. Since World War II, new arrangements have transformed the constitutional system from a regime premised on institutional conflict and limited power to one of shared interests and increasingly centralized authority.

ORGANIZATION OF THE BOOK

Chapter 2 examines the founders' distrust of standing armies and concentrated power. For most of the nation's history, Congress abided these concerns by increasing military spending in preparation for specific wars and dismantling the military after the conflict was over. From the late eighteenth to mid-twentieth century, presidents had to convince Congress to appropriate additional funding to go to war. As a result, Congress retained important leverage over how these funds would be spent. At the end of the war, Congress promptly downsized the defense budget. However, as chapter 3 shows, the rise of the rural defense pork barrel during World War II fundamentally transformed congressional incentives. The chapter documents the extension of World War II military production from large cities with preexisting aircraft industries to smaller towns adjacent to the home plant and the agrarian southern region. Although these decisions were based on sound historical reasons, many rural, semirural, and suburban areas inadvertently became economically dependent on the defense infrastructure that they received. In chapter 4, mapping techniques illustrate the flow of defense dollars from the onset of the Cold War to the first decade of the twenty-first century. The analysis suggests that military spending has systematically spread out into more economically reliant areas, serving in part as an economic development tool in places that lack diversified economies. At the same time, policies have shifted the most devastating costs of war onto a minority of soldiers who volunteer to fight, future populations of taxpayers who will inherit the nation's war debts, and foreign countries where US wars take place.

Building from this evidence, chapters 5–7 introduce and elaborate a new theory of disproportionate economic reliance in congressional politics. The analysis suggests that more economically homogenous, rural and semirural areas with defense industries experience disproportionate reliance on local weapons suppliers as a source of employment and revenue. Local defense dependence encourages political representatives to press for increased military spending and support major wars at greater rates than their partisan and ideological allies in Congress. These members' preferences are reflected in the distribution of defense subcontracts, which flow to more economically dependent, rural areas during critical dissemination stages. The final chapter documents post–World War II presidents' strategies to control the flow of defense resources that Congress appropriates and use them to carry out their military policies.

Presidential War Powers in Historical Perspective

The system will not hurry us into war; it is calculated to guard against it. It will not be in the power of a single man, or a single body of men, to involve us in such distress; for the important power of declaring war is vested in the legislature at large; and this declaration must be made with the concurrence of the House of Representatives: from this circumstance we may draw a certain conclusion that nothing but our national interest can draw us into a war. —James Wilson, Pennsylvania Ratifying Convention, December 11, 1787

In 1789, when Britain sought an alliance with the United States against Spain following Spanish seizure of the port at Nootka Sound (an inlet off of Vancouver Islands), President Washington adopted a policy of neutrality without consulting Congress. The administration was intent on keeping the nation at peace and favored using neutrality as leverage to protect Louisiana and Florida from British conquest, obtain a favorable treaty of commerce with Britain, and acquire rights from Spain to use the Mississippi River. Leading members of Washington's cabinet—Alexander Hamilton, Henry Knox, John Jay, and John Adams—unanimously agreed that neutrality required that Britain be denied a right of passage through US territory to advance against Spain. If Britain should enter the United States without permission, Washington's cabinet strongly encouraged him "to immediately convene the Legislature; to make the most vigorous measures for war; to make a formal demand of satisfaction; to commence negotiations for alliances; and if satisfaction should be refused, to endeavor to punish the aggressor by the sword."[1] Britain did not ask permission or advance troops. Therefore, Washington's administration unilaterally determined a policy of neutrality. Yet, despite Washington's independent commitment to diplomacy—including his 1793 Proclamation of Neutrality following a controversial interpretation of the US-France Treaty of Alliance—his cabinet members also urged congressional involvement prior to potential military action.

Washington's administration advised congressional involvement prior to armed conflicts, but not for diplomatic measures, because going to war was expensive and Congress exercised strict control over its budgetary prerogatives. While the president could pursue peaceful negotiations independently, he relied on Congress to raise funds and mobilize the military. The framers of the Constitution divided military powers between separate governing departments with these goals in mind. They created an executive poised to take initiative in military and foreign affairs, but expected that military power could only be exercised in consultation with Congress. The Constitution's proponents recognized that legislative control over resources, Congress's ties to local voters, and the public costs of war would impose important political constraints on large peacetime armies and unnecessary wars. In the earliest periods of the nation's history, military build-ups required the recruitment of citizen-soldiers and volunteers, investments in European military technologies, and higher taxes, while resulting in the loss of revenue, just as the Constitution's framers expected. Given the extent of these burdens for a geographically isolated republic, congresses sharply cut military spending after armed conflicts and denied presidents the resources necessary to carry out their military policies independently. Legislators' tight budgetary control over the type of armed forces at the president's disposal reinforced Congress's constitutional responsibilities in the context of the nation's war policies.

The first part of the chapter suggests that constitutional framers sought to structure political institutions to empower the national government and enable it to effectively repel external enemies, while at the same time guarding against permanent armies and unnecessary military excursions. Statements of both supporters and opponents of the proposed Constitution convey a general understanding that large military budgets and needless wars would drain national revenue and provoke public resentment. While the two factions disagreed as to whether a strong federal government would prove to be an oppressive force in the lives of citizens, neither side anticipated a context in which ongoing military spending would be construed as beneficial among large swaths of voters, or where members of Congress would perpetuate military spending indefinitely.

The second part of the chapter documents the relations between congresses and presidents in military actions and wars throughout several important historical junctures. In *The Imperial Presidency*, the legendary Arthur Schlesinger Jr. argues that earlier presidents demonstrated greater deference to Congress in military matters because they "saw their constitutional principles in context" and understood that wars were expensive and controversial.[2] However, in addition to these internal restraints, earlier presidents also lacked external means to conduct military operations independently. While chief executives have always sought to direct military policy with as few restrictions as possible, their freedom of action is contingent on the levels of available defense resources that Congress has historically provided.

From the late eighteenth to mid-twentieth century, presidents relied on Congress to appropriate additional funding to go to war, and Congress promptly limited the military budget after an armed conflict was over. In the earliest years of the republic, the nation lacked a unified military, professional army, and functional procurement system. Deprived of resources and authority, presidents regularly requested legislative authorization prior to military deployments. However, as soon as Congress authorized more military personnel and established a standardized procurement system, mid-nineteenth-century presidents capitalized on an ability to move existing troops without congressional authorization and obtained legislative approval only after military hostilities appeared inevitable. At the turn of the century, presidents gained leverage from modern naval resources that Congress authorized during industrialization, in addition to existing weapons arsenals equipped with supplies left over from previous wars. While these resources allowed early twentieth-century presidents to circumvent congressional approval in limited regional conflicts, these presidents could not conduct more extensive military expeditions without obtaining ongoing congressional cooperation.

LIMITING PEACETIME ARMIES AND UNNECESSARY WAR

Lessons from the Eighteenth-Century Continental Army

The First Continental Congress formed in 1774 when representatives of several colonies met to discuss mutual grievances under King George III. The following year, the Second Continental Congress assumed the responsibility to direct foreign affairs and conduct the Revolutionary War, while the states retained all of their legislative powers.

George Washington's Revolutionary War experience fueled dissatisfaction with the lack of power in the Continental Congress and its inability to raise funds. As early as 1870, after Charleston fell to the British, Washington complained in a private letter to a member of Congress about the present state of finances and lack of power in Congress "competent to the great purposes of war."[3] With the adoption of the Articles of Confederation one year later, Congress gained the exclusive authority to declare war and conduct foreign affairs, but still lacked means to raise armies. Congress had to impose requisitions on the states in order to raise funds, although it had no authority to compel compliance among reluctant state legislatures (articles VI–IX). The arrangements continued under the articles much as they had under the Continental Congress.[4]

On March 4, 1783, six months prior to the signing of the Treaty of Paris and the culmination of the war, General Washington expressed forebodings to Alexander Hamilton of "the sufferings of a complaining army on one hand, and the inability of Congress and tardiness of States on the other." He implored Hamilton that "unless Congress have powers competent to all *general purposes*, that the distress we have encountered, the expense we have incurred, and the blood we have spilt in the course of an Eight years war, will avail us nothing."[5] On June 8, 1783, he submitted a public letter to the states lamenting the inefficiencies and resource shortages that hindered the war effort.[6] He found irredeemable fault with the articles, which lacked centralized control over the military and produced collective action problems among States, creating a danger to military supply levels and troop morale:

> The inefficiency of measures, arising from the want of an adequate authority in the Supreme Power, from a partial compliance with the Requisitions of Congress in some of the States, and from a failure of punctuality in others, while it tended to damp the zeal of those which were more willing to exert themselves; served also to accumulate the expences of the War, and to frustrate the best concerted Plans. . . . The discouragement occasioned by the complicated difficulties and embarrassments . . . would have long ago produced the dissolution of any Army, less patient, less virtuous and less persevering, than that which I have had the honor to command.[7]

In addition to impediments to the war effort, states experienced difficulties maintaining order after the war had ended. State authorities were unable or unwilling to quell public uprisings and Congress lacked the authority to do so.[8] States' refusal to comply with requisitions frustrated Congress's efforts to pay down the national debt and made additional borrowing impossible. Further, state legislatures tended to exacerbate the nation's economic problems by continuing to issue additional paper money. Poor economic conditions contributed to a growing demand for political reform.[9] Alexander Hamilton later bemoaned that, under the articles, "We have neither troops, nor treasury, nor government."[10]

While the Revolutionary War experience provoked a felt need for more effective governance in matters of war, the colonial experience under King George III also bred a pervasive antimonarchical, antiarmy sentiment.[11] As a result, most framers present during constitutional ratification shared nuanced concerns for effective governance and individual liberty, or centralized control over the military and freedom from large standing armies. The more extreme positions, however, are commonly associated with the Constitution's supporters, who called themselves "Federalists," and their opponents, whom their rivals pejoratively labeled "Anti-Federalists."[12] Although these two factions sharply diverged over how best to structure government to obtain these ends, records of the debates over constitutional ratification suggest that the document's defenders and opponents each sought to guard against excessive military activity, which they associated with loss of revenue and burdensome public costs. The consistent application of the same themes—the internal costs of military mobilization and fear of standing armies—reflects not only the nation's rejection of monarchy, but also its deficient procurement infrastructure, lack of significant naval force, isolated position, and domestic aspirations that characterized the eighteenth-century republic.

The Constitution's Army Clauses

The ratification debates over how best to empower government to provide for the national defense and prevent the concentration of political power ultimately led the constitutional framers to devise separate institutions to declare war and conduct it. In accordance with Washington's plea for effective legislative control over resources and adequate authority in a "Supreme Power," the constitutional framers arranged political institutions to transfer power to provide for the general defense from the states to Congress and empower a singular executive as commander-in-chief of the armed forces.

Echoing George Washington's most pressing concerns, leading Federalists found a "manifest inconsistency" in the Articles of Confederation that vested "the Federal Government [with] the care of the general defense" but left "in the State governments the *effective* powers by which it is to be provided."[13] To correct these deficiencies, the framers vested unlimited power to raise armies and appropriate the resources needed to support them in Congress.[14] Federalist writings express the view that, since Congress would be responsible to prepare for the nation's defense, it also had to be supplied with requisite means to secure that end.[15] Frustrated with the military experience during the Revolutionary War under the Continental Congress,

Alexander Hamilton argued that imposing limitations on appropriations creates "constitutional shackles" that incapacitate the nation's ability to prepare for its own defense.[16] Advocating on behalf of ratification, James Madison advanced a similar defense of Congress's unlimited power to raise troops as a necessary precaution given the unpredictable nature and scope of future threats.[17]

The opposition to the Constitution's army clauses centered on this transfer of military power from the states to the federal government. Leading critics of the proposed Constitution feared that unlimited centralized authority to raise military forces would invite internal domestic costs that were "improvident" and "dangerous" to republican liberty.[18] Throughout ancient and modern history, "almost all" European and Asian nations had lost their liberty because of the establishment of a standing army.[19] By this line of argument, it was hardly sensible to chart the same course.[20]

Arguments against Congress's authority to raise armies emphasized the power of the central government to overpower its own citizens; the potential for excessive use of force against other nations was either unforeseen or regarded as unimportant. Opponents of the Constitution's army clauses expressed fears that the new government would impose unwarranted burdens on citizenry, creating an untenable fissure between governing and governed that would eventually degenerate to military despotism. Standing armies required recruitment of citizen-soldiers that not only interfered with citizens' private pursuits, but was also "expensive" and "inconvenient"—a considerable burden on taxpayers, a drain on public revenue, and a gross interference with commercial and political aspects of republican life.[21] Cognizant of the need for small peacetime garrisons to repel potential attacks coming from Spain, Britain, or the Native Americans, a leading opponent of the Constitution's military clauses denounced an "unqualified" and "indefinite" power to raise and maintain armies during peacetime. The argument pointed to a danger "to be apprehended from their overturning the constitutional powers of the government and assuming power to dictate in any form they please."[22] If Congress established a large peacetime army and used its power over the militia to disarm citizens, then the central government would effectively hold a national monopoly on force and the means to make itself independent of the people.[23]

In response to these charges, the Constitution's leading proponents emphasized the document's institutional safeguards against tyranny. Railing against the "Anti-Federalist" reliance on parchment barriers—written proscriptions on government power—Hamilton famously advanced a structural argument that institutional mechanisms would provide *inherent* safeguards against the potential abuse of political power. "If . . . it shall be resolved to extend [a] prohibition to the *raising* of armies in times of peace," he warned, then "we must expose our property and liberty to the mercy of foreign invaders . . . because we are afraid that rulers, *created by our choice, dependent on our will*, might endanger that liberty by an abuse of the means necessary to its preservation."[24] In this view, an electoral check on Congress obviates the need for written restraints on the legislature's power to defend the nation. Legislators' dependence on the people would prevent members from demanding excessive sacrifices of their constituencies or threatening their liberties.

The Constitution's defenders maintained that, while "dependence on the people is . . . the primary control on the government," the document also provides important "auxiliary precautions." To guard against the concentration of overwhelming or tyrannical power in one place, the Constitution separates and divides powers in different branches, supplying each with the "necessary means and personal motives to resist encroachment of the others.[25] "Ambition [is] . . . made to counteract ambition," as each branch jealously defends its own constitutional responsibilities against infringement. In addition to legislators' ties to their voters, the division of war powers between the president and Congress creates another check on Congress's willingness to maintain standing armies in peacetime: The legislature will presumably seek to guard its own constitutional prerogative to spend money and declare war rather than vesting permanent funds in the executive department. To allay his opponents' fears of an "elective monarchy," Hamilton pointed out that the Constitution's two-year limit on military appropriations expressly prevents Congress from granting the executive a permanent supply of military funds. For himself and other Federalists, however, this was perhaps a superfluous guarantee, given that he could not foresee any reasonable legislative incentive for doing so.[26]

Consistent with Washington's desire for a "supreme power" and Hamilton's preference to infuse "energy" in the executive, the framers empowered a singular executive as commander-in-chief of armed forces.[27] Not surprisingly, Hamilton found the propriety of the provision, "so evident in itself and . . . so consonant with the practice of state constitutions . . . that little need be said to explain or enforce it. . . .The direction of war most peculiarly demands those qualities which distinguish the exercise of power by a single hand."[28] As James Iredell elaborated at North Carolina's ratifying convention, the commander-in-chief provision was consistent with the precedent already established in state constitutions that had vested military authority in governors. The obvious need for "secrecy, dispatch, and decision" in military operations dictates that "the command of armies ought to be delegated to one person only."[29] Iredell, Wilson, and Hamilton all emphasized institutional safeguards that would prevent concentration of military power in the executive. For example, while Charles Pinckney feared that the "executive powers of the existing Congress might extend to peace and war . . . which would render the Executive [an elective] Monarchy,"[30] Iredell found the president's power "sufficiently guarded" against gradual accretion or abuse because Congress retained control over defense resources: "A very material difference may be observed between [the President's] power, and the authority of the king of Great Britain under similar circumstances. The king of Great Britain is not only the commander-in-chief of the land and naval forces, but has power, in time of war, to raise fleets and armies. He also has the authority to declare war."[31]

Opponents also pointed out that Congress would at times be compelled to raise armies that "then the President is to command without any control."[32] While Federalists had no explicit answer to alleviate those fears, the response was largely implicit in the Federalists' line of argument. First, the debates that took place during constitutional ratification reveal a common understanding that Congress could prevent any abuse of authority in the president. Second, and related, Federalist assessments reflect eighteenth-century conditions, in which Congress lacked both a "pretense" and a plausible electoral motivation to perpetuate military resources in peacetime.

Under the colonial government, state legislatures had successfully used their power over funds to check governors—appointed agents of the British king—in military affairs. Accordingly, many of the arguments put forth during the constitutional convention reflect an understanding that Congress would exercise its power over revenue to control military policy. At the Pennsylvania ratifying convention, James Wilson and Edmund Randolph's pointed debate over whether the House of Representatives should possess sole control over appropriations hinged on a shared premise that control over revenue could be employed to direct military affairs.[33] Similarly, several objections to the proposal to grant two-thirds of the Senate the power to override the president's diplomatic treaties suggest that Congress could already control the conduct of war through the appropriations process. Nathaniel Gorham considered "the precaution unnecessary, as the means of carrying on the war would not be in the hands of the President, but of the Legislature," while Gouverneur Morris found "the power of the president in this case harmless." As preeminent constitutional law scholar Abraham Sofaer concludes, the debate "reflects a recognition that the President could not realistically pursue a war (or any other diplomatic policy requiring "means") that even one branch of Congress was resolved against."[34]

While debates over ratification reveal a pervasive impression that Congress would use its power of the purse to influence military affairs, records also suggest that proponents of keeping the nation at peace and repressing war found solace in the parochial legislature. George Mason, an avid proponent for "clogging war" and "facilitating peace," was "against giving the power of war to the executive, because [he was] not (safely) to be trusted with it; or to the Senate, because [they were] not so constructed as to be entitled to it."[35] Hamilton turned his audience's prejudice for legislative supremacy on its head by challenging the premise that the parochial legislature would unnecessarily accumulate military resources: "But the question again recurs, upon what pretense could [the president] be put in possession of a force [large enough to awe the people into submission] in time of peace?"[36] Hamilton's rejoinder implies that legislators would have to convince their constituencies of either interest or necessity in order to perpetuate military resources in peacetime—a "pretense" that was not clearly discernible in the nascent eighteenth-century republic.[37]

Congressional control over military resources reflects a structural view of liberty commonly held among Federalists: The representative structure of Congress would prevent members from raising armies during peacetime. Arguments made in support of ratification replayed the themes of legislative control over resources and dependence on the people, which would presumably prevent the executive usurpation that their opponents feared. In order for the executive to use military force or employ coercion, the legislature must raise troops and appropriate resources, which would require widespread public sacrifices.

While the extent of the president's discretionary power to command or move *existing* troops is debatable, it is clear that Congress was expected to supply troops necessary for battle. Given the pervasive costs of doing so in a period of relative security from imminent attack, Federalists advanced arguments suggesting that the institutional design would limit executive discretion over military matters and reduce the likelihood of war. By contrast, the central opposition to the Constitution's army clauses reflects a historical understanding that an electoral check on legislatures is insufficient if Congress exploits its unlimited authority and acquires a monopoly on force, which the executive could then control with impunity. The opponents of ratification feared an indefinite military buildup because they presumed that it would inflict intolerable costs on the populace and facilitate the demise of the republic.

Defenders and critics of the proposed Constitution disagreed on the seriousness of international threats that the nation faced, the potential need for standing armies to repel foreign aggressors, and the prospect for liberty under a consolidated national government. However, each side associated large-scale military mobilization and permanent armies with internal, domestic costs. At minimum, both sides understood that taxation, military service, and loss of federal revenue interfere with citizens' private occupations, exhaust federal resources, incur public resentment, and ought to be avoided in peacetime to the greatest extent that liberty and security will allow. Neither line of argument anticipated developments that would promote a profitable military industry, reduce the public costs of war, and inadvertently strengthen executive war powers.

CONGRESS'S HISTORICAL BUDGETARY CONTROL

Prior to World War II, congresses regularly dismantled the armed forces and withdrew military spending after going to war. At the same time, major wars, land acquisitions, and an industrializing economy also contributed to representatives' willingness to gradually increase defense investments. Throughout this period, Congress developed an increasingly professional army, invested in steel markets for domestic weapons purchases, built up naval forces that transported wars to foreign territories, and authorized the ability to print money. While presidents took advantage of their heightened ability to employ existing resources and direct minor military operations independently, the absence of a permanent military establishment consistently limited executive authority over matters of war and defense.

Limited Resources and Congressional Advantage

Although many Federalists saw the nation's military weakness as one of the major defects of the confederation, the Federalist Congress never created a large standing army. In fact, military historians typically characterize the period of early Federalist control (from 1789 to 1801) by the absence of a peacetime establishment, continual reliance on state militias, and deficient military procurement infrastructure.[38] Congress maintained a peacetime establishment of approximately 3,000–3,400 personnel during John Adams's term—an exceptionally small army by comparative standards. While the earliest US presidents—Washington, Adams, Jefferson, and Madison—sought to direct the course of foreign affairs with limited interference, these leaders lacked the resources to conduct major military engagements without congressional cooperation. The political environment placed greater emphasis on diplomacy and required ongoing congressional spending to support military operations.

Following George Washington's tenure, John Adams worked closely with Congress to prepare for military conflicts while favoring diplomatic solutions. In 1798, when war with France appeared likely, President Adams called Congress into special session and urged that it provide a navy, harbor defenses, and raise emergency forces.[39] Congress responded by authorizing a series of statutes granting supplemental funding for a naval armament and for the defense of ports and harbors; authorizing the president to raise a provisional army and to provide cannons, arms and ammunition; suspending commerce with France; and authorizing the president to seize certain French armed vessels and intercept US ships sailing to French ports.[40] Pledging to pursue peaceful, diplomatic means, the president generally used the forces provided to him defensively and successfully avoided direct war with France.

Despite his deference to Congress in matters of war, Adams also exercised greater independence in military affairs once Congress had procured sufficient resources. In one of the most notorious cases of executive contravention of a congressional act in the early republic, Adams issued an order to "intercept any suspected American ship sailing to or from a French port." In doing so, Adams either disregarded or deliberately stretched statutory language authorizing seizure of US vessels sailing *to* French ports as part of a general prohibition on commercial relations with France.[41] Following these orders, US captain George Little seized a Danish ship sailing from a French port. He was accused of treason and sued for damages for violating explicit statutory authorization. Writing for the Supreme Court, Chief Justice Marshall held that the captain was liable, as congressional statutes supersede inconsistent presidential orders.[42] However, the president had already acquired the means with which to enforce the command.

After Adams narrowly avoided war with France, Thomas Jefferson came to power and reduced the size of the army. However, despite Jefferson's "pathological" antipathy for standing armies, he ultimately left the Federalist army largely intact.[43] He demonstrated similar deference to Congress in matters of war and exhibited a comparable readiness to conduct more limited initiatives independently. For example, when Jefferson sent a small squadron of frigates to the Mediterranean to protect against ongoing attacks by Barbary pirates, he explicitly referenced authorizing legislation and deferred to Congress to abandon the Mediterranean or retain its cruise ships.[44] In response, Congress passed a series of statutes explicitly granting the president authority to equip armed vessels to protect commerce and carry out "warlike operations against the regency of Tripoli, or any of the other Barbary powers."[45] Exercising greater prerogative, Jefferson proclaimed a "qualified war" in response to a British attack on an American ship in 1807. However, lacking adequate resources, he limited his response to a proclamation ordering all British ships out of American waters and backed these actions with economic sanctions rather than military force.[46]

Jeffersonian-Republican aversion to standing armies left the incoming president, James Madison, with a small regular army and larger but hopelessly disorganized state militias. Despite Madison's efforts to steer clear of foreign entanglements, neutrality proved increasingly difficult as Napoleon's forces ravaged through Europe. Both France and Britain implemented prohibitive trade restrictions, making commerce with either nation an act of allegiance to one country and hostility to the other. Further, British ships regularly patrolled the Atlantic and subjected American merchant vessels to search and seizure. Turning to practice of impressment in order to expand their fleet, they captured many American sailors and forced them into the British navy. Like Jefferson, Madison was reluctant to go to war, but requested additional troops to defend US ships against a British blockade in 1811. The costs of military mobilization were so high that Congress vacillated and refused to raise taxes, despite the predominantly prowar attitude among Republican majorities.[47] Leery of full-fledged war, Madison initially used economic pressures to force Britain to relax its blockade. It was not until this method appeared unavailing that he sent a message to Congress with a litany of complaints against England and request for an official declaration of war. The Republican-controlled, prowar, nationalist House led by Speaker Henry Clay voted to go to war, followed later by a more divided Senate.

To carry out the war, Madison sought to seize Canada from the British, presumably to force England to acknowledge US sovereignty and lift disruptions to American trade. Despite expectations of an easy victory, American forces were poorly equipped for war. The United States entered the war with undisciplined state militias, a tiny navy, virtually no military command structure, and an utterly dysfunctional procurement system.[48] Congress increased the size of the army only immediately before declaring war against Britain, but legislators were still reluctant to provide a navy and refused to authorize new ships, arguing that a small navy would not stand up against Britain's large fleet.[49] Although state militias were more readily available, leading historian Sean Wilentz characterized these forces as "barely trained and poorly supplied . . . [earning] a strong reputation among the officer corps for uselessness."[50]

Politics exacerbated these logistical problems. Northeastern Federalists strongly opposed the war and resisted conscription; four states even refused to send militias. Throughout the conflict, Congress controlled the armed forces at the president's expense by refusing increases in the size of the army and navy, micromanaging military procurement policies, and imposing specific mandates and limits on appropriations.[51] In Abraham Sofaer's estimation, "Congress [had] the upper hand [because it] controlled the extent and type of armed force at the executive's disposal."[52]

The war exacted severe economic costs and ended in stalemate in 1816. Further, British forces set fire to several northeastern states and the capitol, provoking threats of secession among New York Federalists.[53] After the war, Congress "scrambled" to get rid of 30,000 infantrymen and immediately reduced the army to 10,000 men, despite Madison's request to retain 20,000 personnel.[54] In 1817 President James Monroe confronted a Congress that viewed additional military preparedness as politically inexpedient and strategically unnecessary. Without a compelling rationale for a military establishment, Congress reduced the size of the army to its pre-1812 level and confined its duties to internal policing.

Professional Armies and Polk's "Undeclared" War

Throughout the nineteenth century, US military forces engaged in periodic battles over land against the Native Americans. These domestic conflicts led Congress to increase the size of regular peacetime armies and to appropriate funds for the "suppression of Indian hostilities." The onset of the Second Seminole War, the longest and most expensive Native American war lasting from 1835 to 1842, also coincided with the development of increasingly professional armies and gradual increases in the military budget. Two additional developments aided presidents' leverage and flexibility in the command of armed forces: First, following the War of 1812, an Ordnance Department centralized command of weapons developments and standardized the procurement system, contributing to greater contractor reliability and a more stable, uniform weapons arsenal.[55] Second, following the Second Seminole War in 1842, the legislature demobilized forces by decreasing the size of regiments rather than eliminating entire units. This strategy reflects the first deliberate attempt to maintain an expansible army.[56]

In 1846 President James Polk asserted greater willingness than his predecessors to move existing forces in a manner that precipitates war. Louis Fisher's analysis of presidential war power makes sense of this shift based on levels of available military resources: "The power of the Commander in Chief is at its low point when there is no standing army because a president cannot deploy troops until Congress raises them. But when a standing army does exist, ready to move at the president's command, the balance of power can shift decisively."[57] This shift helps explain Polk's emboldened actions in the Mexican-American War.

Texas won its independence from Mexico in 1836, spawning nearly a decade of debate concerning whether the United States ought to recognize the independence of Texas. As president, Andrew Jackson had initially declined to do so, given his fears of reprisal from Mexico and expressed deference to congressional prerogatives in matters of war.[58] However, in 1845, Congress passed a joint resolution to annex Texas from Mexico and admit it into the union. Subsequently, President Polk ordered General Zachary Taylor to move his forces—1,500 personnel—from Fort Jesup (on the Louisiana border) to a point "on or near" Rio Grande in order to repel a potential Mexican invasion. After receiving a message from the War Department detailing an attack on a US detachment, Polk drafted a message to Congress declaring that a state of war existed. Congress responded by passing a formal declaration of war, increasing the size of the army, appropriating $10 million, and authorizing the president to call 50,000 volunteers to support existing forces in Mexico for a one-year term.

The Mexican War demonstrates that, with available armies, presidents can move troops to increase the likelihood of war and alter the congressional debate over the appropriation of funds. Unlike the War of 1812, where 90 percent of infantrymen belonged to fledgling state militias, the army of 1846 consisted almost entirely of volunteer and regular forces, many of which Congress had retained after the Second Seminole War.[59] Greater numbers of active duty soldiers, standardized procurement policies, and Congress's joint resolution to annex Texas contributed to Polk's willingness and ability to move existing troops without advance congressional approval. After the war, however, Congress reduced the army to a smaller peacetime force than the 10,000 personnel authorized in 1815—an action that left forces "stretched very thin," especially given the need to police the newly acquired Texas and California regions.[60] Regular forces and militias were periodically employed against Native Americans and to quell civilian disturbances up until the Civil War.

Meanwhile, the US Navy had also become an instrument with which to rescue American citizens and protect American property abroad, and military actions against pirates, looters, and insubordinate natives regularly took place without congressional authorization.[61] However, various armed conflicts transpired without presidential authorization as well—such as the bombardment and destruction of Greytown, Nicaragua, in 1854 at the initiative of an intemperate naval captain who grew impatient waiting for an apology after a native insulted an American diplomat. Unauthorized military actions like the destruction of Greytown typically consisted of hostilities against nongovernmental groups and were so limited that they did not require any additional appropriations or even "rise to the dignity of formal congressional concern."[62]

Industrialization and Regional Expansion

In 1861, after the election of Abraham Lincoln, seven southern states seceded from the union, and a quarter of the US Army joined the Confederate forces. In response, President Lincoln issued a proclamation calling forth state militias, suspending habeas corpus, blockading southern ports, and providing unappropriated funds for the purchase of military equipment. Lincoln issued his proclamation before Congress convened in a special session. However, he pled his case to the legislature after the fact, expressing doubts about the legality of his actions and requesting formal statutory authorization. Regardless of the sincerity of Lincoln's appeal, he was at the mercy of the legislature to appropriate money and raise troops in order to carry out the civil war against Confederate forces.

To support the war effort, Congress drafted over 2 million soldiers into the Union Army and increased military spending over seventeenfold.[63] To achieve a military buildup of historic magnitude, the Civil War Congress relied on unprecedented acts of emergency prerogative, including an income tax, increased borrowing, and the printing of legal tender. Printing paper money allowed for a dramatic increase in federal borrowing, enabling the president to successfully prosecute the war against the South and facilitating a historic shift in power from the states to the federal government.[64] The ease of government borrowing allowed for new investments in domestic weapons procurement infrastructure, which supplemented weapons imported from Europe. Although federal spending unleashed a boom in the arms production industry and facilitated large profits for domestic war suppliers, military appropriations immediately ceased after the Civil War ended. One military historian directly attributes the discontinuation of the contract system to the "tightfistedness of Congress."[65] It was not until the late 1880s and 1890s, when domestic suppliers for steel and raw materials emerged, that Congress gradually began to authorize development of new naval vessels.

Congress's peacetime investment in naval resources coincided with the emergence of an industrial economy and a historically unparalleled interest in regional expansion. The United States established rights to a coaling station in Samoa and made several attempts to annex Hawaii after the native government threatened to withdraw US rights to a site for a naval station at Pearl Harbor.[66] The navy sought to secure coaling stations in the Caribbean while private firms promoted efforts to build an isthmian canal in Panama.

In 1896 the Cuban insurrection against Spanish occupiers destroyed sugar and tobacco plantations, adversely affecting US importers and exporters.[67] Public sentiment in the United States strongly favored the rebels; expansionism, business interests, and the goal of Cuban independence all contributed to overwhelming legislative support for war with Spain. Senator John Mellon Thurston captured the national interests in Cuban independence on the Senate floor in 1898, proclaiming that "war with Spain would increase the business and earnings of every American railroad, it would increase the output of every American factory, it would stimulate every branch of industry and domestic commerce."[68]

While presidents Cleveland and McKinley resisted mounting congressional pressure for war in favor of diplomatic measures, a series of events undermined these efforts toward diplomacy. The destruction of the US battleship *Maine* in the Havana harbor, the loss of 260 lives, and the administration's conclusion that Spain was responsible for the explosion eventually led President McKinley to proclaim that the right to intervene in Cuba "may be justified by the very serious injury to the commerce, trade, and business of our people and by the wanton destruction of property and devastation of the island."[69] In 1898 Congress passed a joint resolution recognizing the independence of Cuba, demanding that the Spanish government relinquish its authority and withdraw from the territory and authorizing the president to use land and naval forces to carry the resolution into effect.

Despite longstanding congressional support for war with Spain and months of negotiations preceding the outbreak, military historians conclude that the country was not adequately prepared for the conflict.[70] Many of the nation's new fleets remained untested, and the United States still lagged nearly a decade behind Europe's military technology. The extensive modernization and buildup of naval forces rapidly outpaced the dwindling and ill-equipped army, leading to a reliance on antiquated weapons systems left over from the Civil War and substantial dependence on Congress for the mobilization of a large volunteer contingent.[71] The Navy successfully fought the most decisive battles of the Spanish-American War, contributing to both US victory and to Congress's willingness to promote further naval expansion and modernization.[72]

As a result of the Spanish-American War, the Navy acquired more bases for its operations, such as Guantanamo Bay in Cuba, which allowed for more regional interventions to protect expanding investments and trade. The following year, in 1899, Congress authorized the procurement of a new, modern battleship, while many of the "emergency" ships added for the war in 1898 were returned to civilian status. By 1907, at the end of Theodore Roosevelt's administration, a decade of congressional investment in naval mobilization allowed the president to dispatch a fleet consisting of four squadrons of four battleships each for worldwide travel. The massive display of sea power, known as the Great White Fleet, demonstrated to the world that the US navy was capable of operating not only in the Pacific, but also in a global theater.

Greater US military presence in the Pacific presented new strategic and logistical problems for the War Department. Between 1900 and 1917, War Department leaders Elihu Root and Henry Stimson and military chief-of-staff Leonard Wood initiated major reorganization initiatives to meet these challenges. In 1903 the department reorganized command of the army and formed a corporate general staff to control and integrate planning. Permanent bureaucratic control over contracting created new opportunities for Congress to exert influence in military procurement processes.[73] Civilian department heads strategically shifted their activities to industrial mobilization and investment in domestic procurement infrastructure to meet the new supply needs of the army and win support from members of Congress with constituencies engaged in steel manufacturing.

In the context of these War Department transformations, heightened civilian control over contract decisions, and a historically unprecedented peacetime naval buildup, President Theodore Roosevelt issued a policy known as the "Roosevelt Corollary" to the Monroe Doctrine. The policy called for noninterference in the internal affairs of other countries, provided that a nation "keeps order and pays its obligations."[74] However, Roosevelt also warned that "flagrant cases of wrongdoing or impotence"—specifically those that provoke intervention by a European power—may ultimately require US military preemption. Roosevelt had already used the armed forces to gain control of the canal in Panama (a former province of Colombia), citing past revolutions, insurrections, and riots as evidence that Colombia was incapable of maintaining order without US interference.[75] The Senate responded by ratifying the president's treaty, and the US Treasury purchased the assets of the Panama Canal Company.

Military revitalization and regional interests emboldened early twentieth-century presidents to station forces abroad and issue limited military engagements independently. While presidents could issue minor troop deployments and carry out regional interventions that did not require large troop counts or heavy combat, they continued to rely on Congress to conduct more extensive military operations. For example, when Roosevelt sought to intervene in the Dominican Republic in 1905 to prevent further accumulation of European debt, the Senate successfully blocked the president's independent negotiations, defeated a proposed treaty, and forced a series of compromised actions. President William Howard Taft stationed small contingents in Nicaragua, Honduras, and Cuba, but he also demonstrated caution in issuing larger military operations. In 1911 Taft cited his power as commander-in-chief to position troops along the Mexican border to prepare for a timely response to an uprising, but also refused to intervene in Mexico without explicit congressional approval.[76]

Subsequently, President Woodrow Wilson sent 330 marines to Haiti in a military occupation that lasted from 1914 to 1934; he dispatched approximately 400 marines to the Dominican Republic in 1916, imposed a military government and stationed forces there until 1924; and, in 1916, he responded to the Mexican bandit Pancho Villa's violent attacks on Columbus, New Mexico, by sending 5,000 US Army personnel to the Mexican border with Senate approval, but without formal legislative authorization. However, the expedition was severely compromised by the war in Europe and lack of federal funds, and Wilson ordered the troops to withdraw the following year. As Louis Fisher points out, the prolonged interventions in Haiti and Nicaragua caused so much domestic opposition that the United States did not openly intervene in the Caribbean or Latin America until 1965, when Lyndon Johnson sent troops to the Dominican Republic.[77]

Congress continued to pursue gradual naval buildups and modest increases in troop strength up until the massive mobilization effort during World War I. Although Wilson initially pledged to keep the nation out of war, he shifted his position in 1915, after a German U-boat sunk a British ship and killed 128 Americans on board. In 1917 he asked Congress for a declaration of war, citing continued German hostilities. Although the president was the leading voice in favor of war, he relied on Congress to commit to an unparalleled defense buildup in preparation for US entrance in the global conflict.

After issuing a formal declaration of war, Congress drafted over 4 million soldiers to support the war effort and increased military appropriations more than twentyfold between 1916 and 1919. For the first time in the nation's history, private businesses took the lead in defense production, providing a windfall for industries such as DuPont (manufacturing chemicals and gunpowder) and Bethlehem Steel. The newly created War Industries

Board empowered prominent businessmen to coordinate the purchase of war supplies. However, after the war, Congress immediately dismantled the agency and reduced military spending to 6 percent of the wartime output. Despite the mobilization of private industry in a military buildup of historic magnitude, careful observers have noted that World War I military mobilization was a "confusion of half-measures" that resulted only in incremental changes in the nation's military-industrial base.[78] Given the limited scale of industrial mobilization for the war effort and few geographic constituencies affected, the military-industrial apparatus was only a temporary war expedient. Congress quickly restored a peacetime economy and limited military spending until World War II.

CONSTRAINING EXECUTIVE INDEPENDENCE

The availability of military resources shapes the extent to which presidents seek congressional cooperation for their military policies. During the debates over constitutional ratification, leading Federalist arguments revealed a common understanding that congressional control over defense resources would restrain the president's ability to exercise force independently. As many Federalists expected, earlier congresses regularly scaled back military spending after armed conflicts, which limited the president's ability to act independently in military affairs. At the same time, the need to police new territories, emergence of domestic weapons suppliers, increased federal borrowing power, and ability to print paper money coincided with incremental adjustments in military spending levels.

While the earliest US presidents sought to steer the course of military and foreign policies with as few restrictions as possible, these leaders also lacked available armies and a standardized procurement system. They demonstrated greater deference to Congress in military matters largely because they lacked the means to direct these operations independently. The political environment placed greater emphasis on diplomacy and required ongoing congressional support to conduct armed engagements.

Once Congress began to raise small armies to protect new territory during the mid-nineteenth century, President Polk seized upon his ability to move existing troops. Professional armies have historically enabled presidents to precipitate armed conflicts, rendering Congress a reactive body and altering the legislative debate over both the appropriation of additional funds and the formal authorization of war.

At the turn of the century, domestic sources of military procurement, business interests in regional expansion, increased borrowing power, and deficit spending made it easier for Congress to gradually increase defense budgets without provoking resentment from voters. In this political environment, Congress authorized an unprecedented peacetime naval buildup, passed legislation heightening civilian control over defense contracts, and worked with War Department officials to reduce reliance on European imports and invest in domestic arms production. In the early twentieth century, presidents Roosevelt, Taft, and Wilson began to make use of newly available military resources, along with weapons arsenals left over from previous wars, to direct small regional troop deployments without legislative authorization. At the same time, however, congresses consistently withdrew wartime spending following armed engagements, and presidents continued to rely on the legislature to support major military operations and commit the nation to war.

From the late eighteenth to mid-twentieth century, Congress regularly mobilized the military for war and divested war funding when the conflict was over. However, as the following chapters will argue, the World War II military mobilization transformed the underlying congressional incentives that the Constitution's framers anticipated. The geographic dispersion of defense production created new economic and political interests in continued military spending that has fundamentally altered Congress's budgetary control over the military.

WORLD WAR II AND THE POLITICS OF DEFENSE SPENDING

World War II Military Mobilization: Origins of the Rural Defense Pork Barrel

Despite periodic increases in military spending in the late nineteenth and early twentieth centuries, Congress did not maintain a large military establishment until after World War II. Although the army grew in real numbers, the ratio between the peacetime military establishment and population remained below the level of the 1790s until the onset of the Cold War. The rise of Nazi Germany and Japan's attack at Pearl Harbor led Congress to create large armies and to fund an extensive weapons arsenal. However, the geographic dispersion of defense infrastructure from large cities into lightly settled areas with underdeveloped economies also made the military apparatus particularly difficult to dismantle.

The nation's military-industrial transformation began in 1941, after President Franklin Roosevelt's Lend-Lease program authorized the transfer of US-manufactured arms and ammunition for the World War II effort. The conversion of US industrial capacity for war purposes provided the Allied powers with thousands of tanks, planes, and ground vehicles, millions of tons of raw materials, and thousands of tools for military production. By late 1943–44, US defense production rivaled the combined total of all its allies and adversaries.[1]

While US munitions production helped the Allied forces counter Nazi Germany and defeat the Axis powers, the production efforts also helped combat a decade-long US economic depression. Nearly 9 million US workers—14.6 percent of the labor force—were unemployed when France fell to Germany in 1940. Unemployment rates hovered just below 10 percent when Japan attacked Pearl Harbor in December 1941, six months after Lend-Lease began.[2] In 1944, at the height of US war production, unemployment had fallen to 1.2 percent of the labor force and US gross domestic product increased nearly 100 percent, despite the enlistment of over 16 million Americans in the armed services.[3]

Idle manpower, dormant industrial resources, and shifting business-government relations poised the nation for explosive military production.

As the Axis powers advanced through Europe and after Japan attacked Pearl Harbor, a perfect storm of economic need, political will, and a potent existential threat transformed the nation to a full-scale military economy. President Roosevelt capitalized on the willingness of Congress and the courts to go along with continued deficit spending and a series of policies that minimized the risks of capital investment for military conversion on behalf of the war effort. In carving out a greater government role in business affairs, Roosevelt not only advanced military goals but also extended the premise behind many of his New Deal programs, which were designed to lift the nation out of a major economic depression. As a result, the military industry grew out of ongoing partnerships between public and private actors, including heavily subsidized defense infrastructure and procurement policies that cater to the profitability and staying power of major military corporations.

The origins of the defense sector are rooted in the geography of World War II military mobilization and the transformation to a full-scale war economy. Defense-sector development followed a "path dependent" process, meaning that temporary wartime decisions became self-reinforcing and the costs of changing course increased over time.[4] Initial centers of economic activity often serve as a magnet for future industry locations, and the geography of production becomes self-perpetuating.[5] Just as high-tech industries flock to Silicon Valley and financial firms invest heavily in Wall Street real estate, defense industry managers prioritize physical proximity to existing infrastructure in order to draw on available resources, limit start-up costs, and achieve economies of scale.[6] Unlike standard markets, however, political factors also structure and reinforce defense-sector geography. As this chapter will show, government actors heavily subsidized the extension of military-industrial capacity from large coastal cities to geographically remote locations during World War II. In doing so, they inadvertently unleashed new economic and political interests that made these temporary war expedients particularly difficult to reverse.

At the earliest stages of the war, military production took place almost exclusively in large coastal cities with preexisting aircraft capacity. At the peak of wartime output, however, new defense facilities spread out across the national landscape into many lightly settled areas with less developed economies. The extension of war production occurred in three stages: First, aircraft industries expanded their production from large cities to small towns and communities near the home plant to help meet the government's ambitious procurement demands. Second, aircraft industry managers and federal agencies licensed automobile companies in the Midwest to manufacture parts and supplies. Finally, executive agencies leased government-owned facilities to private companies in southern and inland locations.

The geographic extension of defense activity to rural and suburban areas outside of central cities fueled defense employment, contributed to population shifts, and laid the foundation for excessive economic vulnerabilities that surfaced after the war. Although no one deliberately set out create widespread economic dependence on war investments, this became an unintended consequence of a national mobilization strategy where multiple actors pursued their own independent goals. Private industries took advantage of cheap land in suburbs and towns near the home plant to meet spatial requirements and increase output in light of enormous government demand. Executive agencies and military personnel prioritized industry dispersion and secrecy and capitalized on untapped labor in formerly agrarian regions that lacked industrial economies. The military mobilization that resulted met immediate war production goals, but inadvertently gave rise to the rural defense pork barrel that emerged after the war.

The development of rural defense infrastructure coincided with shifting government-industry relations and new defense procurement policies that promote unparalleled industry stability. Nearly all of the largest military corporations in the 1940s and 1950s continue to rank as leading defense firms in the 1990s and 2000s, despite changing geopolitical realities and shifting procurement needs. Congress helps keep defense industries in business by retaining procurement policies established during the war, which cater to industry profits at the expense of competition and cost control. Negotiated bids, guaranteed earnings on investments, subsidized mergers, and market concentration contribute to stability in defense production, employment, and revenue. These arrangements help prevent plant closures and widespread layoffs where defense industries might otherwise shut down during periods of excess capacity.

ORIGINS OF THE RURAL DEFENSE PORK BARREL

While the United States entered World War I with almost full employment, World War II coincided with a sluggish domestic economy, an unemployment rate of 15 percent and latent industrial capacity. As a result, dormant resources and idle manpower could be redirected to wartime purposes with minimal disruption to peacetime life. Historian David M. Kennedy has commented at length on the influence the economic depression had on the scale and scope of US military production during World War II. In Kennedy's assessment, not only did the war stimulate economic growth and lift the nation from a major economic depression, but these dismal economic conditions also allowed for total military mobilization on behalf of the war effort.[7]

Despite a down economy, industries were initially reluctant to make a total conversion to military production. Businesses viewed arms production as unprofitable given the historical lack of stability and continuity in defense production during peacetime.[8] To forge a partnership with the business community, the Roosevelt administration adopted a series of policies that minimized the risks of capital investments for businesses that converted to military production. First, a newly established Defense Plant Corporation (DPC) gave money to firms to build new facilities and purchase equipment. Private operators also leased plants from the government, which retained the ownership title during the war but eventually sold most of its facilities at a loss. Second, Congress and the administration agreed to reimburse whatever a company spent and guarantee an added profit for arms production—a "cost-plus" incentive to business that has remained a ubiquitous feature of military procurement and research and development. Finally, war spending rose thirty-five-fold from 1940 to 1945. The proliferation of available funds not only assisted the war effort, but also provided a stimulus to business, employment levels, and national productive capacity.

Unlike textbook capitalist economies—where risk and financing are assumed by the entrepreneurial actor in hopes of profitable returns—economic risks shifted from business to the government. As two scholars put it, government investments, subsidies, and guaranteed profit margins allowed companies to "function in a world of socialized risks and private profit."[9] However, unlike standard command economies, the US government never needed to co-opt business for the war effort. Rather, increased spending, subsidized wages, and guaranteed cost-plus earnings ensured relatively low-risk profits flowing to major defense industries. These policies, in turn, helped meet President's Roosevelt's ambitious military procurement goals. Given this coincidence of interests, it is little surprise that World War II military contracting quickly "became a hunting license" as firms engaged in a "cutthroat scramble for scarce resources."[10] Airframe and engine manufacturing in the United States increased 4000 percent between 1940 and 1945, and the government directly financed 90 percent of the total output.[11]

To examine the geographic origins of the nation's military-industrial base, I compiled information on the primary locations that engaged in war production in 1940, 1944, and 1950 (located in appendixes 3.1–3.3).[12] Given various data limitations, the database only consists of industries engaged in military aviation, as opposed to other types of defense production. However, aviation was so central to the war buildup that it is widely considered "the foundation of the military-industrial complex."[13] In May 1940 President Roosevelt announced an unprecedented request for 50,000 planes a year for the war effort.[14] This ambitious procurement goal called for greater annual production rates than the aircraft industry had produced in its entire history.[15] While the president's request immediately required large-scale expansion and rapid production, the characteristics of the aircraft industry limited the geography of military assembly at the earliest stages of the war. However, at the peak of war production in 1944, decisions by industry managers and executive agencies fueled an expansion of defense activity to areas without previous military-industrial capacity. These actors' wartime preferences continued to shape the nation's military-industrial map in 1950, despite many postwar plant closures.

In 1940 government defense investments reflected a pronounced coastal bias, favoring major metropolitan areas with existing aircraft capacity. Aircraft facilities clustered around a few major industries, including Lockheed Aircraft, Douglas Aircraft, and Northrop Aircraft in Los Angeles, California; Boeing in Seattle, Washington; United Aircraft in Hartford, Connecticut; Curtiss-Wright in Paterson, New Jersey; Grumman in Long Island City, New York; and Curtiss-Wright in Buffalo, New York. While several of the nation's interior regions—Kansas City, Kansas; Wichita, Kansas; Robertson, Missouri; and Cincinnati, Ohio—contained industry subsidiaries and light airplane companies, the major coastal metropolises still received over 96 percent of military procurement dollars in 1940.[16] Prior to the wartime expansion, large coastal cities held a near-monopoly on military aircraft contracts.

By 1944 the geography of military production changed dramatically. While the five largest aircraft companies averaged 3,500 employees each prior to 1940, average aircraft industry employment ballooned to more than 100,000 workers per company within four years.[17] Further, existing industries did not rely solely on in-house expansion. By 1944 every region, two-thirds of states, most of the nation's larger cities, and many suburbs and towns were involved in military production. At the same time, domestic unemployment plummeted to 1.2 percent, while GDP increased nearly one-hundred-fold.[18]

The expansion of military production took several forms: Most commonly, existing aircraft industries extended their operations by establishing new facilities in neighboring locations. These industries also licensed (nonmilitary) manufacturing companies to supply parts and assist in national defense production. In addition, new federal agencies created to assist with war mobilization underwrote the construction of new facilities, primarily in interior regions of the country that lacked diverse industrial economies. Despite their distinct geographic calculus, both private-sector and government actors established military industrial capacity in small cities, suburbs, and towns across the nation.

In the private sector, major aircraft companies typically favored increasing the utilization of existing plant space. Where space limitations precluded expansion, companies extended capacity by acquiring new sites in adjacent vicinities. In 1944 branch plants had spread into the outskirts of large cities, occupying suburbs, towns, and small communities surrounding Los Angeles, Seattle, Hartford, Long Island City, and Buffalo. These new plants were typically located far enough away from cities to meet large space requirements, yet remained within the metropolitan district and sufficiently near the original site to benefit from its supply channels and other facilities.

For example, in Los Angeles, Douglas Aircraft Company acquired a site on the Long Beach Municipal Airport and constructed a large assembly plant. Lockheed Aircraft acquired hundreds of facilities in the Los Angeles area scattered across small towns from Maywood to Van Nuys. Boeing Aircraft Company selected sites in Renton, Everett, Bellingham, and Aberdeen, several miles from the home plant in Seattle. United Aircraft Company extended production to Southington and Willimantic, near central operations in Hartford. Grumman Aircraft Company made use of existing space, cheap rental units, and available labor in small communities surrounding Long Island City, including Bethpage, Babylon, Lindenhurst, and Port Washington. Bell Aircraft Corporation not only leased additional space in Buffalo, but also completed an assembly plant at Niagara Falls Airport in Wheatland, while Curtiss-Wright also extended its productive capacity to Buffalo Municipal Airport.

However, in spite of the expansion in home and branch plants, the administration's ambitious production goals still surpassed industry capacity. To increase war output even more, defense industries licensed automobile companies to manufacture airframes, engines, and propellers. Unlike aircraft companies, the auto industry was familiar with mass-production techniques and faced a period of reduced output. Accordingly, business executives, the administration, and Congress called upon the nation's major manufacturing industries to produce military supplies.

Auto conversion occurred primarily in traditional Midwestern manufacturing hubs surrounding the Great Lakes region. Indianapolis (Chevrolet, General Motors), Chicago (Buick, Dodge), Detroit (Continental Motors,

Packard Motor), Cleveland (Ford Motor), and Milwaukee (Nash-Kelvinator) all converted their facilities for subassemblies, glider production, engine production, and light-transport units. Like the aircraft sector, demand for output led the auto industry to spread its operations into smaller towns and communities adjacent to cities with large defense plants.

The available historical records suggest that, from 1940 to 1944, industries that had converted their facilities for defense production generally opted to expand their operations in geographically proximate areas. The geography of military production extended from major cities in predominantly coastal areas to manufacturing centers throughout the Midwest and small towns on the outskirts of original plant sites. However, the complete decentralization of military output across every region and a vast majority of states was not simply a result of increased demand or private-sector decisions. Rather, the federal government also played an unprecedented role in restructuring industry locations and dispersing the nation's military output. The Plant Site Board—an executive agency established to determine the locations of new defense sites—bought and leased facilities in interior locations of the country and funded the transfer of material and production away from predominant coastal areas.

Prior to World War II, government was not positioned to play an active role in the selection of new production sites. However, as the principal source of funds for the construction of new facilities and as the major market for the industry's output, executive officials enjoyed considerable latitude over new industry locations.[19] The National Resources Planning Board even acknowledged the federal government's commanding role in decentralizing military-industrial capacity to regions "characterized by severe unemployment" and in "predominantly agricultural areas," while emphasizing that military goals remained the most pressing factor governing procurement decisions.[20]

Government-owned, company-operated facilities are military production sites selected by federal agencies under the advisement of the Army and Navy departments, as opposed to locations favored by the private sector.[21] Under the direction of military leaders, the Plant Site Board and DPC bought and leased facilities to businesses throughout interior and southern regions, often at a guaranteed profit. By eliminating overhead costs and subsidizing the geographic diffusion of industry, DPC transferred companies' military production to Fort Crook, Nebraska (Martin), Kansas City, Kansas (North American), Oklahoma City (Douglas), Tulsa (Douglas), Chicago (Douglas), Indianapolis (Curtiss-Wright), Dallas (North American), Fort Worth, Texas (Consolidated), Grand Prairie, Texas (North American),

Louisville, Kentucky (Consolidated, Curtiss-Wright), and Marietta, Georgia (Bell Aircraft). Further, modification centers—joint business-government ventures—extended to new locations, such as Daggett, California (Douglas), Phoenix (Goodyear), Tucson (Consolidated), and Dallas (Lockheed), and Elizabeth City, North Carolina (Consolidated).

A Defense Zone, defined by the War College as the area enclosed by a line 200 miles inland from the coasts and the Canadian and Mexican borders, reinforced the government's interest in interior locations. In direct compliance with Defense Zone requirements, new production centers emerged in Omaha, Nebraska (Martin), Kansas City, Kansas (North American), Wichita, Kansas (Cessna Aircraft), Kansas City, Missouri (United Aircraft), Evansville, Indiana (Republic Aviation), Memphis, Tennessee (McDonnell), Nashville, Tennessee (Stinson Aircraft), Lockland, Ohio (Curtiss-Wright), and Beaver, Pennsylvania (Curtiss-Wright). Given these trends, it is no surprise that states with the largest percent of private funding were overwhelmingly coastal areas, while the mobilization of inland locations was almost entirely government funded.[22]

There are many legitimate reasons why the administration and the armed services sought to disperse military production in wartime. Most important, military demands for security place a premium on more remote locations in the center of the country, away from coastal areas that are more susceptible to external attack. In addition, interior locations also offer cheaper land, access to airfields, and untapped labor supplies. As a result, the dispersion of industry extended economic activity and employment opportunities to regions and localities that may not otherwise have established defense infrastructure or received an economic stimulus from the flow of federal defense dollars.

As the war effort drew more heavily on the nation's population, the availability of labor became a major consideration in the selection of new locations, even overshadowing preferences for inland locations. The federal government invested in areas less than the prescribed 200-mile distance from the coast, including Allentown, Pennsylvania (Consolidated), Burlington, North Carolina (Fairchild), Birmingham, Alabama, and New Orleans (Consolidated). These government decisions amplified industries' expansion into small cities and towns, and even very small communities, with cheap land, available floor space, and high unemployment.

Unprecedented defense industry expansion coincided with new residential patterns that persisted after the war. Table 3.1 exhibits the metropolitan areas and surrounding locations with major defense production sites during World War II, the population of each census-designated area in 1940 and

Table 3.1. *Population change in cities and towns with major war industries, 1940–1950*

	Population		
	1940	1950	Percentage change
Los Angeles, CA	1,504,277	1,970,358	31.0
Outskirts (average)	30,423	48,968	60.7
Outskirts (excluding towns with plant closure)	29,311	55,057	87.8
Seattle, WA	368,302	467,591	27.0
Outskirts (average)	29,710	37,727	27.0
Outskirts (excluding towns with plant closure)	4,488	16,039	257.4
New York City, NY	7,454,995	7,891,957	5.9
Outskirts (average)	116,355	139,648	20.0
Outskirts (excluding towns with plant closure)	13,652	19,401	42.1
Buffalo, NY	575,901	580,132	0.7
Outskirts (average)[a]	44,558	49,614	11.3
Binghamton, NY	78,309	80,674	3.0
Outskirts (average)[a]	31,568	34,483	9.2
Hartford, CT	166,267	177,397	6.7
Outskirts (average)[a]	21,207	32,025	51.0
New London, CT	30,456	30,551	0.3
Outskirts (average)[a]	23,652	23,429	−0.9
Philadelphia, PA	1,931,334	2,071,605	7.3
Outskirts (average)[a]	1,977	7,127	260.5
Chicago, IL	3,396,808	3,620,962	6.6
Outskirts (average)[a]	17,355	20,551	18.4
Detroit, MI	1,623,452	1,849,568	13.9
Outskirts (average)	26,643	40,902	53.5
Outskirts (excluding towns with plant closure)	37,853	56,648	49.7
Cincinnati, OH	455,610	503,998	10.6
Outskirts (average)[a]	26,366	30,200	14.5
Cleveland, OH	878,336	914,808	4.2
Outskirts (average)[a]	1,108	6,317	470.1
Dallas, TX	294,735	434,462	47.4

(continued)

Table 3.1. *continued*

| | Population | | |
	1940	1950	Percentage change
Fort Worth, TX	177,622	278,778	56.9
Outskirts (average)[a]	1,595	14,594	815.0
Phoenix, AZ	65,414	106,818	63.3

Note: Information drawn from appendices 3.1–3.4. Primary sources include Cunningham 1951; National Resources Planning Board, *Industrial Location and National Resources* (Washington, DC: Government Printing Office, 1941); 1947 Census of Manufacturers, prepared by Bureau of Census (Washington, DC: US Government Printing Office, 1952); Location of manufacturing plants by industry, county, and employment size: 1954, prepared by the Bureau of Census and the Office of Area Development (Washington, DC: US Department of Commerce, 1959). *Census of Population:1950*, vol. 1, *Number of Inhabitants: United States Summary*, Table 24, Prepared by the US Bureau of Census. (Washington, DC: US Government Printing Office, 1952, pp. 48–65), accessed at: http://www2.census.gov/prod2/decennial/documents/23761117v1ch03.pdf.
[a]No major plant closures reported.

1950, and the percent population change after the war. For ease of presentation, the table displays the average population change for all of the suburbs, towns, and communities engaged in defense activity within each separate metropolitan region. (Detailed information listing the population trends for each census-designated area with defense infrastructure is located in appendix 3.4.) Since postwar plant closures should dampen shifts in residential patterns, the table reports both the average population change and average change excluding locations that dismantled their defense facilities after the war.

The table illustrates the disproportionate population growth that occurred in suburbs, towns, and southern cities that received defense investments, as opposed to large, industrialized cities where the bulk of defense activity took place. Los Angeles was arguably the heart of World War II defense production, with hundreds of defense facilities spread throughout the metropolitan landscape. While the metropolitan area population grew 31 percent between 1940 and 1950, the smaller cities and towns within the metro region that engaged in World War II defense production experienced far greater expansion (61% growth on average, 88% average growth in areas without plant closures). The rapid development of two Lockheed Aircraft facilities in Burbank corresponds with 129 percent population growth, while Douglas Aircraft expansion in El Segundo is associated with a 114 percent population increase (see appendix 3.4). Downey's (Vultee, North American) population grew 138 percent, while Hawthorne (Northrop) expanded almost 100 percent. Other areas without previous defense infrastructure—including Fresno, Van Nuys, and Santa Ana—expanded by roughly 50 percent after Lockheed established defense plants in these areas.

In nearly every metropolitan area, the small cities and towns with wartime industries in 1944—and continued military capacity in 1950—experienced explosive population growth. Central cities with previous infrastructure exhibit far more modest changes. While New York City's population grew by almost 6 percent, smaller outskirts such as Lindenhurst, New York, and Fairlawn, New Jersey, attracted new residents at disproportionately greater rates (20% growth on average, 42% growth in areas without plant closures). In fact, even more remote midwestern locations such as Wayne, Michigan (123% population growth) and Brooklyn, Ohio (470% population growth) far exceeded residential expansions in central auto manufacturing cities, like Detroit (14% population growth) and Cleveland (4% population growth).

Population growth in suburbs and towns with defense infrastructure also outpaced broader residential patterns in places of comparable size. From 1940 to 1950, population growth in suburban areas expanded by 23.9 percent over the previous decade, on average.[23] In-migration to suburbs (fueled by the growth of the automobile industry) coincided with 22.9 percent growth in central cities (relative to the previous decade) and population declines in nonmetropolitan areas.[24] On one hand, most cities with extensive defense infrastructure experienced less pronounced growth than the national average, suggesting that population flows to central cities occurred independently of defense production. On the other hand, as table 3.1 exhibits, suburban locations *with defense infrastructure* rapidly outpaced average levels of suburban growth from 1940 to 1950. The trend is most consistent in areas that retained defense plants in 1950, including suburbs of Los Angeles, Seattle, New York, Hartford, Detroit, Philadelphia, Cleveland, and Dallas.

The only evidence of population decline in a war industry location occurred when defense facilities shut down after the war. For example, Paterson, New Jersey, failed to expand after the devastating closure of a major Wright Aeronautical plant following World War II (–0.2% population change). Norwich, Connecticut, may have also experienced out-migration after Hamilton Standard Propellers shut down (–0.9% population change). The discontinuation of wartime facilities typically corresponds with more stagnant population distributions from 1940 to 1950. More lightly settled areas that attracted new Boeing facilities outside of Seattle, Washington—including Aberdeen,

Bellingham, Hoquiam, Everett, Chehalis, and Tacoma—each experienced considerably less pronounced growth in 1950 than the central city of Seattle (27% population growth). However, nearly all of Boeing's branch plants shut down in the postwar era, catalyzing the (temporary) retrenchment of industrial capacity and employment in these regions. The only Boeing branch plant that did not close in the period immediately following World War II is the facility in Renton, several miles from the home plant in Seattle. Unlike surrounding regions that faced dormant capacity in the postwar era, Renton enjoyed continual utilization of its Boeing plant and expanded its resident base by 257 percent in 1950.

Finally, direct military investments in southern and southwestern cities that lacked defense infrastructure prior to World War II experienced appreciable expansion. The populations in Phoenix (63% population growth), Dallas (47% population growth), and Fort Worth (57% population growth) grew at faster rates than other cities of comparable size, such as Hartford (6.7%), Buffalo (0.7%), and Seattle (27%). While cities throughout the South and Southwest generally experienced population growth after World War II, prompted largely by the development of air conditioning, the average southern cities grew approximately 36 percent between 1940 and 1950.[25] By contrast, southern cities with major defense installations—Phoenix (63% growth), Dallas (47% growth), and Fort Worth (57% growth)— grew at faster rates than the average for the region. Still, none of these cities grew as rapidly as the small town of Grand Prairie, Texas (815% population growth), where the federal government bought and leased a major bomber assembly plant during the war.

The table shows that small towns and communities engaged in war production consistently experienced disproportionate local development, which was often built around a single industry. By contrast, large cities where most defense production took place were more robust to structural changes in the defense economy. While war industry managers typically retained their principal locations after World War II and closed smaller facilities in more peripheral locations, they also reopened numerous branch plants at the onset of the Korean War in 1950. At the same time, government bureaus sponsored the reutilization of facilities in interior locations that the private sector had abandoned. Continued government ownership of plants throughout interior and southern regions reflects persistent national security interests in the dispersion of military-industrial capacity and access to airfields in geographically remote locations. These decisions also reinforced economic and political interests in the nation's defense investments.

Prior to World War II, the bulk of arms production took place in government arsenals and shipyards. Military officials advertised bids for products from the private sector, and the military purchaser awarded the contract to the lowest bidder. By one estimate, 87 percent of defense contracts followed these competitive regulations in early 1940, just prior to US defense buildup.[26] In September 1940 Congress passed new procedures for defense contractors that continue to govern military procurement processes, including guaranteed cost-plus profits, tax breaks, advance and progress payments, negotiated contracts (as opposed to full and open competition), and government financing of plants and equipment. These incentives encourage industries to continue producing weapons as quickly as possible, regardless of expense.

Breaking a 150-year tradition, the United States did not fully demobilize its armed forces after World War II. Despite the considerable retrenchment in 1945, the United States maintained a military establishment of immense proportions by any historical standard. As a result, in 1950, President Truman was able to call upon US forces stationed overseas, use existing military technologies, and engage troops in Korea without consulting Congress or seeking a declaration of war. The United States' entrance in the Korean War and the nation's broader struggle against the Soviet empire facilitated massive military rearmament and a culture of peacetime military spending, creating tremendous demand for munitions from private defense industries.

As a result of arrangements established during World War II, the US military industry consists of close relations between a few major sellers and a sole government buyer. Unlike traditional free markets, these unique buyer-seller relationships are governed by procedures that limit private risk and curb market competition.[27] However, unlike standard monopsonies—where multiple sellers deliver to a single buyer—the sole government purchaser does not seek to maximize its profits by squeezing the seller. Rather, given an appropriations process subject only to political limits, government actors are primarily concerned with quality and performance and uniquely insensitive to cost.[28] Critics and commentators have railed against the waste and excess that flow from cost-plus arrangements, where contractors are reimbursed for program expenses and typically lack incentives to cut costs.[29] However, government willingness to cover potential cost overruns and provide financial incentives to industries may be an inherent feature of the defense market. Extensive use of cost-plus arrangements encourages bids for high-risk endeavors favored by Congress and defense bureaucracies, including research and development and procurement of complicated weapon systems with unpredictable cost margins.

In addition to procurement policies that bolster industry profits, most defense contracts are determined on the basis of political and administrative criteria other than open competition among two or more defense companies. Sole-source awards, follow-on contracts, and "negotiated" bids determine the bulk of defense allocations, while only about 34 percent of defense dollars are allocated based on full and open price competition.[30] The prevalent use of negotiated contracting arrangements and high costs to market entry (limiting the number of viable competitors) have contributed to the continued financial success of major defense firms, despite periods of overcapacity and changing procurement needs.

Table 3.2 lists the leading defense firms in each decade from 1940 to 2006 based on the dollar volume of prime contract awards.[31] As the table illustrates, nearly all of the leading military corporations in the 1940s and 1950s rank among the top fifteen defense contractors in the 1990s and 2000s (excluding companies with a principal civilian function, such as energy or automobiles). The table also documents the extent to which these companies retained their prominence through mergers and acquisitions. Lockheed Aircraft, Martin Corporation, Douglas Aircraft, and Grumman underwent strategic mergers, forming Lockheed Martin, McDonnell Douglas, and Northrop Grumman, respectively. United Aircraft became United Technologies in the 1970s and retained its principal World War II production units, including Sikorsky Aircraft, Hamilton Propellers, and Pratt and Whitney. McDonnell Douglas, Lockheed, and General Dynamics acquired Consolidated-Vultee's major business units, while General Dynamics purchased the defense divisions formerly held by leading auto companies like General Motors and Chrysler. Boeing Aircraft acquired North American and Rockwell products in 1996, merged with McDonnell Douglas the following year (under the name The Boeing Company) and retained prominence as the number 2 aerospace firm, ranked behind only Lockheed Martin. The one major exception to the pattern of industry stability is the decline of the Curtiss-Wright Corporation in the 1960s, which Eugene Gholz attributes to antagonistic relations between the firm and the Defense Department bureaucracy.[32]

At the same time, several new firms have emerged as leading military contractors. Raytheon, Honeywell, and TRW gained prominence for specialization in missile production during the 1980s and 1990s. In the late 1990s and 2000s, the Department of Defense began to draw heavily upon companies with expertise in information technology, including Science

Table 3.2. *Leading defense corporations, 1944–2006 (by decade)*

Rank	World War II (1940–44)	Mergers/acquisitions/function
1	General Motors	Civilian function (auto)
2	Curtiss-Wright	Lost prominence in aerospace, specialized as supplier
3	Ford Motor Co.	Civilian function (auto)
4	Consolidated-Vultee	Absorbed by General Dynamics, McDonnell Douglas and Lockheed
5	Douglas	Merged with McDonnell
6	United Aircraft	Became United Technologies
7	Bethlehem Steel	Civilian function (steel, shipbuilding, mining)
8	Chrysler	Civilian function (auto)
9	General Electric	Civilian function (energy)
10	Lockheed	Merged with Martin Marietta
11	North American	Absorbed by Boeing
12	Boeing	Merged with McDonnell Douglas, absorbed Rockwell and North American
13	AT&T	Civilian function (telecommunications)
14	Martin	Merged with American Marietta, Lockheed
15	Dupont	Civilian function (chemicals)

Rank	Korean War (1951–53)	Mergers/acquisitions/function
1	General Motors	
2	Boeing	
3	General Electric	Civilian function (energy)
4	Douglas	
5	United Aircraft	
6	Chrysler	
7	Lockheed	
8	Consolidated-Vultee	
9	North American	
10	Republic Aviation	Absorbed by Fairchild
11	Curtiss-Wright	
12	Ford	
13	AT&T	

(*continued*)

Table 3.2. *continued*

Rank	Korean War (1951–53)	Mergers/acquisitions/function
14	Westinghouse	Civilian function (electricity)
15	Grumman	Merged with Northrop

Rank	1960	Mergers/acquisitions/function
1	General Dynamics	Absorbed Chrysler and General Motors defense divisions
2	Lockheed	
3	Boeing	
4	McDonnell	Merged with Douglas
5	North American	
6	Martin	
7	United Aircraft	
8	AT&T	
9	RCA	Absorbed by GE
10	Douglas	Merged with McDonnell
11	Hughes	Merged with General Motors
12	Raytheon	Missiles
13	Sperry-Rand	Civilian function (electronics); absorbed by Northrop Grumman
14	IBM	Civilian function (telecommunications)
15	Republic Aviation	

Rank	1976	Mergers/acquisitions/function
1	Lockheed	
2	North American-Rockwell	Absorbed by Boeing
3	General Dynamics	
4	General Electric	
5	McDonnell Douglas	Merged with Boeing
6	Grumman	
7	AT&T	
8	United Aircraft	
9	Boeing	
10	Litton	Absorbed by Northrop Grumman
11	LTV	Absorbed by Lockheed Martin

Table 3.2. *continued*

Rank	1976	Mergers/acquisitions/function
12	Hughes	
13	Sperry-Rand	
14	Textron	Absorbed by Bell Helicopter, Cessna Aircraft, Lycoming Engines
15	Westinghouse	

Rank	1987	Mergers/acquisitions/function
1	McDonnell-Douglas	
2	General Dynamics	
3	Lockheed	
4	General Electric	
5	General Motors–Hughes	Merged with Raytheon
6	Martin Marietta	
7	United Technologies	Retained Sikorsky Aircraft, Hamilton Propellers, Pratt & Whitney
8	Raytheon	
9	Rockwell	Absorbed by Boeing
10	Boeing	
11	Grumman	
12	Unisys	Information technology
13	Tenneco	Civilian function (auto parts)
14	Litton	
15	Honeywell	Consumer products, engineering, aerospace

Rank	1996	Mergers/acquisitions/function
1	Lockheed Martin	Absorbed LTV
2	McDonnell Douglas	
3	General Motors	
4	Raytheon	
5	General Dynamics	
6	Northrop Grumman	Absorbed Litton, Sperry-Rand
7	United Technologies	

(*continued*)

Table 3.2. *(continued)*

Rank	1996	Mergers/acquisitions/function
8	Boeing/ Boeing North America	Acquisition
9	Litton	
10	General Electric	
11	Westinghouse	
12	Textron	
13	SAIC	Information technology
14	United Defense	Merger of FMC and Harsco, absorbed by BAE
15	TRW	Missiles

Rank	2006	Mergers/acquisitions/function
1	Lockheed Martin	
2	Boeing	
3	Northrop Grumman	
4	General Dynamics	
5	Raytheon	
6	Halliburton	Oil and gas
7	L-3 Communications	Information technology
8	BAE Systems	Absorbed United Defense
9	United Technologies	
10	SAIC	
11	Computer Sciences	Information technology
12	Humana	Health care
13	ITT	High-tech engineering and manufacturing
14	General Electric	
15	Honeywell	

Sources: US Department of Defense, Statistical Information and Analysis Division, Procurement Reports and Data Files for Download: Historical Data and Reports (various years); Burnett and Scherer 1990, 293.

Note: The corporations are ranked by volume of prime contract dollars.

Applications International Corporation (SAIC), L-3 Communications, and Computer Sciences.

The level of market concentration suggests that subsidized industry restructuring keeps major companies profitable by limiting market competition. Federally subsidized mergers and acquisitions make it easier for existing companies to corner their markets, limit the number of viable competitors, and avoid lowering prices or going out of business. Consequently, several problems have emerged: Eugene Gholz and Harvey Sapolsky argue that a stream of defense industry mergers in the 1990s exacerbated excess capacity, which contributed to inefficient production methods and excessive government spending.[33] Jacques Gansler suggests that defense industry stability in the post-Vietnam period (when the defense sector faced declining procurement budgets) contributed to chronic underutilization of resources, financial and labor problems, billions of dollars in pending procurement claims, a dearth of available suppliers, and US dependence on foreign military sales.[34] However, these inefficiencies may be inherent features of a market where the sole government purchaser prioritizes defense-sector stability at the expense of competition and cost control.

CONCLUSION: THE AMERICAN WARFARE ECONOMY

During World War II, 16 million Americans fought overseas, while millions more supported higher taxes, rationing, price controls, and unprecedented government intervention in the economic sphere. Greater government willingness to experiment with Keynesian techniques, including increased deficit spending, government assumption of economic risk, and measures to stimulate private profits, also helped meet President Roosevelt's ambitious defense production goals.

As a result of the military-industrial mobilization, new defense facilities spread out to many rural and semirural areas outside of large cities. The proliferation of small towns and communities built around war-related industries was not the result of deliberate planning. Rather, the emergence of the rural defense economy was a historical idiosyncrasy catalyzed by an unprecedented military mobilization in which various actors pursued their own goals. Given enormous government demand for defense output and cost-plus incentives, aircraft industries expanded their productive capacity to suburbs, towns, and communities near cities with existing defense infrastructure. Government interests in industry dispersion, military secrecy, and available manpower also led the DPC to establish new defense infrastructure throughout more remote interior and southern locations. Both industry and federal actors prioritized space requirements, access to airfields, and proximity to military bases. The war mobilization laid the foundation for defense infrastructure in areas that lacked diversified economies, and precipitated population flows to emergent military-industrial communities. Meanwhile, guaranteed earnings, subsidized industry mergers, and acquisitions helped companies remain profitable and avoid closures throughout the following decades, regardless of periods of reduced output.

The conventional wisdom suggests that overlapping interests among military corporations, Pentagon bureaucracies, and members of congressional defense committees create an impenetrable "iron triangle" where the actors in charge of defense spending are poised to rig the system to their own advantage. This familiar story suggests that the elites charged with policymaking reap substantial benefits from defense spending at the expense of the average American taxpayer who ends up footing the bill. However, this view of a duped public levied with excessive tax burdens eclipses the systematic extension of defense dollars across regions, states, and localities; the outsized economic and political importance of these distributions in more industrially homogenous communities; and the reduced the costs of military spending and war among the general public. Chapter 4 examines these trends in detail.

From Shared Sacrifice to Local Subsidy: Dispersing Defense Benefits and Externalizing War Costs

When World War II ended, the nation emerged with a full-scale war economy. The financial sector was invested in providing war funding, the industrial sector was producing weapons and military equipment, and large percentages of the workforce were either employed in defense industries or in the armed forces. Even if the Truman administration and Congress had made dismantling the military economy a top priority, it would have taken years to complete the conversion. Instead, unlike earlier wars, the scale, scope, and expansive geography of the military mobilization transformed political incentives surrounding US defense production. Members of Congress perceived more benefits in perpetuating defense spending than in reducing costs by demobilizing as had occurred after previous wars.

While mutually dependent relations among defense corporations and political actors help facilitate industry profits and meet an expansive government demand for munitions, key structural features of the military economy also cater to local and national majorities. First, in nearly every decade since World War II, defense dollars have extended to increasing numbers of beneficiaries across regions, states, and communities. As upcoming chapters discuss at length, many of these areas also grow to depend on defense dollars in order to sustain their local economies. Second, the extension of defense revenue and employment opportunities coincided with policies that limit the public sacrifices necessary to maintain a military economy and exercise force abroad. As a consequence, constituencies incur increasing benefits from ongoing defense spending at diminished perceptions of public expense.

Just as World War II defense investments expanded to suburbs, towns, and interior and southern regions, small increments of defense dollars have spread out in almost every decade from Eisenhower's presidency to the George W. Bush administration—even though the bulk of defense dollars remain geographically concentrated around major defense-production sites. Given the nation's uneven economic development, these funds have varying levels of impact and importance across distinct local economies. To account for this variability, a new theory and measurement tool is employed to capture heightened economic reliance in areas where the defense sector accounts for a larger proportion of the overall local economy.

The analysis illustrates the flow of defense funds from major metropolitan locations along the Northeast, Midwest, and Pacific coast to cities and towns throughout the Deep South and Sunbelt regions that capitalized on defense production as an economic-development tool. Even after the fall of the Soviet Union, the scope of military allocations expanded well beyond 1970s levels, despite modest reductions in weapons spending and the reduced-threat environment of the 1990s. Following the attacks of September 11, 2001, the US "war on terrorism" precipitated an additional defense-contracting expansion and military profits extended into more and more sparsely populated areas including the Desert, Mountain, and Plains regions.

The geographic expansion of benefits flowing from defense contracting coincided with policies that systematically reduce the public costs of warfare to the broad public. The all-volunteer force and use of private military and security contractors contribute to substantially lower US troop counts and fewer American military casualties. These policies reduce public opposition to the exercise of force abroad—at least until US troop casualties mount, victory appears less likely, and public support for ongoing military engagements erodes.[1] At the same time, increased deficit spending pushes financial costs onto future generations and obviates the traditional need to tax current populations in order to fund major wars. Finally, new military technologies allow policymakers to use force with reduced risk to American lives, instead imposing potential harm to civilians, economic losses, damage to infrastructure, and disruption of peacetime life on foreign nations where US wars take place.

To be clear, the analysis does not suggest that the economic benefits of defense spending and reduced costs of war for most Americans have directly caused defense budgets to escalate or fueled more belligerent foreign policy decisions. Rather, the broad expansion of defense benefits and shifting of war costs are critical preconditions for heightened presidential authority over a permanent military establishment. This political environment makes it easier for congresses and administrations to push for greater levels of defense spending and exercise force abroad without fear of electoral reprisal.

MEASURING DISPROPORTIONATE DEFENSE DEPENDENCE

To examine geographic patterns of defense spending following World War II, I compiled a database with information on decennial defense contract distributions throughout US cities and towns from 1966 to 2006.[2] I extracted the contracting data from the US Department of Defense Statistical Information and Analysis Division. However, the raw procurement information at the DoD website is sorted by contract identification number rather than by location. This yields hundreds of thousands to millions of entries per year. To aggregate the data in usable format, I worked with a computer programmer to write a script that parsed the information according to place, county, and state Federal Information Processing Standards (FIPS) codes (currently labeled American National Standards Institute [ANSI] codes). Since the FIPS codes were not standardized until 1980, I corrected all of the codes for the 1966 and 1976 fiscal years. Problems with inexact syntax and missing data yielded hundreds of missing entries per year, which I recoded by hand. In cases where a place no longer exists or lacks a FIPS code, I coded the entry based on information from an adjacent area. Based on these aggregations, the number of FIPS-designated places that received defense contracts in a given year ranges from 5,334 in FY1976 to 15,508 in FY2006. (Puerto Rico, Guam and other non-US territories were excluded from the analysis.)

The previous chapter suggests that defense allocations are likely to have a disproportionate impact in regions and localities with less developed economies. During World War II, the modest flow of defense dollars to peripheral locations such as El Segundo, Glendale, and Hawthorne is associated with greater population growth than much larger defense investments in the central city of Los Angeles. Further, the rise of government-owned facilities in developing regions such as Phoenix, Arizona, and Fort Worth, Texas, corresponds with outsized population growth relative to other southern cities, as well as more industrious northeastern cities of comparable size. All of this suggests that the postwar survival of a major facility is far more critical to economic welfare in a newly industrializing area such as Bethpage, New York (a previously unincorporated, agricultural community on Long Island), than in an economically diverse urban hub such as New York City.

To gauge the relative importance of the defense industry across different settings, I apply a measure of population density per county as a gauge for local and regional economic diversity. Specifically, lower levels of population density indicate less industrial diversity and greater reliance on major local industries to generate and sustain employment and revenue. Economics research commonly recognizes the link between population density and economic development. Dense cities—not simply cities—increase labor productivity, spur human capital and knowledge transfers, facilitate external economies of scale, and draw more diverse industries.[3] The US

Department of Agriculture (USDA) Economic Research Service reports that many rural areas—defined by lightly settled development patterns—face fewer employment opportunities and more stunted economic growth, increasing economic dependencies in these regions.[4] In fact, nonmetropolitan rural areas commonly bid for government facilities, such as prisons, which have in turn become economically important for many rural areas.[5]

To examine the validity of the proxy, I compared a list of counties ranked according to population density with a diversity index (the CS-Index) that geographer Elizabeth Mack and her colleagues developed. The CS-Index is a multivariate measure tapping into county-level resources, educational attainment, and levels of entrepreneurship.[6] The CS-Index draws on 2003 data from the Bureau of Economic Analysis (BEA) at the county level—the smallest level of aggregation for which these data are available. Using population density as an alternative metric for economic diversity allows me to gauge local defense-dependence over previous decades. (In chapters 5 and 6, I also use population density to examine economic dependence at the congressional-district level.)

While the CS-Index includes 3,074 contiguous US counties, the authors display only the twenty most and least economically diverse locations. Comparing these rankings with a list of counties sorted by population density in the coterminous United States allows me to gauge the extent to which the measures tap into the same underlying characteristics.

The juxtaposition suggests that the two variables are capturing nearly identical geographic features. The top three most industrially diverse counties according to the CS-Index—Los Angeles (CA), Cook (IL), and New York (NY)—are all in the top 1 percent of the most densely populated US counties. In addition, the twenty most industrially diverse counties in the CS-Index are all within the top 10 percent of counties with the highest population density. The least industrially diverse counties in the CS-Index demonstrate an even closer approximation to counties with the lowest population density. The three least economically diverse counties in the CS-Index—Sherman, Oregon; Loving, Texas; and King, Texas—are among the 5 percent of US counties with the lowest population density. However, when Sherman County is excluded, the twenty least economically diverse counties exhibit an even more precise match to the low density measure (within the 1% of counties with the lowest population density).

Given the similarity of the measures—and the greater availability of population density data both over time and across geographic units—I use population density as a proxy for industrial diversity. Lower population density indicates less industrial diversity and, therefore, greater economic reliance on local defense industries. I consulted the US Census Bureau for information on county population and land area per square mile from 1960 to 2005, and I computed the population density for each US county (population/land area per square mile). The database includes the population density for 3,142 counties, including boroughs and parishes in Alaska and Louisiana (respectively). I used Geographic Information System (GIS) software to map the volume of defense dollars and projects per place superimposed on county-level population density.[7]

DISPERSING DEFENSE BENEFITS

Military spending in the post–World War II era followed cyclical trends, generally increasing during major wars and declining following periods of armed conflict.[8] The defense budget hit relatively low ebbs following US withdrawal from the Vietnam War in the mid-1970s and again after the collapse of the Soviet Union during the reduced-threat era of the 1990s. However, US defense expenditures also increased and receded relative to a substantially higher baseline in the decades following World War II than throughout the nation's prior history.

At the onset of the Cold War, policymakers and defense bureaucracies incorporated Keynesian techniques pioneered in Roosevelt's New Deal, using military appropriations to stabilize and stimulate the economy. Policymakers in the Truman administration viewed military appropriations not only as an instrument to counter Soviet aggression, but also as a means to ensure full employment, smooth out the business cycle, and relieve economic downturns.[9] Despite Eisenhower's suspicions of the military-industrial complex and his fear that military spending exacerbates deficits and strains the private economy, defense spending expanded in the late 1950s and the early 1960s. At the same time, the South and West experienced a large infusion of federal funds, and many conservative southern Democrats in Congress who had opposed the New Deal domestic bureaucracy became vocal advocates of a large military bureaucracy.

Figures 4.1 and 4.2 display the nationwide distribution of defense dollars in 1966 and 2006.[10] Larger pentagons represent greater levels of defense spending and lighter shades indicate more sparsely populated, rural geography. The maps illustrate several trends. First, the geography of Cold War military spending is not simply a product of political and economic decisions; it also rooted in pre-established defense-sector development. Major World War II defense sites located in coastal and Great Lakes regions remained predominant military contract recipients during the Cold

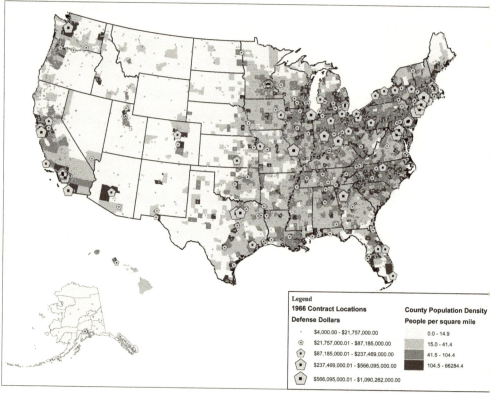

Figure 4.1. *Allocation of FY1966 defense dollars.*

The figure shows the volume of DoD dollars allocated per city or town and county-level population density compiled by the author and displayed using Geographic Information System (GIS) software. *Source*: US Department of Defense, Statistical Information and Analysis Division, "Procurement Reports and Data Files for Download: Historical Data, 1966–2006," US Department of Defense, Washington, DC (http://siadapp.dmdc.osd.mil/procurement/Procurement.html).

War. However, mirroring the 1944 defense expansion, defense dollars also spread out to increasing numbers of local constituencies and more remote locations—although defense dollars did not multiply or expand nearly as dramatically as the number of defense contracts (see figures 1.4–1.5). Second, the nation's defense expansion is characterized by regional shifts. Since World War II, the South and West have gained increasing shares of defense dollars, while the Northeast and industrial Midwest suffered relative losses. These regional trends may have contributed to increasing southern internationalism in the Cold War era.[11] Finally, more lightly settled rural, semirural, and suburban areas have systematically gained defense dollars. The extension of defense funds to more sparsely populated areas without

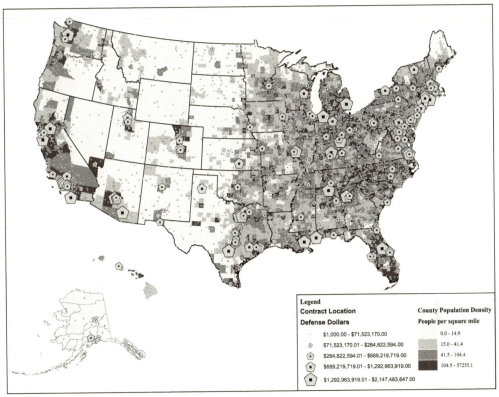

Figure 4.2. *Allocation of FY2006 defense dollars.*

The figure shows the volume of DoD dollars allocated per city or town and county-level population density compiled by the author and displayed using Geographic Information System (GIS) software. *Source*: US Department of Defense, Statistical Information and Analysis Division, "Procurement Reports and Data Files for Download: Historical Data, 1966–2006," US Department of Defense, Washington, DC (http://siadapp.dmdc.osd.mil/procurement/Procurement.html).

a diverse industrial base generates disproportionate defense dependence, where local growth or decline is largely predicated on continued defense production.

As figure 4.1 illustrates, the distribution of defense dollars in FY1966 extended across every state and a preponderance of counties, while clustering around major World War II contracting sites on the East and West coasts, the Great Lakes region, and in several locations in the South. In fact, most of the leading World War II defense contracting sites—New York City, Los Angeles (Lockheed, North American, Douglas), Wichita (Boeing), St. Louis (Curtiss-Wright), Dallas–Fort Worth (Lockheed, North American Consolidated-Vultee), Marietta (Bell), Philadelphia (Piasecki Helicopter),

Seattle (Boeing), and East Hartford (United Aircraft)—continued to draw the largest concentrations of defense dollars two decades after the war. Despite subsequent declines in the Great Lakes and the industrial Northeast, major manufacturing cities—including Buffalo (Curtiss-Wright), Cleveland (Martin), Cincinnati (Ford), Columbus (Chrysler), Detroit (GM), Baltimore (Martin), Indianapolis (GM), and Chicago—continued to rank as leading defense production sites during the Kennedy/Johnson years.

At the same time, many suburbs, towns and agricultural-turned-military locales surrounding these cities developed their local economies based largely on defense infrastructure that was established during the war. For example, Bethpage, Oyster Bay, and Farmington (outside New York City); Sunnyvale, Burbank, Anaheim, Long Beach, Culver City, and El Segundo (near Los Angeles); Morton (adjacent to Philadelphia); Southington, East Windsor, and Bloomfield (near Hartford); and Renton, Bellingham, and Tukwila (surrounding Seattle) developed as major contracting sites based on the constant flow of smaller increments of defense dollars. Meanwhile, Smyrna and Kennesaw (adjacent to Dobbins Air Force Base and the Atlanta Naval Station near Marietta); McConnell Air Force Base, Fort Riley, and Fort Leavenworth (outside Wichita); Fort Leonard Wood and Independence (outside St. Louis); Grand Prairie, Garland, Irving, and Addison (near Dallas–Fort Worth); and Fort Carson and Peterson Air Force Base (in Colorado Springs) drew larger shares of defense dollars and attracted defense industry development in these areas.

Nearly all of the largest defense contract recipients in 1966 had already developed productive capacity during the World War II military buildup.[12] However, in addition to the inertial effect of World War II military mobilization on the Cold War defense economy, congressional politics and economic development also played a significant role. During the Great Depression, the South was an overwhelmingly agrarian region within an industrialized nation. However, government investments in defense infrastructure during and after World War II laid the foundation for an industrial southern economy in a postwar era. In the decades following World War II, southern Democrats in the House and Senate vied for military contracts as a basis for revitalization of their regional economy.[13] By 1956 southerner William Faulkner declared, "Our economy is no longer agricultural. Our economy is the Federal Government."[14]

The powerful House Speaker Sam Rayburn of Texas ran a decentralized leadership in the 1940s and 1950s, permitting committee chairs to exercise unprecedented influence. Rayburn's leadership style empowered defense committees to handle the Pentagon's budget, giving these members a greater role in the military procurement process. Senator Richard Russell, a Democrat from Georgia and Armed Services Committee chair from 1954 to 1968, stacked his defense committee with Democratic allies from defense-dependent states, including Georgia, Mississippi, Alabama, Texas, Washington, and Missouri. House and Senate Armed Services committee members, predominantly comprised of southern Democrats, adopted tough-on-defense, internationalist postures.[15] These legislators also worked to draw military contracts to their constituencies during a period of Republican realignment and heightened electoral vulnerability.

In 1969 Mississippi Democrat John Stennis took over as chair of the Senate Armed Services Committee. In the House, Mississippi Democrat Sonny Montgomery, an ardent internationalist and defender of the national security state, served as an influential Armed Services Committee member. Both legislators represented Pascagoula, Mississippi, a prominent site for the naval industry by the 1970s and one of the fastest-growing defense locations in the nation. Alabama senator John Sparkman played an instrumental role in convincing the US Army to choose Huntsville as a location for a missile-research program and successfully fought to block the closure of the Redstone Arsenal in 1949. Since the 1960s, Huntsville has consistently drawn large defense contracts, while smaller amounts have flowed to proximate areas such as Fort Rucker, Anniston, and Maxwell Air Force Base.

Senate Armed Services committee member John Tower, the first Republican US senator from Texas since Reconstruction, oversaw military contracts flowing to Bell, Lockheed, and Boeing plants in Dallas and Fort Worth from 1961 to 1985. At the same time, many lightly settled areas surrounding Dallas–Fort Worth—Grand Prairie, McKinney, Fort Hood, Fort Bliss, El Paso, Lockland Air Force Base, Garland, Corpus Christi, Plano, Hurst, and Richardson—continued to thrive on smaller increments of defense appropriations. Representative George Mahon (D-TX) represented defense-dependent constituencies in the Texas panhandle, including Lubbock and Amarillo, from 1935 to 1985. As chairman of the Appropriations Committee, Representative Mahon not only set the defense budget, but also helped establish Reese Air Force Base (six miles west of Lubbock) and Webb Air Force Base (south of Lubbock). In Mendel Rivers's Charleston, South Carolina, district, federal funds flowed to an air force, naval base, and missile center, in addition to McDonnell Douglas, Avco, General Electric, and Lockheed plants.

Areas throughout the South and West and along the Atlantic coast continued to procure relatively large concentrations of defense dollars in the 1970s. While the defense budget fell following the nation's withdrawal from

Vietnam, the Great Lakes region and the Northeast corridor experienced the most severe procurement losses. Curtiss-Wright closed its operations in Buffalo; Wright-Patterson Field failed to attract industry suppliers in Dayton; Chrysler lost out on missile contracts to the air force; and General Motors reconverted to auto production. Only Ford Aerospace succeeded as a defense supplier, after transferring production from Detroit to Texas, California, and Colorado. In the landmark study *The Rise of the Gunbelt*, Ann Markusen and her colleagues argue that this transition to a military economy spawned new regional development patterns. Sunbelt regions gained the most defense dollars and enjoyed outsized economic growth, while Midwest regions lost their share of defense funds and suffered considerable decline.[16]

While these trends uncover persistent regional disparities, they also eclipse important local variation. In fact, the largest volume of defense dollars allocated in 1976 went to St. Louis, Missouri, home of Curtiss-Wright Aerospace and Sen. Stuart Symington, a leading Democrat on the Senate Armed Services Committee. At the same time, previously minor defense sites outside of large cities, such as Hawthorne, Sunnyvale, and Burbank (Los Angeles suburbs) and Bethpage, New York (a small Long Island community), as well as southern sites in Pascagoula, Mississippi, and Newport News, Virginia, procured disproportionately large concentrations of defense funds, rivaling Los Angeles, Seattle, Hartford, and Fort Worth in defense-contract dollars.

These trends accelerated during the defense buildup of the 1980s. More lightly settled regions throughout the South and West continued to gain military dollars, while Great Lakes and northeastern regions experienced relative losses. Marietta and Huntsville emerged as leading defense recipients, rivaling prominent 1970s sites like Pascagoula, Bethpage, Sunnyvale, and El Segundo in the volume of defense dollars received. Only New York, Connecticut, and Massachusetts counterbalanced the strong southern and western currents—although upstate New York continued to experience defense declines. Perhaps in response to these trends, a New York delegation comprised of representatives Joseph Addabbo (D-NY), Sam Stratton (D-NY), Thomas Downey (D-NY), and senators Al D'Amato (R-NY) and Patrick Moynihan (D-NY) became vocal legislative advocates for (often-controversial) military projects built by Grumman (in Bethpage and surrounding Long Island regions) and General Electric (in Schenectady, Binghamton, and neighboring upstate New York areas).[17]

Regional economic imperatives may also have preempted ideological shifts in partisan positions on defense issues. In the early 1950s, House and

Senate Democrats supported military spending more than congressional Republicans. However, Republicans favored defense spending as strongly as Democrats by the late 1950s and 1960s, and the parties switched positions in the 1980s.[18] The issue realignment is consistent with the regional importance of defense production, particularly for the developing southern economy. Despite a historical aversion to federal power, in the 1950s southern Democrats embraced the national security state and joined northern Democrats in support of large defense budgets. As the South became more solidly Republican, defense spending increasingly benefited the core of the realigned Republican Party—the South and West. Even though the effects of the Reagan military buildup cut across party lines, defense losses throughout the Northeast and Midwest disproportionately affected Democrats.

By the 1980s, the parties had adopted positions that reflect the relative importance of military spending for their core constituencies. The foreign policies advanced by presidents Ronald Reagan and George H. W. Bush promoted the political imperatives of the nation's newest industrializing regions and the heart of emergent Republican Party.[19] In contrast, Democrats became more critical of military spending after their voters lost defense shares and as alliances between their northern and southern contingents began to fray. However, Democratic leaders continued to prioritize local defense interests, even while they criticized the president's military agenda. For instance, House Appropriations Defense Subcommittee chairman Joseph Addabbo opposed President Reagan's massive defense buildup, but fought hard to promote funding for weapons programs that benefited the defense economy in his district.[20] House Speaker Tip O'Neill (D-MA) railed against President Reagan's military policies, but worked tirelessly to fund weapons that brought funding to his voters.[21]

Despite defense reductions after the collapse of the Soviet Union, most places faced a period of stagnated defense activity in the 1990s. Few areas experienced considerable retrenchments. In fact, the most significant losses occurred in the manufacturing belt—including Troy, Michigan, Cleveland, Ohio, and throughout upstate New York. In contrast, many constituencies in the South and West continued to benefit from military contracting, while averting most of the losses. Some areas even acquired relative gains. Most notably, Huntsville, Alabama, Grand Prairie, Texas, and Lewisville, Texas, grew their military sectors during a period of reduced output. Arlington, Virginia, also gained enormous defense shares based largely on its proximity to the Pentagon and thriving defense economy.

While the most densely populated counties continued to rank as leading defense recipients in the 1990s—Los Angeles, California; Fairfax, Virginia;

Middlesex, Massachusetts; and Maricopa, Arizona—the proportion of defense dollars flowing to more rural and semirural locations also accelerated. Despite a smaller overall defense procurement budget, defense dollars were more widely dispersed, extending to two-thirds of counties and increasingly flowing to more lightly settled areas outside of large cities. Given the reduced threat environment of the 1990s, these allocations suggest that the military contracting is not only expansive; it is also highly systematic. Defense dollars have increasingly shifted from the manufacturing belt to the Sunbelt, while smaller amounts extended from large cities into more remote areas.

There are a number of factors that might explain the unequal allocation of benefits and geographically targeted cuts: First, industries benefit from economies of scale by concentrating production efforts. Given the unique facets of the defense economy, this may be easier to achieve in less densely populated areas such as suburbs, towns, and other low-density settlements. Since the World War II defense buildup, small towns and communities adjacent to large cities have offered cheap land and available manpower close enough corporate headquarters to benefit from the same supply chain. During the Cold War, defense industry managers also expanded production to geographically remote areas near military bases, capitalizing on access to airfields and available testing facilities.

Second, the 1990s also marks a strategic shift to procurement of radar equipment, telecommunications, and electronics. The Department of Defense favored companies best adapted to emerging military needs, including Lockheed Martin, Boeing, and Northrop Grumman, as well as new technologically adept firms like Raytheon and TRW. During the 1990s, these industries conducted many of their operations in northern Virginia, allowing for strategic proximity to the Pentagon and influencing contract distributions in McLean, Arlington, Falls Church, and Manassas. Major firms also clustered around key areas in the South and West with pre-existing defense infrastructure, including Huntsville, Fort Worth, and Grand Prairie. These military relocations are consistent with the argument that the assembly-line auto culture of the Midwest locked out aerospace companies in the early Cold War years and operated as an impediment to defense activity in the region.[22]

Finally, there may be political and economic reasons why policymakers, defense bureaus, and defense industry managers favor certain geographic locations over others. Since the onset of the Cold War, defense companies have enjoyed strong political support in areas where the military sector is particularly crucial to the overall local economy. For example, defense industries gained aggressive political allies in southern states and districts, including legislative advocacy for military programs, representation on defense committees, and direct access to defense bureaucracies. As documented in the previous chapter, executive agencies provided the initial defense investment in the South by buying and leasing facilities to industries and eventually handing them over to the private sector at a loss. However, these emergency wartime measures had unintended, but lasting consequences. Throughout the Cold War, industrializing areas in the postwar South relied on military contracts for economic growth to a greater extent than fully industrialized regions.[23] Not surprisingly, these economic imperatives influenced political preferences and legislative strategies in the region.[24] Defense industries may concentrate production efforts with this political climate in mind.

In the wake of 1990s defense reduction, the twenty-first-century "war on terrorism" coincided with enormous growth in defense contracting. Figure 4.2 illustrates the proliferation of defense dollars across the national economic landscape, covering 85 percent of the nation's counties. While defense dollars remain highly concentrated in historically predominant defense sites, smaller appropriations increasingly spread across more rural locations, including Desert, Mountain, and Great Plains regions with relatively little defense infrastructure. While most locations experienced greater defense activity in 2006 than in any previous decade, military contracts exploded in small towns and communities with outsized defense economies—including Corpus Christi and Amarillo (Texas), Fort Lewis (Washington), Fort Bragg (North Carolina), and Newport News (Virginia). Large amounts of federal funds also flowed to suburbs and towns in the Northeast and Great Lakes regions, including Northrop Grumman's headquarters in Bethpage, New York (former home to Grumman Aircraft Engineering); Raytheon headquarters in Tewksbury and Waltham, Massachusetts; a major Boeing plant in Ridley Park, Pennsylvania; and General Dynamics facilities in Sterling Heights, Michigan, and Dayton, Ohio.

In the 2000s, the most sparsely populated areas of the nation—Desert, Mountain, and Plains states—increased their shares of military contracts at greater rates than previous decades. Defense dollars and projects flowed to military plants located near air force bases, airfields, missile ranges in Utah (Clearfield, Hill AFB), Colorado (Littleton, Colorado Springs, Peterson AFB), New Mexico (Kirtland AFB, White Sands Missile Range, and Albuquerque), Oklahoma (Tinker AFB, Oklahoma City), Hawaii (Hickam AFB), and Alaska (Anchorage, Elmendorf AFB). This defense expansion not only stimulates economic activity, but also generates and intensifies local dependencies on defense activity in more sparsely populated areas with less diverse economies.

Taken cumulatively, the data show that defense contracting spread out to increasing numbers of regions and localities in the post–World War II decades, regardless of the amount of procurement funds available. The number of cities, towns, and communities that received defense contracts increased threefold over four decades—from over 5,000 locations in 1966 to more than 15,000 places in 2006—even though the level of weapons spending did not increase nearly as dramatically. Despite declines in the procurement budget following US withdrawal from Vietnam, the number of places that received defense contracts in 1976 paralleled 1966 allocations, when policymakers contended with an alleged missile gap and passed the Gulf of Tonkin Resolution authorizing the Vietnam War ($n = 5,334$ in 1966; $n = 5,534$ in 1976). After the Cold War, during the reduced threat years of the 1990s, the number of places that received defense contracts rivaled the number of defense contracts recipients during the Reagan buildup of the 1980s ($n = 8,113$ in 1986; $n = 8,071$ in 1996). While defense procurement spending in the 1980s exceeded 2006 expenditures by a slight margin, the number of places that received defense dollars and contracts nearly doubled in 2006 in the context of the Iraq War ($n = 15,508$). In short, smaller increments of defense dollars have consistently flowed to greater numbers of local beneficiaries. Distributing defense dollars across a wider expanse effectively divides up the defense pie into smaller pieces, spreading defense benefits more thinly but also across greater numbers of constituencies.

In addition, increasing accumulations of defense dollars have systematically flowed to suburbs, towns, and formerly agricultural areas, particularly in the South and West—even though large cities on the northeastern and western coasts remain the nation's leading defense recipients. While the proliferation of defense benefits gives more local constituencies a stake in the military economy, the impact of defense distributions varies considerably in different economic settings. Smaller portions of the defense budget—tens of thousands, or even tens of millions of dollars per year—may not have a major effect in large cities, like New York City, Chicago, or Boston. However, these allocations are likely to have a more pronounced influence in towns, suburbs, and communities outside of large, diversified cities. Efforts to concentrate military production and achieve economies of scale also affect a greater proportion of the local residents in more sparsely populated areas than in densely populated urban settings. As the analyses in chapters 5–7 will show, disproportionate economic reliance in more rural areas with a large defense economy places a political premium on protecting defense interests and securing contracts for weapons suppliers.

EXTERNALIZING WAR COSTS

In 1792 James Madison advanced an argument that structural restraints in a republican form of government would help prevent unnecessary wars. With implicit reference to the nascent American republic, Madison suggested that a polity concerned with limiting wars and perpetuating peace must give the populace an electoral check on policymakers, while imposing the direct costs of war on the electorate: "[War] should not only be declared by the authority of the people, whose toils and treasures are to support its burdens, instead of the government which is to reap its fruits: but . . . each generation should [also] be made to bear the burden of its own wars, instead of carrying them on, at the expense of other generations."[25]

Madison's argument builds on foundations established by Niccolò Machiavelli in 1515. Machiavelli saw war as an essential component of political life, and he argued at length about the importance of a conscript army and the dangers associated with mercenary and auxiliary forces.[26] Mercenaries, he claimed, lack allegiance to the state and are reluctant to fight, while foreign armies may retain an allegiance to an opposing power. His argument suggests that subjects or citizens are more reliable than hired arms and most effective when a leader has gained the support of the people.

Madison's essay accepts the premise that war is inevitable, but challenges the structure of European monarchies and ancient principalities. Historically, rulers who declared war and directed military conflicts received glory for victories and sacrificed little for defeat, while the public ultimately funded the wars and fought and died at the monarch's caprice. However, a representative government vested with the power to declare war, raise armies, and tax and spend would be less likely to initiate questionable military ventures when its members' electoral fortunes hinge on the public appeal of their actions. Further, the people would be less likely to support unnecessary wars when they must ultimately bear the sacrifices.

As Madison predicted, the US representative governing system requires a base level of popular support for a prolonged war effort. From the American Revolution through the Eisenhower administration, large numbers of Americans were asked to sacrifice in wartime by joining the armed services and carrying a heavier tax burden. Administrations and congresses were then held accountable for wars and military actions during the next election cycle. However, since World War II, elected officials have conducted and financed wars in a way that makes it easier to sustain popular approval. The use of draft deferments allowed middle-class families to avoid military service during the Korean and Vietnam wars, while the subsequent shift to all-volunteer armies and private military and security companies (PMSCs) helped circumvent the need for a military draft or even a large volunteer contingent. At the same time, heavier emphasis on deficit spending allowed policymakers to avoid tax hikes or domestic spending reductions in order to finance large military buildups and wars. The ability to obviate or reduce public sacrifices during wartime evades Madison's prescription, imposing the bulk of the war costs on a small minority of active duty soldiers and volunteers, future generations of taxpayers, and foreign nations where US wars take place. While these developments do not necessarily motivate more military spending or spur a greater inclination to go to war, they do make it easier to sustain a military economy and exercise force abroad.

Fighting America's Wars: From Citizen-Armies to Security Contractors

From the late eighteenth to the late twentieth century, American military service was tied to citizenship. Small wars required participation from state militias, professional armies, and the recruitment of volunteers. Larger wars called for universal conscription, which compelled a segment of citizens to enlist in the military. Historically, high levels of public service in the military during wartime, either through compulsory or voluntary means, involved citizens in the foreign policy of the state in one of the most direct ways possible. James Madison assumed that the impact of military service on citizens' lives would influence levels of public engagement and legislative involvement in foreign policy decisions, reinforcing institutional checks on military expeditions. However, a purely voluntary structure where only a small segment of the populace experiences the heaviest costs of war weakens this democratic accountability. Reliance on a market system with private security forces available to executives for deployment at any time erodes these electoral checks even more.[27]

To assess historical levels of citizen involvement in the armed services, figure 4.3 displays US troop counts as a percent of the US population in major wars from the War of 1812 to the Iraq War of 2003. The figure shows that, historically, sustained US military actions required larger numbers of volunteers, reservists, or conscripted soldiers in the armed services (relative to the US population) in the centuries before the end of the Vietnam War than the decades that followed.

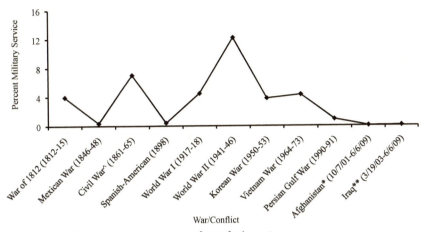

Figure 4.3. *US troop count as percent of population, 1812–2009.*

^ Union forces only; * including NATO international security forces; ** highest total troop count
(October 2007 surge).
Sources: US Department of Defense, Statistical Information and Analysis Division (SIAD), "Principal
Wars in Which the United States Participated: US Military Personnel Serving and Casualties 1775–1991,"
US Department of Defense, Washington, DC (http://siadapp.dmdc.osd.mil/personnel/CASUALTY/
castop.htm); Brookings Afghanistan Index, compiled by Campbell and Shapiro (2009, 10); Brookings Iraq
Index, compiled by O'Hanlon (2009, 24); US Bureau of Census, "Population and Housing Unit Counts,
1890–1990," US Government Printing Office, Washington, DC, 2000.

In fact, prior to 1973, every US war lasting for more than two years included the enlistment of at least 4 percent of the nation's population in the
armed services. Only the Mexican War (1846–48) and Spanish-American
War (1898)—continental conflicts of shorter duration—contained lower
troop counts. Despite its brief length, US entrance in World War I from 1917
to 1918 placed more than 4 million US soldiers in combat. During World
War II, more than 16 million Americans shared in the sacrifice by serving
in the military. The overseas troop count during World War II comprised
over 12 percent of the US population—the largest troop commitment in the
nation's history (excluding the combined total of Union and Confederate
soldiers that fought in the Civil War). Even the Korean War, an undeclared
conflict, included more than 6 million US troops sent into battle, or nearly 4
percent of the population. In the following decade, US entrance in Vietnam
required a military draft that enlisted over 8 million men and women in
combat and sparked mass protests, public unrest, and political upheaval.
In the immediate aftermath of the Vietnam War, President Nixon instituted
the 1973 All-Volunteer Force (AVF), eliminating the draft and transforming
military service from a legal duty tied to citizenship to a voluntary act.

Subsequently, President Clinton pioneered the use of the private sector

in the Balkans conflict and the 1999 Kosovo War. Both humanitarian interventions provoked opposition from the military and neither secured formal
authorization from Congress. However, PMSCs offered a market alternative
that reduced the need to draw on uniformed personnel, call forth reservists
or mobilize volunteers, quelling potential sources of domestic opposition.
A military consulting firm trained the Croatian military in its secessionist
war against Serb-dominated Yugoslavia in 1995, reducing the number of US
soldiers deployed in a contentious civil conflict characterized by war crimes
and ethnic cleansing. Private security forces also provided a police force for
Haiti and logistical support in nearly every multilateral mission of the 1990s,
while limiting the direct costs of these actions to the American public.

The use of the private sector accelerated during the George W. Bush administration. While over 100,000 uniformed US military personnel risked
their lives in Iraq and Afghanistan, private military contractors outnum-
bered uniformed US soldiers, according to a 2011 report by the Congressional Research Service (CRS).[28] Pentagon contractors included a mixture of
Americans, Iraqis, Afghans, and other third-party nationals hired to provide
security and perform traditional military (and DoD) functions. According
to 2008 Congressional Budget Office estimates, the number of military contractors in Iraq exceeded the number of US soldiers by 2007.[29] Contractors
may have been a particularly crucial component of the Iraq War strategy because the country went to war with little international support and without
enough American soldiers to carry out the mission.

While it is easier to acquire the necessary popular support to begin wars
without a military draft or large numbers of new recruits, evidence also suggests that public support for an ongoing war declines when US casualties
mount, regardless of whether US soldiers are draftees, reservists, or volunteers.[30] However, public tolerance for casualties is also much higher when the
people perceive a large stake in the cause of the war or believe that US victory
is likely.[31] To examine the rates of military casualties among US soldiers, figures 4.4a–b display US military deaths in wars and major hostilities from the
Revolutionary War in 1775 to the Iraq War in 2003 based on the total number
of US fatalities and as a percent of the population (respectively). To adjust to
scale, figure 4.4c exhibits the number of US military deaths as a percent of
the population in eleven military engagements in the post–World War II era.

As illustrated in figure 4.4a, the number of American fatalities in the Civil
War and World War II dwarf every other military conflict in US history. However, these wars are unique in an important aspect: Both were perceived largely
as existential struggles—the former for the survival of the Union and the latter
for the defeat of fascism following an attack on US soil. Presidents Lincoln and

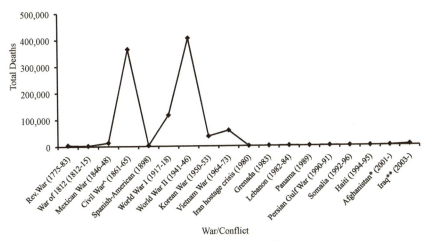

Figure 4.4a. *US military deaths in wars and selected military engagements, 1775–2009.*

^ Union forces only; * including NATO international security forces (October 7, 2001–June 6, 2009);
** including US military deaths from March 19, 2003, to June 6, 2009.

Sources: US Department of Defense, Statistical Information and Analysis Division (SIAD), "Principal Wars in Which the United States Participated: U.S. Military Personnel Serving and Casualties, 1775–1991," "Worldwide US Active Duty Military Deaths: Selected Operations, 1980-1996," "US Military Casualties: Operation Enduring Freedom," and "US Military Casualties: Operation Iraqi Freedom," US Department of Defense, Washington, DC (http://siadapp.dmdc.osd.mil/personnel/CASUALTY/castop.htm).

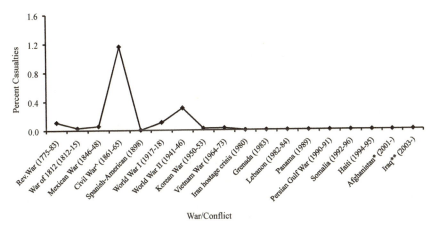

Figure 4.4b. *US military deaths in wars and selected military engagements as percent of population, 1775–2009.*

^ Union forces only; * including NATO international security forces (October 7, 2001–June 6, 2009);
** including US military deaths from March 19, 2003, to June 6, 2009. Information drawn from figure 4.4a.

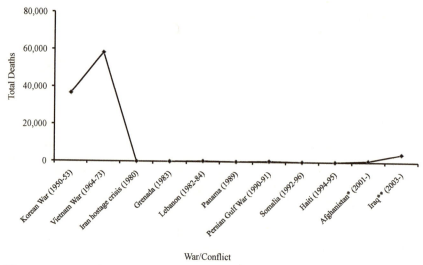

Figure 4.4c. *US military deaths in wars and selected military engagements post–World War II.*

* Including NATO international security forces (October 7, 2001–June 6, 2009); ** including US military deaths from March 19, 2003, to June 6, 2009. Information drawn from figure 4.4a.

Roosevelt successfully called upon the nation (or the Union forces) to make collective sacrifices order to combat a potent threat to a way of existence.

While the Revolutionary War and the Iraq War yielded similar numbers of US military deaths, the extent of the national burden is obscured by population growth over time. Figure 4.4b displays US military deaths as a percentage of the total population. The figure reveals several important factors: First, a higher percentage of US citizens sacrificed their lives for freedom from the British Empire during the Revolutionary War than for Korea, Vietnam, Afghanistan, and Iraq. Second, following World War II, US military actions produced far fewer fatalities in relation to the national population, regardless of the scope or duration of the conflict. In fact, a greater percentage of citizens lost their lives in World War II than in all subsequent wars combined. Third, as a percentage of US citizens killed in battle, the nation faced a disproportionate burden during the Civil War and (to a lesser extent) during World War II than all other military conflicts.

Since World War II, American troops have engaged in armed combat on many occasions, but have only experienced sustained ground combat and suffered more than 1,000 deaths in actions in three cases: Korea, Vietnam, and Iraq. As displayed in figure 4.4c, US military fatalities numbered into the tens of thousands in Korea and Vietnam. Subsequently, the elimination of the draft, use of private security contractors, development of more so-phisticated military technology, and medical advancements have contrib-uted to drastically lower numbers of US military deaths in major ground wars like Afghanistan (nearly 700 fatalities in 2009) and Iraq (approaching 4,400 fatalities in June 2009).

War fatalities are not only declining, but are also disproportionately borne by poorer and less educated families and communities. Doug Kriner and Francis Shen argue that the shift away from universal conscription in World War II to selective recruitment in Korea and Vietnam—where more affluent and educated classes could obtain draft deferments—and greater reliance on military volunteers in Iraq correspond with a widening socio-economic "casualty gap."[32] Just as poorer and less educated citizens are more likely to lose their lives in America's wars, more-affluent citizens are increasingly shielded from wars' most devastating effects.

Despite the historically low number of US military casualties for a ground war of its capacity and pronounced class bias in the composition of US fight-ing forces, public support for the Iraq War may have declined for several reasons: First, the unexpected duration and complexity of the war resulted in 900 percent more US military deaths than any troop engagement since Vietnam. Second, the precipitous drop in public tolerance for the Iraq War after US forces suffered 1,500 casualties—a historically low figure—also indicates that the populace placed less value on the stakes in Iraq than in previous wars (even publicly contentious wars) like Vietnam and Korea.[33] Third, the public may also have become more leery of the prospect of vic-tory as the war dragged and sectarian violence escalated.

Despite the erosion of public support for the Iraq War and targeted elec-toral checks, the limited sacrifices required of most Americans contributed to the base level of public approval necessary to initiate and prolong the war. The ability to draw on a small cadre of military volunteers and reserve forces for repeated tours of duty, combined with even larger reservoirs of private-sector support, is likely to influence elected officials who may not otherwise be willing to risk the potential backlash in public opinion com-monly associated with large troop counts.

Paying for America's Wars: From Debt Reduction to Heightened Federal Borrowing

While fewer numbers of Americans risked their lives in Iraq than in pre-vious ground wars of comparable duration, Americans also made fewer economic sacrifices—even at the onset of the war when a majority of the public supported the mission. Historically, the nation's leaders worked to pay down war debts during peacetime. From the Washington through the Eisenhower administration, presidents sought to maintain the nation's ability to borrow on credit and avoid imposing heavy obligations on future generations by promoting balanced budgets and prioritizing debt reduction.[34] However, increased reliance on federal borrowing and the systematic growth of the US economy after World War II made it easier to fund wars and defense buildups without asking voters to pay higher taxes or face cuts in domestic spending programs.

To assess levels of federal borrowing and the size of the national economy, figures 4.5a–b display US debt obligations in each fiscal year from 1940 to 2008 in constant (2008) dollars and as a percentage of gross domestic product (GDP). The national debt represents government borrowing to pay for the expenses that it could not afford through collected revenue. This includes money owed to individuals and foreign governments, in addition to money borrowed from Social Security and other trust funds. While the national debt reflects all sorts of federal expenditures—not simply defense spending—these figures help gauge levels of federal borrowing during US wars and major defense buildups. Although these levels may reflect government borrowing unrelated to defense, it also documents government willingness to fund expenditures on credit, as opposed to imposing tax hikes or mandating reductions in other programs.

As figure 4.5a illustrates, US debt increased dramatically from 1940 to 1945, growing from $600 billion to over $3 trillion over the course of World War II. The debt declined to just over $2 trillion under Truman, despite expenses incurred during the Korean War, and hovered at roughly the same rate through the mid-1970s. The debt began to increase very gradually in the mid- to late 1970s, during a period of economic recession and the aftermath of the Vietnam War. However, debt obligations remained well below $3 trillion until the 1980s, during President Reagan's unprecedented peacetime defense buildup. In fact, the federal debt grew to nearly $5 trillion under Reagan and increased steadily under George H. W. Bush and Bill Clinton, approaching $7 trillion in the mid-1990s. Despite the demise of the Soviet Union, the debt did not taper off until 1996 and did not decline until the 2000 fiscal year. From 2001 to 2007, the national debt increased from $7 trillion to over $10 trillion. Although only a fraction of this debt can be attributed to military ventures, an ability to spend on credit allowed policymakers to conduct extensive wars in two global theaters without imposing additional taxes to support these operations.

Figure 4.5b displays public debt as a percentage of GDP. Since GDP is a measure of the nation's total economic output, the figure represents the per-

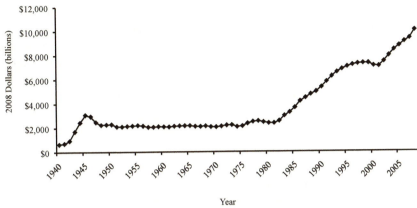

Figure 4.5a. *US debt obligations, 1940–2008 (in billions of 2008 dollars).*

Sources: US Bureau of the Public Debt, "Historical Debt Outstanding, 1940–2008" (http://www.treasurydirect.gov/govt/reports/pd/histdebt/histdebt.htm); Office of Management and Budget, "Historical Tables: Budget of the United States Government, Federal Debt at the End of Year: 1940–2012" (table 7.1), US Government Printing Office, Washington, DC (http://www.whitehouse.gov/omb/budget/Historicals).

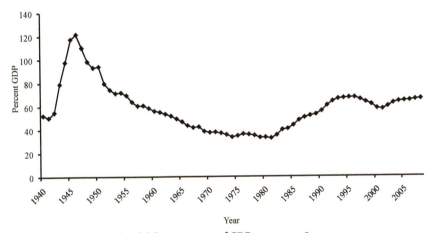

Figure 4.5b. *Gross federal debt as percent of GDP, 1940–2008.*

Source: US Bureau of Economic Analysis, National Economic Accounts, "Current Dollar and Real Value GDP, 1940–2008" (http://www.bea.gov/national/xls/gdplev.xls).

centage of the US economy necessary to pay off foreign loans from 1940 to 2008. As a percent of GDP, US debt grew to more than 120 percent in 1946, at the end of World War II, then declined slowly through the mid-1970s and hovered below 40 percent until the 1980s. In the early 1980s through the mid-1990s, national debt as a percent of GDP roughly doubled, growing from 33 percent to 67 percent—a far more muted increase than the actual dollar value.[35] Since 2001, debt obligations in relation to GDP has increased gradually and then flattened, hovering over 65 percent.

Unlike figure 4.5a—where debt obligations in real terms exhibit the most dramatic increase from 1980 to 2008—debt spending as a percentage of GDP displays a sharp peak during World War II followed by a period of rapid decline in the decade after the war and modest fluctuations in subsequent years. While the disproportionate debt obligation incurred during World War II reflects the massive spending increase in support of military production, the Great Depression and smaller size of overall national economy also contribute to this effect. Conversely, the decline in debt obligations as a percent of GDP observed in subsequent decades is largely a reflection of the overall strength of the modern US economy. Excepting a brief economic decline from 1946 to 1950, US GDP increased systematically from 1940 to 2008, growing from $1.2 trillion to over $13.4 trillion, or 895 percent.[36] GDP substantially outpaced federal spending, even while government spending exceeded federal revenue. As long as the national economy continues to grow, defense spending represents a smaller share of the overall economy, despite considerable increases in the actual size of the military budget.

During World War II, the American people were expected to sacrifice both overseas and domestically. Federal campaigns and propaganda efforts encouraged citizens to support higher taxes, purchase war bonds, and abide by government rationing and price controls. However, since the 1980s, administrations and congresses have been able to avoid a major revision in fiscal policy—such as increasing taxes and cutting spending on nonmilitary programs to fund large defense buildups—largely because military expenditures and wars represent a declining portion of GDP compared to past conflicts. At its peak, World War II spending accounted for roughly 45 percent of GDP, the Korean War comprised 15 percent, and the Vietnam War peaked at 10 percent. Although the expenses for the Vietnam War and the 1980s defense buildup were slightly higher in real terms than the Korean War, they were smaller as a proportion of the national economy. Despite real increases in defense spending compared to any period during the Cold War, the entire military budget in 2008 was below 5 percent of GDP, and the cost of the war was roughly 1 percent.

Given the nation's economic strength, which has contributed to a virtually unlimited ability to borrow on credit, the government has not needed to implement wage and price controls to curb inflation since the Korean War. Nor have policymakers increased taxes or cut civilian spending in order to cover mounting military bills since the 1980s. Instead, administrations, congresses, and US Treasury officials have relied more heavily on borrowing and emergency supplemental appropriations. While lower taxes and more domestic spending make it easier to spur economic growth and sustain support for military operations, this fiscal strategy comes at a disproportionate cost to future generations of taxpayers who must eventually fund growing debt obligations.

THE BROKEN WINDOW FALLACY

What would become of glaziers if panes of glass were never broken? —Frederic Bastiat (1850)

In a famous parable, a little boy carelessly breaks a window belonging to a shopkeeper. Consequently, the broken window provides work for the glazier hired to replace the glass; the glazier can then buy bread, benefiting the baker, who will buy shoes, benefiting the cobbler, and so on. Bystanders begin to conclude that the apparent act of vandalism is actually a public good: it causes money to circulate and stimulates industry. Of course, the fallacy in the argument is that the spectators only considered the benefits of purchasing a new window, while ignoring the costs of the shopkeeper who might have otherwise spent money on goods for himself.

Like the broken window parable, defense spending and war stimulate widespread economic activity, while the majority of Americans shoulder few direct burdens. Government investments in military technologies fuel defense employment, deter potential attacks on US soil, and facilitate weapons developments that make it easier to identify enemy targets at reduced risk to US military personnel. At the same time, all-volunteer armies and private military and security contractors shift the duty of military service onto a diminishing subset of the population. Deficit spending also relaxes the financial burdens associated with large defense budgets and wars among the current base of American taxpayers. Defense companies, constituencies engaged in weapons production, and national political majorities all benefit from these arrangements, regardless of devastating costs borne elsewhere.

Like the shopkeeper with the broken window, the costs of maintaining a military economy have not disappeared simply because political majorities are more insulated from their immediate effects. Foreign nations where the United States fights its wars incur harm to civilian life, including damage to economic infrastructure, lost productivity, and loss of civilian lives. Although fewer Americans fight and die in the nation's wars than any previous historical period, a small segment of volunteers shoulder this burden. The financial expense of war and periods of increased defense spending also have opportunity costs in the United States. Funds spent on military procurement could be spent on other purposes, including investments in infrastructure, health care, or education. The borrowing used to finance military procurements will also constrain future US taxpayers who might have chosen to spend the money in other ways.

In addition to shifting the public costs of military buildups and wars, defense contracting also benefits increasing segments of the population. More lightly settled towns and communities attracted greater shares of defense dollars in each decade since the onset of the Cold War, even while large cities located on the East and West coasts receive the bulk of these funds. The geographic expansion of defense production has self-reinforcing consequences. The following chapters will show that the extension of defense infrastructure throughout rural, semirural, and suburban areas creates excessive dependencies on local weapons suppliers. Disproportionate economic reliance encourages political representatives to prioritize defense interests and seek more military spending. Contractors and defense bureaucracies also work to distribute weapons contracts with these economic and political imperatives in mind.

Local Defense Dependence and Congressional Weapons Spending

After the fall of the Soviet Union, policymakers worked to reduce defense spending, and leading Pentagon officials attempted to cancel many high-cost weapons systems designed to fight the Cold War. Although Congress gradually decreased the overall defense budget in annual omnibus legislation, legislators failed to enact nearly every specific cut to defense procurement programs that came to the floor for a vote. In an address to the Senate Armed Services Committee in 1992, Secretary of Defense Dick Cheney admonished members of Congress for promoting the economic interests of their voters regardless of changing military priorities, testifying that: "Congress has . . . squabbled and sometimes bickered and horse-traded and ended up forcing me to spend money on weapons that don't fill a vital need in these times of tight budgets and new requirements." Many of Congress's military priorities, he claimed, "are not related to defense, but mostly related to politics back home in the district."[1]

Dick Cheney's frustrations have not escaped the attention of commentators and concerned citizens. Academics and journalists have documented a number of specific cases in which members of Congress fought to increase the defense budget or to procure strategically questionable weapons programs in order to secure jobs and spending in their districts.[2] Further, case studies and media reports suggest that "home-district money," "jobs," and "pork" helped prolong the lifespan of several weapon systems that Dick Cheney tried to terminate—including the V-22 Osprey helicopter, the SSN-Seawolf submarine, and the B-1 stealth bomber.[3] Legislators representing areas threatened by defense layoffs also worked to extend the lifespan of outmoded weapons systems during the Cold War and stealth aircraft in the twenty-first century "war on terrorism."[4]

Yet political scientists have found little evidence suggesting that economic interests affect legislators' defense-spending decisions systematically, or among more than a small handful of members. Rather, most statistical research suggests that legislators representing areas that stand to benefit

93

from defense spending are no more likely to support large defense budgets or controversial weapons systems than other members and senators.[5] These studies suggest that members of Congress make decisions about levels of defense spending and the types of weapons systems available based on their ideological dispositions, and independently of economic circumstances or other institutional interests.

However, previous work has several limitations. Quantitative studies typically rely on a blunt metric of defense "benefit," such as the absolute number of military bases, airfields, or naval yards, or the total prime contract revenue in a state or district.[6] This approach assumes that defense dollars are equally important to the constituencies with the capacity to receive them. Neither quantitative work nor case studies account for the relative importance of defense spending for a constituency's overall economy. In addition, statistical work largely neglects the civilian employees of defense industries that bid for weapons contracts.[7] Scholars have not accounted for privately owned weapons industries because the data are not readily accessible, and most employment information related to defense contracting is classified.

Researchers themselves commonly recognize these problems. For example, Bruce Ray explains the null relationship between statewide prime contract revenue and members' "hawkishness" on foreign policy decisions by noting that political science measurements may be too crude to capture congressional preferences for defense programs systematically.[8] Richard Fleisher explains the lack of relationship between Senate votes for the B-1 bomber and the percentage of B-1 expenditures flowing to a state by pointing out that for most senators voting against the program did not harm the state's economy.[9]

Unlike earlier approaches, the concept of defense dependence outlined in the previous chapter helps refine and clarify the conditions in which the local economic circumstances are likely to influence legislators' military spending decisions. First, an original database documenting the nationwide locations of leading US defense industries captures the overall size of the local defense-industry presence. Second, *disproportionate reliance* is conceptualized based on the relative concentration of defense facilities to other industries. A defense plant located in a more economically homogenous, rural area will typically employ a larger proportion of local residents and contribute more to the local economy than a defense company situated in a densely populated, urban setting. The framework is consistent with Michael Bailey and David Brady's research showing that senators representing more homogenous states weigh constituency characteristics more heavily than senators with a heterogeneous electorate.[10] The same logic suggests that members of Congress representing more economically homogenous districts with defense facilities will prioritize military spending more than members representing areas with an equal defense-sector presence scattered among a more diverse economic landscape.

Original data presented here provide new evidence suggesting that local reliance on defense jobs is a key driver of military spending preferences in the US House of Representatives. Local dependence on weapons suppliers encourages representatives to support various types of military procurement spending, despite the partisan and ideological divisions that typically characterize congressional behavior. Evidence also indicates that economic interests reinforce partisan positioning in Congress and may strengthen ideological beliefs systems favoring American military hegemony.

A TALE OF TWO DISTRICTS

While political science research typically suggests that legislators' ideological beliefs shape their military spending decisions, this explanation is too simplistic. Local economic reliance on the defense sector also contributes to congressional support for military spending and may reinforce some members' hawkish ideologies.

Local economic reliance does not simply imply that members of Congress representing areas with defense interests will seek more military spending. Rather, representational strategies will differ across rural and urban settings with an equal defense sector presence. As stated earlier, more economically homogenous constituencies typically experience greater dependence on the major companies in their district. Further, they also tend to have clearer, more pervasive preferences than diverse, urban settings with multiple, cross-cutting local interests. Providing district support is a more straightforward process for representatives in rural, semirural, or suburban locations than for their urban counterparts.

To illustrate this difference, imagine a Democratic representative in a lightly settled region with multiple air force bases, several major weapons industries, and a naval shipyard that also serves as largest employer in the county. Given the importance of defense jobs for this constituency, it is not particularly surprising that the member is a vocal congressional defense hawk and a ranking member of a prestigious defense committee.

Now envision a fellow Democrat representing the adjacent central city—a more densely populated, urban setting that served as the former base for a defense industry headquarters. This district has many remaining defense facilities that operate within a more diversified economy and alongside a growing commercial technology sector. Unlike her colleague, this member sits on the Ways and Means Committee and prioritizes international trade issues. She has a mixed voting record on defense issues, giving much lower priority to the multiple defense industries scattered across the city's more robust economic landscape.

These examples describe two veteran members of the 112th Congress, representatives Norm Dicks (D-WA, 6th District) and Jim McDermott (D-WA, 7th District). Representative Dicks represents the Bremerton/Tacoma region of western Washington, where local residents rely on Boeing industries, airfields and the Puget Sound Naval Shipyard—the largest employer in Kitsap County—to fuel their local economy. In contrast, Representative McDermott represents the adjacent city of Seattle, where multiple Boeing industries are situated within a more diverse economic landscape. While McDermott's constituency stands to benefit from military spending, local defense interests are far more crucial for the voters in Dicks' district.

Of course, the notion that economic incentives shape members' defense decisions does not invalidate conventional wisdom that legislators' ideologies guide their military policies. Rather, the emphasis on local economic imperatives is consistent with the view that legislators generally rely on their worldviews to make geopolitical decisions, and voters hold them accountable by the same metric. However, shared interests among voters and representatives ultimately form a core foundation for these belief systems. Legislative support for large military budgets are likely to gain more traction politically in areas with the greatest economic stake in these decisions—even while members like Norm Dicks genuinely equate their electoral interests with their ideological commitments. One need not question the sincerity of these members' national security goals to recognize the symbiosis between ideological beliefs and local interests. Many policymakers genuinely equate their own institutional interests with the common good.[11]

If economic reliance on defense spending shapes legislative preferences, then congressional support for weapons programs will not be driven only by broader national security goals. Rather, the shared goal of economic security will also cultivate support for such policies, regardless of partisanship or ideology.

IDEOLOGICAL SHIFTS AND PARTISAN POSITIONING

While legislators' well-known preoccupation with securing reelection suggests that both Republicans and Democrats from defense dependent districts will be more likely to support increased defense funding, one might also expect to see differences between the parties' respective voting patterns. Republican Party leaders, including Republican presidents, have long sought to position the party as "pro-defense." All Republican members of Congress are undoubtedly cognizant of the collective party strategy to enhance the party's "brand name" on defense issues, regardless of the composition of their district.

The previous chapter suggests that the 1980s party switch on defense issues corresponded with the growing importance of defense spending in emerging Republican constituencies, particularly in the South and West. While congressional Democrats supported defense spending more than their Republican colleagues in the 1950s, the parties reached a "consensus" in favor of large defense budgets in the late 1950s and 1960s, but switched positions by the 1980s. Although there are multiple explanations for the partisan shift—including efforts to rebrand the party labels after the unpopular Vietnam War—defense spending notably promoted core economic imperatives of the newly realigned Republican Party.[12]

After the Republican electoral realignment, the 1994 Republican "Contract with America" championed the need for large defense budgets, highlighting national defense priorities as a "conservative" cause. Successful Republican leadership on this issue should encourage Republican members to champion defense spending initiatives and oppose defense cuts. The following year, the 1995 Republican Party takeover in the US House of Representatives resulted in greater ideological homogeneity in both the Republican and Democratic parties and increased levels of partisan voting.[13] If parties in Congress stake out opposing positions on debates over defense spending levels, then partisan factors will exhibit strong influences on congressional voting on defense-spending decisions.

Given these partisan incentives, Republican Congress members should be predisposed to vote in favor of more military spending, all else equal. Accordingly, economic considerations may have a larger impact on Democrats, who do not have the same partisan predisposition.

MODELING PATTERNS OF CONGRESSIONAL
SUPPORT FOR DEFENSE EXPENDITURES

To conduct the analysis, I located roll-call votes taken in the US House of Representatives on defense spending measures from 1993 to 1998. I focused on this five-year period for several reasons. Most critically, the analysis of disproportionate economic reliance employs an original database consisting of the nationwide locations of leading US defense industries, which are accessed from a variety of sources (see below for further elaboration). These data are prohibitively difficult to collect and cross-check in early periods, given the lack of comprehensive historical records on the locations of weapons industries. In addition, congressional debate on these subjects is often more limited and one-sided during periods of heightened military threat, including the period immediately following the terrorist attacks of September 11, 2001. The absence of a significant military threat throughout much of the 1990s offers a unique opportunity to analyze variability in congressional behavior on such matters.

The House of Representatives provides an appropriate focal point for this study for several reasons: The House offers a larger case selection than the Senate and a more precise measure of constituency reliance. Not only do the shorter terms of its members link members more closely to their constituencies, but also the districts are smaller and often more homogenous than those of the Senate, allowing for greater variability across cases.

Dependent Variables

The database consists of 36 roll-call votes taken in the US House of Representatives from 1993 to 1998 and extracted from *CQ Weekly*. The votes include three specific types of defense spending initiatives: controversial weapons expenditures (n = 17), defense cuts (n = 11), and policies on arms sales to foreign nations (n = 8). Each bill forces congressional members to take a position on a matter that influences the status of the military economy.

The dependent variable is the members' average position ("defense score") on all three types of defense policies during the 103rd, 104th, and 105th congresses, respectively. A "pro-defense" vote (pro–weapons spending, anti–spending cuts, and pro–ease of arms sales) was coded "1"; an "antidefense" vote was coded "0." The average district scores are continuous measures ranging from 0 to 1, where higher values indicate more support for defense spending. Separate scores were also generated for controversial weapons programs, general defense cuts, and arms sales in order to test for variation in members' support across different types of military spending.[14] Appendix 5.1 provides a table of descriptive statistics for dependent and independent variables. Appendix 5.2 lists these bills, resolutions, and amendments.

Controversial weapons expenditures are defined as disproportionately high-cost weapon systems with debatable strategic utility that top Pentagon officials, including the secretary of defense, Joint Chiefs of Staff, and/or the president, targeted for spending caps, cancellation, or spending cuts. The weapons systems that meet these criteria include the SSN-Seawolf submarine, B-2 stealth bomber, V-22 Osprey helicopter, F-22 stealth fighter, Trident D-5 missiles (armed with nuclear warheads), and other ballistic missile systems. Top members of the Pentagon have targeted each program for cuts or cancellation, criticizing the systems as prohibitively costly or otherwise inappropriate in an era faced with threats of terrorism or other forms of unconventional conflict.[15]

Defense cuts consist of legislation proposing spending freezes and overall reductions in defense spending. This includes bills, amendments, and resolutions providing an across-the-board cut in DoD activities or reducing the level of funding allotted for army, navy, or air force weapons procurement.

Arms sale policies are defined as measures restricting or easing US arms sales to foreign nations or legislation tightening or relaxing restrictions on US arms contractors. These votes force members to take a position that either grows or rolls back the weapons industry. Examples include a bill to prohibit the use of funds to finance the sale or transfer of a defense article or service to a foreign nation, and an amendment omitting a government tax on the foreign sale of US weapons.[16]

Explanatory Variable: Disproportionate Economic Reliance

Economic reliance: The percentage of defense-sector employment within a district would provide an optimal measure of economic dependence on the defense sector. However, the Bureau of Labor Statistics yields "nondisclosable" results on defense employment queries.[17] Given these data limitations, an interaction term, *low density*facilities*, is employed to assess the conditional influence of a large defense-sector presence within a more sparsely populated setting. The measure serves as a proxy for a district's economic reliance on defense revenue.

Defense facilities: Information on the nationwide locations of major defense industries affords a reasonable measure of local defense-industry presence. To create this measure, I collected original data on the nationwide locations of Boeing Company, Lockheed Martin, Raytheon, TRW Inc., Northrop Grumman Corporation, and Alliant Techsystems during the 1990s. These six companies were all top DoD manufacturers during the period under study and primary producers of the controversial weapons systems examined.[18] I collected information on each industry's major locations by referencing 10-K reports (annual business and financial documents) submitted by each company for the 1995 fiscal year.[19] I also consulted past research compiled by the Center for Media and Democracy on the locations of major missile defense industries.[20] These search methods yielded the city-based locations of 606 US defense facilities spread across forty-eight states (excepting Vermont and Delaware). I hand-coded the relevant districts by referencing the Congressional District Atlas for the 103rd Congress of the United States (based on 1992 redistricting plans).[21]

A count variable indicates the number of defense facilities in a district. However, this measure does not gauge a district's economic *reliance* on the defense sector. To capture local dependence on the major defense companies in a district, I apply the proxy for local economic homogeneity introduced in chapter 4.

Population density: As the previous chapter suggests, population density provides a reasonable gauge for local economic diversity that is available both historically and at the congressional district level. The variable captures the same underlying characteristics as the CS-Index, a multivariate measure for economic diversity calculated at the county level. To create the measure, I calculated the overall district population divided by area per square mile. I also calculated the inverse of this measure in order to create a variable for low density, where higher values indicate more sparsely populated areas. Lower levels of population density indicate less industrial diversity, and hence, greater reliance on local defense facilities for employment and revenue.

Control Variables

The models include a number of covariates specific to district composition and congressional representation:

Military population: Drawing from Scott Adler's congressional district data file, the models control for the uniformed military population in each congressional district.[22]

Defense committee membership: A dummy variable is coded "1" if a member belongs to a defense committee with jurisdiction over weapons programs and "0" to indicate that a member does not belong to a relevant defense committee.[23]

Campaign contribution (lagged): To examine potential legislative alliances with defense industry lobbyists, the model captures the volume of campaign contributions from the defense industry given to each congressional member in the previous election cycle.[24]

Partisanship: Given distinct partisan positioning on defense issues, a dummy variable is employed to control for members' partisanship (coded "1" for Republican and "0" for Democrat).[25]

Ideology: DW-NOMINATE scores are employed to capture members' members' predisposed preferences or leanings.[26] The scores consist of members' aggregated voting patterns and control for a variety of pressures that may yield more conservative voting behavior in rural areas. While scholars have demonstrated several conceptual and empirical problems with the use of aggregated voting patterns in models predicting voting behavior, the scores are applied to provide a more rigorous test of local economic reliance.[27]

Modeling Techniques and Empirical Limitations

Since the dependent variable (members' defense scores) is a continuous measure, multiple regression using ordinary least squares (OLS) affords an appropriate analysis. I ran the model three times, for the 103rd, 104th, and 105th congresses. District composition is virtually identical in this period, so the results should hold relatively constant. To ease interpretation of the results, I report the expected values and estimated differences of a pro-defense spending vote when low density and defense facilities are set to high and low values using CLARIFY.[28]

While the OLS analysis provides the most appropriate test of economic reliance given current data availabilities, there is a serious limitation to this approach. Unfortunately, since data restrictions preclude a longer time series, I am unable to include fixed effects that control for district-level effects and time-invariant characteristics. Therefore, I cannot empirically rule out the possibility that defense-industry managers strategically locate their facilities in areas where representatives have more pro-military views. However, evidence presented in the previous chapters indicates that this is unlikely.

Earlier chapters suggest that economic reliance on the defense sector stems from a historical accident: Business executives and federal agencies made short-sighted decisions during the World War II military mobilization that advanced their immediate aims to increase output as quickly as possible and meet emergency military needs. Aircraft-industry managers spread production into geographically proximate areas outside of large, coastal cities. Executive agencies and military personnel prioritized more geographically remote inland and southern locations. These decisions were made based on legitimate reasons, including cheap land, untapped labor, access to airfields, and military secrecy. However, they also inadvertently laid the foundation for widespread economic reliance on defense infrastructure, which only became apparent after the war. Of course, defense-industry managers may have built up existing defense sites with political factors in mind after the war was over, as observed in the postwar South. However, business executives did not control the overall wartime economic mobilization or the military's specific investment decisions.[29] The available historical evidence indicates that military priorities fueled the initial defense expansion, which created sunk costs and encouraged economies of scale. Local economic dependence was a historical accident and not a deliberate industry strategy.

ECONOMIC RELIANCE AND CONGRESSIONAL WEAPONS SPENDING

Table 5.1 displays expected values and estimated differences of congressional support for military spending. (The regression analyses associated with the expected values are located in appendix 5.3.[30]) The entries in the table reflect members' estimated level of support for defense spending as a percentage ranging from 0 percent ("anti-defense") to 100 percent ("pro-defense").

The table displays the change in members' estimated support for defense spending when the number of defense facilities and population density in a district are set to high and low values. Representatives' partisanship, committee assignment, campaign contributions from the defense sector, and other factors referenced above are held constant at their respective mean values. For comparison, the table also shows the estimated changes in members' voting preferences for defense expenditures when their partisanship changes from Democrat to Republican, while members' district characteristics and ideology scores are held constant at their respective mean values.

As the theory of local defense dependence predicts, excessive economic reliance yields stunning levels of congressional support for weapons spending. As shown in the upper-left-hand quadrant, controlling for partisanship and other factors, members of Congress from a rural district with the maximum defense-sector presence support the military expenditures under examination 95 percent of the time ($p < .001$)! By contrast, members from a densely populated, urban area with no defense facilities only support these weapons expenditures at a low rate of 32 percent ($p < .001$). The difference is striking: Representatives from the most economically reliant districts support military spending at 66 percent greater rates than members from districts with no conceivable economic gain ($p < .001$). The difference in weapons-spending preferences between members whose voters have the most and the least to lose from the vote outcome would determine the success or failure of the programs under consideration. The change in district composition could transform the military budget and the types of weapons systems in the US arsenal.

At the same time, the right-hand column shows that members of Congress from districts with a maximum defense presence are 25 percent more likely to favor military spending than members from districts with no major

Table 5.1. *Estimated influence of economic reliance on US House members' support for weapons spending, 1993–1998*

Change in economic reliance		Change in defense facilities	
Urban, zero defense facilities (min)	.32 (.05)***	Medium density, zero facilities (min)	.59 (.009)***
Rural, 16 defense facilities (max)	.95 (.05)***	Medium density, 16 facilities (max)	.79 (.043)***
Difference	.63 (.069)***	Difference	.20 (.048)***
Percent change	66%***	Percent change	25%***
Change in partisanship		Change in population density[a]	
Democrat	.43 (.009)***	Urban, 2 facilities (5th percentile)	.48 (.021)***
Republican	.83 (.01)***	Rural, 2 facilities (95th percentile)	.65 (.008)***
Difference	.40 (.013)***	Difference	.17 (.024)***
Percent change	48%***	Percent change	26%***

Note: Table 5.1 entries are calculated by the author from the multiple regression analysis in appendix 5.3 using CLARIFY. The dependent variable is legislators' average level of support for weapons spending measures (scaled continuously from 0 = anti-defense spending to 1 = pro-defense spending). Entries are expected values and estimated differences in expected values. The standard errors of the expected values are in parentheses. All control variables are held constant at their sample means.
[a] Denotes change in low density from the 5th decile (urban) to the 95th decile (rural)
***$p < .001$

defense facilities, given an average population density ($p < .001$). Despite partisanship and other political pressures, the prospect of constituency gain encourages members of Congress to support increased spending for weapons development.

The results are also consistent with the theory that rural areas experience greater dependence on the defense industry than their urban counterparts with an equal defense presence. Given an equal number of defense facilities, members from more sparsely populated areas are 26 percent more likely to support increased defense expenditures than members from the most densely populated, urban areas ($p < .001$).

As expected, partisanship yields considerable influence on these vote outcomes. All else equal, Republicans are 48 percent more likely to support the weapons expenditures examined than their Democratic colleagues ($p < .001$). However, even the influence of partisanship—a deeply ingrained institutional mechanism—does not rival the magnitude of influence that disproportionate local reliance exerts on congressional support for the weapons expenditures under study.

These findings suggest that members from districts that are disproportionately reliant on the defense sector are considerably more likely to prefer larger defense budgets than members from districts that have a lower economic stake in the programs. In fact, the effect of economic reliance yields a stronger influence on members' preferences than the sum of *low density* and *defense facilities* alone, suggesting that the interaction term is greater than the sum of its parts. Of course, the models do not reveal why members representing economically reliant districts are more likely to vote for large defense budgets. As Dick Cheney's indictment of Congress indicates, some members may press for more military spending in crude attempts to promote the economic interests of their voters. However, a more nuanced interpretation suggests that these members also have worldviews that favor American military supremacy and that are likely to be reaffirmed and rewarded politically in places that have a large economic stake in these decisions. In either scenario, a district's economic imperatives yielded strong legislative support for defense programs, despite highly partisan battles over budget-cutting and increasing partisan unity in the 103rd and 104th congresses.

ECONOMIC RELIANCE AND PARTISANSHIP

Figure 5.1 illustrates the estimated effect of local economic reliance on Democratic and Republican House members' support for weapons spending. For comparison, the figure also displays the effect of an increasing number of defense facilities in a district and the influence of more rural geography (respectively) among Democratic members. Ideology and other constituency factors are held constant at their sample means. (The expected values are calculated based on the regression analyses located in appendix 5.4.)

Increasing economic reliance corresponds with greater levels of support for weapons programs among both Democratic and Republican members during the 103rd Congress. However, the parties also exhibit distinct voting patterns. As indicated by the steeper trend line, a larger defense-sector presence within a more rural setting exhibits a greater influence on Democratic members' support for weapons programs than their Republican counterparts, changing from an estimated 30 percent support in urban districts

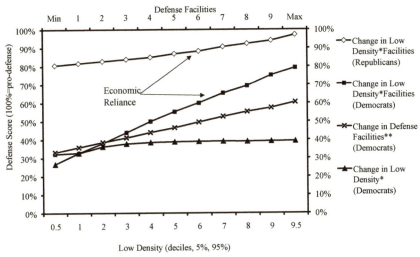

Figure 5.1. *Estimated influence of economic reliance on Democratic and Republican House members' support for weapons spending, 1993–1994.*

*The trend denotes a change in low density (urban to rural) while defense facilities is set at its sample mean; **The trend denotes an increase in defense facilities while low density is set at its sample mean. The figure displays expected values calculated by the author from the multiple regression analysis in appendix 5.4 using CLARIFY. All control variables are held constant at their sample means.

with no facilities to approximately 80 percent support in rural districts with the largest defense-sector presence (50% change). Economic reliance encourages Democratic members to support defense spending to a considerably greater extent than increasingly rural geography alone (13% change), an increasing number of defense industries alone (27% change), or the sum of these two variables.

By contrast, Republican support for weapons spending hits a low point of 80 percent in urban areas with no defense facilities and approaches nearly 100 percent in the most economically reliant districts. Given this strong, uniform Republican support for defense programs, it is not surprising that economic reliance has a larger influence among Democratic members. In fact, nearly every economic and political factor examined in the full regression model (appendix 5.4) shapes Democratic members' support for defense expenditures to a greater extent than their Republican counterparts. The goodness-of-fit statistic diminishes to one-third to one-fifth of its size in the models explaining variance in Republican (as opposed to Democratic) voting patterns on defense policies. As the figure shows, there is far less variation among Republican representatives to explain! Members of the Republican Party are already inclined to vote pro-defense based solely on their

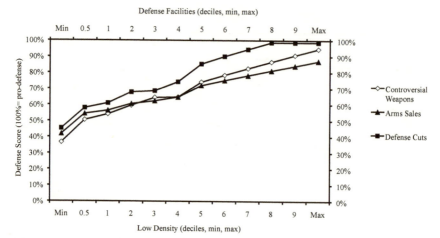

Figure 5.2. *Estimated influence of economic reliance on House members' support for defense spending by vote type, 1993–1998 (pooled).*

The figure displays expected values calculated by the author from the multiple regression analysis in appendix 5.5 using CLARIFY. All control variables are held constant at their sample means.

partisanship. Since House Republicans represent more economically reliant districts than Democrats, on average, members' local economic imperatives may reinforce the Republican Party's "pro-military" stance.[31]

Figure 5.2 illustrates the magnitude of the effect that economic reliance has on members' support for defense spending across policy type. (The expected values are calculated based on the regression analyses in appendix 5.5.[32])

All else equal, economic reliance yields consistent, almost uniform levels of legislative support for all three types of defense investments. Economic reliance yields the largest influence on members' opposition to defense cuts, reinforcing the Republican Party's position on this issue. However, legislative support for controversial weapons and arms sale policies follow similar patterns. In fact, none of these weapons systems would garner a majority of congressional support if voting was restricted to legislators from areas without an economic stake in the program.

These results indicate that the shared threat of economic hardship affects legislative voting on targeted and generalized weapons spending. Former senator David Pryor (D-AR) captured this sentiment of reciprocity when explaining his vote to continue to fund the controversial Seawolf submarine: "When my military jobs get in trouble, if we have not made that [economic] transition . . . I hope the same people that asked me for my help will . . . remember our . . . workers and our plight."[33] Restricting arms sales abroad, canceling expensive weapons programs, and implementing defense cuts all threaten to exacerbate economic vulnerabilities in defense-dependent areas. These economic imperatives promote greater political support for military spending regardless of national defense needs.

PERPETUATING THE MILITARY ECONOMY

Commerce subcommittee chair Hal Rogers (R-KY) captured the severe fiscal effect of the post–Cold War budget crunch by referring to 1995 as "the year to eat bugs and drink rainwater."[34] Yet, despite the need for cutbacks, in 1995–96 the House failed to pass a single proposal for defense cuts that came to a floor vote. The only proposed defense spending reduction that a majority of House members agreed to in a roll call vote in the entire time period under study reduced the amount spent maintaining bases overseas and reallocated the funds for the operation of military bases in the United States.[35]

Debates over military spending continue to persist in wartime. After inheriting two major wars and a fiscal crisis, President Obama announced a strategic shift in defense policy calling for fewer nuclear weapons—much like President George H. W. Bush had done after the Soviet Union collapsed two decades earlier.[36] President Obama received similar resistance from Congress. In spite of the president's priorities, Rep. Norm Dicks successfully fought for funding to build a second munitions wharf for Trident II D5 ballistic missiles, which are used to launch nuclear weapons at the Bangor Naval Submarine Base—part of the Kitsap naval base and a major employer in his Washington district. Seattle representative Jim McDermott continued to mount strong opposition to the ballistic missile platform, imploring Congress to cut the "outdated radioactive relic" and support social programs instead.[37]

Constituency reliance on the defense sector helps explain why it is difficult for Congress to cut the defense budget and why members continue to fund strategically questionable weapons systems: In addition to the partisan and ideological pressures that members of Congress face, representatives also support programs that are critical to widely shared economic interests in their district. Evidence presented here suggests that more economically homogenous, rural constituencies generally experience greater dependence on the major defense companies in their district. Defense sector activity in more remote locations outside of large cities affects a greater proportion of local residents and simplifies the task of representing district interests.

Constituency reliance is particularly important when explaining Democratic members' voting behavior on defense measures because they lack a partisan predisposition to support these policies. Notably, however, Republican members overrepresent more economically reliant constituencies, which may reinforce the party's pro-military stance. Despite partisan divisions, local reliance on the defense sector encourages all members of Congress to extend the lifespan of controversial weapons systems, mount opposition to defense cuts, and relax restrictions on arms sales abroad. Evidence suggests that economic goals in more dependent areas promote legislative support for ongoing defense procurement spending, regardless of changing geopolitical realities and shifting national priorities.

The Distributive
Politics of Defense
Contracting

In 2005 Rep. Howard "Buck" McKeon (R-CA, 25th District) of the Armed Services Committee and Air and Land Forces Subcommittee oversaw more than $550 million directed to Northrop Grumman and Lockheed Martin facilities in the Antelope Valley region for defense projects. In addition, contractors for Northrop Grumman, Lockheed Martin, Raytheon Company, General Dynamics and SAIC targeted the district for twenty-seven major assignments distributed after the prime contract arrangement. Located at the western edge of the Mojave Desert, the aerospace and defense industry in Antelope Valley, California, employ over 20,000 residents—or approximately 40 percent of the labor force. On his webpage, Representative McKeon publicized his success procuring district projects for the B-2 stealth bomber, modifications to the B-1B bomber, the F-117 stealth fighter, and the development of the military's "new generation" fighter, the F-35 Joint Strike Fighter. At the same time, Lockheed Martin, Boeing, and General Dynamics facilities scattered throughout the economically diverse Phoenix-Mesa-Scottsdale metropolitan area were further from Representative Flake's (R-AZ, 6th District) political radar. Despite the defense interests in his district, in 2005 Representative Flake prioritized eliminating earmarks from the Homeland Security Appropriations Bill rather than seeking defense projects for his constituency.[1]

Representatives McKeon and Flake both represent constituencies that stand to benefit from defense contracting. However, despite a large defense industry presence, shared partisan affiliation, and similar conservative credentials, Representative McKeon approaches defense spending very differently than Representative Flake does. Existing perspectives emphasizing partisanship, ideology, and parochialism in Congress cannot explain why Representative McKeon prioritizes defense interests to a far greater extent than Representative Flake—at least not beyond the circular claim that these members have different preferences on defense issues.

Political scientists have found little systematic evidence suggesting that the Department of Defense (DoD) distributes contracts to advance the reelection interests of influential legislators like Buck McKeon—particularly those on the armed services committees and defense appropriations subcommittees.[2] Despite conventional wisdom that politics plays an important role in defense spending, the data demonstrate that prime defense contracts are generally awarded to a limited number of locations with defense industry headquarters, usually in large cities.[3]

By analyzing the contracting data at a finer resolution, however, the effect of economic reliance becomes apparent. Members of Congress prioritize defense interests based largely on the relative importance of military spending for a district's overall economy, and defense contractors also work to extend funding to areas that are excessively reliant on the defense benefits that they receive. This argument builds on the analysis presented in chapter 5, which suggests that members representing areas that are disproportionately reliant on the defense sector are more likely to support weapons spending and work to stave off program cuts. Of course, members can always voice their spending preferences for the record, even though their constituencies may not receive any advantages in the distribution of military contracts. However, if defense agencies and contractors spread benefits strategically in order to increase legislative support for military programs, then defense funds should flow to more economically vulnerable areas. From a political standpoint, single company towns that rely on defense jobs—like Buck McKeon's Antelope Valley district—are more attractive candidates than locations with the mere capacity to receive defense projects, such as the industrially diverse Mesa/Scottsdale metropolitan region.

To examine political biases in defense allocations systematically, I extended the scope of previous studies and tracked prime contracts to the subcontracting level, where most defense dollars eventually go.[4] While researchers have long speculated that politics may influence the distribution of subcontracts, data limitations have prevented a comprehensive analysis.[5] New data presented here overcome this obstacle.

The chapter unfolds in two parts: First, evidence shows that local economic reliance influences defense committee membership in the House of Representatives. Second, the focus on a secondary stage in the contracting process uncovers a striking pattern of defense projects flowing to economically reliant districts—even though defense industry headquarters receive the bulk of prime contract dollars.

The analysis identifies local dependence on the defense sector as one of the most important factors leading members of Congress to seek representation on defense committees and to procure defense benefits. The findings are also consistent with the inference that defense industries spread out their operations across multiple districts in order to stimulate greater political demand for weapons systems. Symbiotic institutional relationships help sustain local economies that rely on defense employment, while encouraging continued political support for weapons spending.

OVERLAPPING INSTITUTIONAL INCENTIVES

Defense contracting is a multistaged process involving Pentagon bureaucracies, defense committees in Congress, and military industries. The Pentagon proposes the initial defense budget requests in the president's bill and submits these requests to Congress. The president's bill goes directly to the House and Senate defense appropriation subcommittees, which debate and amend various provisions. The subcommittees then submit the amended bill to Congress for final budgetary authorization. In an overlapping sphere, the armed services committees authorize all funds and conditions for their use, and they report needs for specific weapons and research and development (R&D) to the DoD. Weapons manufacturers then bid for the contracts to build the weapons systems that Congress has authorized.

The Pentagon determines which companies are awarded prime contracts for weapons production and research grants within the limits of their budgetary authorization. Defense-industry managers (or contractors) then decide whether to carry out defense production in-house, distribute assignments to their own facilities at other locations, or subcontract projects out to other companies. Defense contractors also select the principal location where most of the work on contracted weapons systems takes place.

The conventional narrative suggests that the actors in charge of setting the defense budget and distributing funds for weapons programs have shared interests in defense-sector growth. Ongoing weapons production advances the electoral security of influential legislators in charge of the military budget, contributes to the prestige of defense agencies and military services, and promotes defense-industry profit margins—a mutually advantageous arrangement often referred to as an "iron triangle." However, political scientists disagree about whether legislators belonging to committees with jurisdiction over defense issues seek more military spending than other members, or if defense agencies and military industries distribute contracts with political goals in mind. These issues are each addressed in turn.

Committee Processes

Ambitious leaders must work to accommodate important public demands to help secure their political power. To advance this end, members of Congress use the committee system as a vehicle for prioritizing their goals and optimizing their ability to claim credit to their voters.[6] Members demonstrate a concern for local interests by joining committees with jurisdiction over important local interests and vying for related benefits, such as farm subsidies or highway funding.[7]

The analysis presented in chapter 5 suggests that local economic reliance on the defense sector encourages members of Congress to press for continued military spending and resist program cuts. The same logic indicates that these representatives will also join defense committees at greater rates than their colleagues. Of course, this does not simply imply that members of Congress representing areas with weapons facilities will seek defense committee assignments. Rather, as outlined in the previous chapter, local defense interests affect elected representatives differently in urban and rural settings. Defense industries generally affect a greater proportion of the overall population in more lightly settled areas with less diverse economies, such as Antelope Valley, California (in the Mojave Desert)—as opposed to larger cities like Los Angeles. The growth or decline of a major industry in a small town could revitalize or wreck a local economy.

While important research shows that the Armed Services Committee attracts members from "high-demand" districts—particularly those with large military bases and high levels of military employment—these studies do not consider disproportionate economic reliance or account for the civilian employees of defense contractors.[8] Scott Adler and John Lapinski explain the exclusion by noting the "[practical] impossibility" of accessing reliable employment data related to defense contractors and subcontractors for each congressional district across multiple decades.[9] By identifying the locations of the major defense industries that bid for weapons contracts, data presented here overcome this limitation. This strategy also affords a reasonable measure of economic reliance on defense funds.

The theory of economic reliance predicts that, controlling for the capacity to receive defense projects, members representing more rural areas with less diverse economies will be more likely to join defense committees than their urban counterparts. Congress members from districts that are more dependent on defense employment will join defense committees at greater rates than other members, controlling for the number of defense facilities in a district and other factors likely to lead members of Congress to seek a defense-committee assignment.

The Politics of Defense Contracting

While members' political priorities influence their likelihood of joining certain congressional committees, Richard Hall also demonstrates that different levels of committee participation correspond with Congress members' revealed "preference intensity."[10] These insights suggest that members' preferences shape internal congressional processes, such as committee decision-making. However, there is still some question as to whether such biases among members of Congress affect the distribution of program benefits.

Literature on this question is mixed. Several scholars have found that members of defense committees extract more benefits for their voters, on average, than the typical member of Congress.[11] However, most studies suggest that DoD personnel do not direct additional funds to the states or districts of influential members of Congress, including those belonging to a defense committee.[12] Instead, studies uncovering systematic biases in defense contracting tend to highlight partisan and ideological influences.[13] These findings are consistent with scholarship emphasizing the importance of the president's partisan affiliation and lack of sustained congressional influence in the allocation of federal outlays.[14]

However, previous scholars have lacked access to reliable data on subcontracting.[15] There is reason to suspect that work focusing solely on the allocation of prime contract dollars may have understated political factors that influence defense distributions. Given federal regulations governing contracts and standard operating procedures, the Pentagon itself may be limited in the extent to which it can distribute prime contracts politically. Prime contractors, however, enjoy wide discretion in distributing assignments and selecting suppliers for parts or technical services for weapons programs. While prime contracts typically flow to wealthy, urban areas, these funds might also "trickle down" to other areas in the form of subcontracts.

According to 2010 estimates by the Government Accountability Office (GAO), 60–70 percent of prime contract dollars are typically made available for subcontracts.[16] Further, these secondary distributions are not subject to the same Federal Acquisition Regulation constraints.[17] They are also typically less visible and less controversial. While prime contract distributions may not be susceptible to political manipulation, subcontracting affords more leeway for political distributions.

The size and structure of the military industry promotes shared incentives and unique opportunity to target defense benefits for political gain. As discussed in chapter 3, the federal government is the sole legal purchaser in a market with a small number of active suppliers, which creates an imperative for the Pentagon to keep major defense industries profitable. Given the scale and scope of defense activity illustrated in chapter 4, economic dependence on defense revenue may also exceed local dependence on other types of government spending, elevating the political importance of defense distributions. In addition, Pentagon bureaucracies can negotiate defense procurements when soliciting bids is impractical, providing greater opportunity for political accommodations.[18]

However, contractors enjoy even more discretion. Evidence suggests that military contractors purposely spread assignments for defense programs over wide expanses. In fact, prime contractors commonly include more than forty-five states and 250 congressional districts for a single project.[19] A broad distribution of benefits can encourage legislators to favor a program that might not otherwise receive support. While very small subcontracts may not draw much public attention or political benefit, new data on the "principal place of performance" allows me to target secondary contract assignments that include most of the labor associated with the prime contract. Research focusing exclusively on political influences on prime contract awards does not address these critical dissemination stages.

While earlier work suggests that "economic need" has no meaningful impact on the distribution of prime defense contracts, scholars have not examined a state or district's economic reliance on a particular sector of the economy.[20] In other words, while lower state GDP may indicate greater economic need generally, this does not correspond with a specific need for defense spending, as opposed to other kinds of government assistance. While representatives from more economically homogenous areas may pursue multiple types of government contracts, I expect that more economically homogenous areas with defense facilities will rely specifically on defense revenue to support existing infrastructure.

If national security considerations drive defense allocations, the defense dollars will flow to districts with a substantial number of defense facilities, but a district's economic reliance on defense spending will have no additional effect. However, if economic reliance influences defense contracting, then defense benefits will flow disproportionately to more rural districts, controlling for both the number of facilities in the district and other factors likely to influence defense distributions.

RESEARCH DESIGN AND MODELING TECHNIQUES

Econometric analysis is employed to test the effect of economic reliance on defense committee membership in the House of Representatives and the distribution of defense contract benefits from 1999 to 2005. The time period was selected to optimize data availability, while also spanning periods of both divided and unified government, as well as a period of relative peace before the abrupt need to heighten national security in the wake of the attacks of September 11, 2001. This time period permits me to address concerns about congressional pork barreling in matters of defense and national security spending in the post-9/11 context. Unfortunately, data limitations preclude a longer time series.

Dependent Variables

Defense committee membership: Extending the dataset from chapter 5, a dummy variable was coded "1" if a House member belongs to a defense committee in the 106th–109th congresses and "0" to indicate that a member does not belong to a defense committee.[21]

Prime contracts allocations: Although aggregating prime contract data is relatively straightforward, the lack of accessible data on defense-sector employment makes it prohibitively difficult to account for every contractor that received federal defense dollars within the context of this study. However, isolating six leading defense contractors accounts for about 40 percent of the total defense dollars spent on weapons procurement and R&D on average.[22] I accessed the Federal Procurement Data System to compile data on prime defense contracts awarded to Lockheed Martin, Boeing, Raytheon, Northrop Grumman, General Dynamics, and SAIC from 2000 to 2005, and I transformed the data (classified by zip codes) to the congressional district level for each relevant congressional term.[23] These companies include the top defense corporations in terms of defense contract dollars and total annual revenue, according to the Department of Defense and Washington Technology.[24] (Halliburton Co., ranked number 6 by DoD, is excluded from the analysis because the company provides products and services for petroleum and natural gas exploration rather than military technology.)

Subcontract allocations: Collecting information on subcontracts proved much more challenging. Information made available on the Federal Procurement Data System includes the "principal place of performance"—or the primary location in which a contracted weapon system is built—identifying one critical distribution made after the primary contract arrangement. However, the data are classified by city. Broad city-level data are not particularly suitable for a more specified, district-level analysis. To address this problem, I coded 4,468 cities and towns where defense allocations took place in 1999, 2000 and 2005 (excluding Washington DC, US territories, and foreign countries). I used both congressional district atlases and Geographic Information System (GIS) software to pair cities with congressional districts in the relevant congressional term.[25] Of course, it would be optimal to examine defense subcontracting across multiple, consecutive years. However, data availability is limited, and reformatting the information is prohibitively time intensive. Given the time-bound analysis and various coding challenges, the results presented here ought to be interpreted as preliminary. Despite these limitations, however, the measure lends important insight on a crucial—and previously underemphasized—stage of the defense-contracting process.

Explanatory Variables: Economic Reliance

Economic reliance: I apply the measure of economic reliance described in chapter 5 and employ a variant of the interaction term (*population density*facilities*) combining the number of defense facilities per district and population density per square mile.

Defense facilities: To measure defense facilities, I extended the dataset discussed in chapter 5 and collected new data on the nationwide locations of the six major 2006 defense contractors noted above. I accessed the information from a variety of sources, including company and third-party websites as well as corporate tax reports and other Security and Exchange Commission (SEC) filings from 1999 to 2006.[26] These search devices yield 1,063 defense facilities spread across all fifty states.[27] Each industry location was cross-checked using Google mapping tools referenced by city location and zip code. The data were also transformed to the congressional district level using GIS software, accounting for redistricting plans in each Congress. The variable is coded based on the number of defense facilities per district.[28]

Population density: Following the criteria set forth in previous chapters, a measure of population density per square mile is employed to capture the influence of economic dependence. A rural district with a large number of defense facilities is likely to have a less diverse economy and therefore to be more economically dependent on defense dollars than an urban district with an equal number of weapons suppliers.

Control Variables

Headquarters: Previous research shows that prime defense contracts often channel to locations with corporate headquarters.[29] To control for expected, nonpolitical distributions, a count variable capturing the number of defense industry headquarters in a district controls for these possible allocations.

Gunbelt: As illustrated in chapter 4, the distribution of defense dollars exhibit pronounced regional disparities over time. New England, South Atlantic, East and West South Central, Mountain, and Pacific divisions have enjoyed increasing benefits from defense contracting since World War II, while East and West North Central suffered substantial per capita losses.[30] The model controls for these expected regional patterns, with districts in "Gunbelt" states coded "1" and districts in other states coded "0."

Defense committee membership: Members' positions on defense committees may signal their political priorities and budgetary influence to defense agencies and contractors, biasing the distribution of defense benefits toward these members' districts. Accordingly, a dummy variable indicating defense committee membership is included as both a dependent and independent variable.

Defense committee leadership: A dummy variable signifies the presence of defense committee and subcommittee chairs. The variable is coded "1" for defense committee leaders and "0" for other members.

Defense Contribution (lagged): Extending the measure employed in chapter 5, the model controls for the volume of campaign funds given to each member by the defense industry in the previous election cycle.

Ideology: Poole and Rosenthal's DW-NOMINATE scores serve as a proxy for legislators' predisposed preferences or ideological dispositions. The variable captures members' aggregated voting behavior and controls for a mix of individual and constituency pressures that may result in greater conservatism in more rural areas.

Party: Finally, given the importance of presidential partisanship in the allocation of federal outlays, the model includes a variable capturing members' partisanship (coded "1" for Republican and "0" for Democrat).

Average Distribution of Defense Contracts and Subcontracts

The table of descriptive statistics located in appendix 6.1 provides information on the distribution of the variables under study. The average distribution of defense contracts across congressional districts shows that prime contact allocations are heavily restricted. In fact, a preponderance of congressional districts do not receive any prime defense-contract benefits at all, and the bulk of these distributions are concentrated in 10 percent of congressional districts (5th decile = 0 dollars, 0 contracts; 9th decile = $336 million, 48 contracts; max = $17.6 billion, 862 contracts). While subcontracting allocations are also skewed, these data nonetheless reveal much wider distributions across districts, more in line with the overall composition of defense facilities (5th decile = 1 subcontract; 1 facility, 9th decile = 15 subcontracts, 7 facilities; maximum = 66 subcontracts, 47 facilities).

The average distribution of defense contracts also comports with important research on the Gunbelt regions spanning the South, West and Northeast corridor. On average, districts within Gunbelt states receive over three times the level of prime contract revenue (μ = \$205 million in Gunbelt districts, μ = \$63.4 million in other districts), more than twice as many prime contract awards (μ = 20.93, μ = 8.36), and more than two times as many subcontracts (μ = 6.70, μ = 2.40) as other districts that are not in Gunbelt regions.

Given the Republican Party's recent efforts to label itself as "pro-defense," the proportion of defense-dependent districts that are represented by Republican members is also notable. Although defense facilities are spread relatively equally across Republican and Democratic districts, on average (μ = 2.50 Republican, μ = 2.38 Democrat) Republicans typically represent more defense-dependent areas (μ = 2.01 facilities in low-density districts) than their Democratic counterparts (μ = 1.18 facilities in low-density districts). These partisan biases are consistent with evidence presented in chapter 5 showing that Republicans overrepresented more economically reliant districts during the 1990s.

The table in appendix 6.2 lists the top 20 percent most economically reliant congressional districts in the 109th Congress (2005–6). Economic reliance captures the number of defense facilities in a district conditioned by low population density. Based on this metric, districts that experience excessive dependence on the defense industry span thirty-six states and cut across regions, offering important nuances to established regional trends in defense-sector development. For example, in the 109th Congress Jim Ryun (R-KS, 2), Jerry Costello (D-IL, 12) and Dave Hobson (R-OH, 7) all represented disproportionately reliant constituencies, although the Midwest is not typically associated with defense production.[31] Consistent with the descriptive statistics presented in appendix 6.1, Republicans also represent two-thirds of districts that rely most heavily on the defense sector. The convergence of economic imperatives and ideological positioning may contribute to the Republican Party's "pro-defense" stance.

Modeling Patterns in Defense Committees and Contract Allocations

Systematic statistical analysis offers a more refined analysis of these patterns, controlling for a number of factors that are likely to affect defense-committee membership and the distribution of defense benefits. The analysis of defense committee membership employs a dummy measure as the dependent variable. Therefore, the ordinary least squares (OLS) assumption of uniform distribution of variance is violated. Logistic regression maximizes the likelihood of observing a defense committee assignment based on a district's economic reliance on the defense sector.

The number of prime and subcontracts awarded per district are counts. As count variables, these distributions are highly skewed, with the majority of the congressional districts receiving no prime contract awards and more than one-third of districts receiving no subcontracts (see appendix 6.1). OLS regression is not appropriate because the data are not normally distributed. Instead, negative binomial regression is used to examine the number of defense contracts and subcontracts flowing to a district across each separate congressional term.[32]

For meaningful interpretation, the figures show the effect of district population density on the likelihood of observing defense committee membership and defense subcontract receipts, given a small, medium, and large number of defense facilities in a district. The technique isolates the effect of population density, holding number of district-wide defense facilities constant.[33] In doing so, this method also provides a reasonable control for a district's economic specialization as a defense supplier.

ECONOMIC RELIANCE AND CONGRESSIONAL DEFENSE COMMITTEES

Figure 6.1 illustrates the predicted probability that a member of Congress will join a defense committee as the population density of a district increases, given a small, medium, and large number of defense facilities in a district. The model holds all other control variables constant at their respective mean values (see appendix 6.1). (The predicted probabilities associated with these control variables are located in a logit analysis in appendix 6.3.[34])

Figure 6.1 shows that, given an equal number of defense facilities, defense committees draw members of Congress from more rural areas at greater rates than representatives from densely populated urban areas. As expected, legislators representing districts with a larger number of defense facilities exhibit a greater likelihood of joining a defense committee than members representing districts with fewer weapons facilities, on average. However, members' priorities are also consistently conditioned by the size of the overall local economy. In fact, the presence of a single defense plant in a district with a population density below the mean yields a likelihood of a defense committee assignment comparable to that for a densely populated district with five weapons facilities. Similarly, members representing districts with five defense facilities and a population

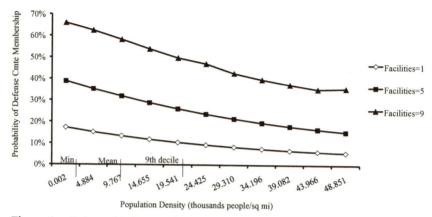

Figure 6.1. *Estimated influence of economic reliance on Defense Committee membership, 109th Congress, first session (2005).*

The figure displays expected values calculated by the author from the logit analysis in appendix 6.3 using CLARIFY. The figure denotes a change in population density (rural to urban) given small, medium, and large numbers of defense facilities in a district. All control variables are held constant at their sample means.

density below the mean exhibit a greater probability of joining a defense committee than representatives from densely populated urban districts that contain nine facilities—a disproportionately large defense capacity. As the theory of economic reliance predicts, members of Congress representing more rural constituencies with a highly concentrated defense-sector presence exhibit the highest probability of joining defense committees—nearly 70 percent—after controlling for rural members' more conservative leanings and other factors likely to influence these decisions.

The results support the inference that the relative importance of the defense industry to a political constituency yields different "preference intensities" among representatives that affect their likelihood of joining defense committees. Members who represent districts that are disproportionately reliant on the defense sector are considerably more likely to involve themselves in defense and national security policymaking than members representing areas that have a lower economic stake in these decisions. The findings are consistent with evidence from previous chapters suggesting that the economic underdevelopment of a more rural constituency places a political premium on existing infrastructure that helps keep the economy afloat. While more urban, economically vibrant, and high-income locations benefit from defense jobs and revenue, the closing of large defense facilities in more sparsely populated areas would cause greater damage to the local economy. Controlling for differences in capacity to receive defense projects, economic reliance on the defense sector shapes the likelihood that local political representatives will prioritize defense issues.

ECONOMIC RELIANCE AND DEFENSE CONTRACTING

The theory of disproportionate economic reliance suggests that more rural districts will receive a greater number of contracts and subcontracts than more urban (and less reliant) districts with an equal number of defense industries. The results (not presented here, but available upon request) show that prime contracts consistently flow to areas with defense industry headquarters. These expected, nonpolitical distributions to defense industry headquarters are the only factor that is consistent and robust to alternative specifications throughout the entire six-year period under study. Consistent with earlier work, evidence suggests that standard operating procedures are the most important factor explaining how DoD personnel distribute defense awards.

However, this narrative paints only a partial picture. Defense contractors might strategically target secondary assignments (or subcontracts) for political purposes after the prime contract arrangement. To examine this possibility, the graph displayed in figure 6.2 exhibits the expected values of the number of subcontracts flowing to a congressional district as population density increases, given a small, medium, and large number of defense facilities. The prevalence of cost-plus contracting—where a defense contractor receives compensation equal to expenses plus a profit—substantially reduces incentives for defense contractors to target rural districts in order to reduce overhead costs, as opposed to optimizing the economic and political benefits of these distributions. The model holds the control variables constant at their respective mean values. (Refer to the negative binomial regression analysis in appendix 6.4 for the predicted rates associated with these variables.)

The results are striking. As expected, rural districts draw greater numbers of subcontracts than densely populated urban areas with an equal number of defense facilities. The curvilinear trend exhibits steep slopes at lower levels of density, which consistently level off in densely populated, urban areas (around the 9th decile) and take on a more linear trajectory. In fact, the most densely populated districts (above the 9th decile) typically receive the lowest levels of expected defense assignments regardless of the number of defense facilities in these areas. A rural district with a large defense-sector presence is expected to secure four times as many subcontracts as an urban district with an equal number of defense facilities and

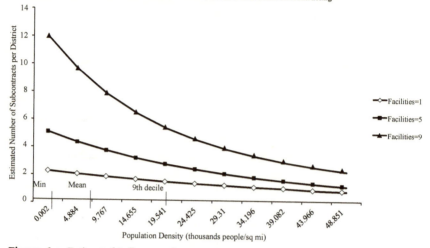

Figure 6.2. *Estimated influence of economic reliance on defense subcontracting 109th Congress, first session (2005).*

The figure displays expected values calculated by the author from the negative binomial regression in appendix 6.4 using CLARIFY. The figure denotes a change in population density (rural to urban) given small, medium, and large numbers of defense facilities in a district. All control variables are held constant at their sample means.

comparable specialization as a defense supplier. Further, a rural area with a single defense industry is estimated to receive nearly as many subcontracts as a heavily urban district with nine defense facilities. The expected differences of one to eight subcontracts per district as population density changes from its minimum to maximum value may appear moderate. However, this disparity often signifies millions of dollars flowing to more rural districts with an equal defense presence. It is reasonable to assume that this difference is meaningful for the preponderance of districts that receive between one and fifteen subcontracts annually, on average (see appendix 6.1).

The results suggest that for densely populated urban areas specialization does not weigh heavily in the allocation of secondary defense assignments. However, more rural districts with defense facilities—not simply sparse, rural areas—are disproportionate subcontract recipients. This finding does not invalidate conventional wisdom that prime contractors distribute projects locally and carry them out in-house; however, it does indicate that economic reliance also plays a role in these decisions. Densely populated cities with more diverse economies are less reliant on these projects and thus less attractive candidates from a political standpoint. Rural and urban areas with equal defense capacity are unequal recipients in the distribution of defense benefits.

Furthermore, the results in the full model suggest that members of defense committees also draw more subcontracts to their districts than other House members ($p < .01$, appendix 6.4). Committee representation may further magnify the political value of a congressional district as a potential subcontract recipient. While local defense capacity is a necessary factor in defense contracting, a district's reliance on defense activity has greater effects on subcontract allocations than the capacity to receive these projects alone. The results suggest that subcontracts are allocated to maximize economic benefits in more rural areas, which typically experience greater dependence on defense dollars to maintain their local economies.

INSTITUTIONAL SYMBIOSIS

By accounting for the economic context in which defense facilities are situated, evidence indicates that economic dependence on the defense sector encourages political representatives to prioritize national security issues by joining relevant defense committees. Constituencies that are more economically dependent on defense suppliers also draw subcontracts at greater rates than other areas with an equal capacity to receive defense projects. While detailed information on the subcontracting process remains largely unavailable, preliminary evidence presented here is consistent with the theory that the defense industry gains politically by extending major assignments to more dependent, rural districts, even while prime contract revenue generally remains concentrated.

Previous academic work on the distributive politics of defense contracting has missed these patterns for two reasons: First, scholars have not accounted for the effect of a district's economic reliance on defense spending. Second, research has focused only on the allocations of prime defense contracts, which are merely precursors to subsequent dissemination. However, probing more deeply into the defense contracting process uncovers new evidence indicating that the degree to which defense procurement policies receive priority among members of Congress varies according to the economic composition of a district. Although Congress members do not directly influence defense distributions, it is clear that the defense industry plays a critical role in the allocation of subcontracts. If the Lockheed Martin corporate headquarters in Bethesda, Maryland, receives a multimillion-dollar defense contract award, then the relevant directors enjoy great discretion in assigning various parts of the project locally, to another Lockheed Martin facility, or subcontracting out to another company.

The results of this analysis suggests a symbiotic relationship among key players, where spreading substantial defense benefits across multiple districts increases political demand for weapons systems among Congress members and contributes to local economies that are more reliant on the defense industry. Defense subcontracting helps meet districts' economic needs for employment and revenue, which in turn generates greater political demand for weapons systems. These overlapping interests encourage defense expenditures in excess of strategic requirements. They also bias defense contract allocations, channeling them to more dependent areas during critical dissemination stages. As the next chapter will argue, local economic reliance not only promotes more military spending, but also leads to greater political support for contentious military operations.

III

YOU AND WHOSE ARMY? EXPANSIVE PRESIDENTIAL WAR POWERS

Economic Reliance
and War

In debates surrounding constitutional ratification, James Madison claimed that the American republic would avoid the fate of European monarchies and military dictatorships by maintaining competition and balance among distinct branches of government. A single actor cannot capriciously commit the nation to war or command armies against his own people as long as the legislative department controls the resources and funding necessary to carry out these actions. However, interbranch competition in warfare only remains viable if the legislative branch uses its power over funding to *limit* the resources available to the executive. As the last two chapters show, patterns of local defense dependence promote ongoing military spending, regardless of national security circumstances or other policy goals. Congressional interests in perpetuating the military economy empower the very actor that the division of war powers was meant to restrain, and prevent Congress from mounting an effective defense against the president's military actions.

Many historical examples support the inference that Congress's blank-check policy promotes more executive independence in military affairs. Perhaps most notoriously, in 1973 President Richard Nixon directed an unauthorized bombing campaign in Cambodia and Laos and deliberately misled Congress and the American public about it. Nixon was already withdrawing US ground troops from Vietnam as the war sputtered to an inglorious end, and evidence of his involvement in the Watergate burglary had crippled his presidency. In an unprecedented assertion of congressional power, the House and Senate passed an amendment to cut off funds for the bombing, but not far enough in advance to prevent Nixon from obtaining resources from other lines of the budget and not in large enough margins to override the president's veto.[1]

Independent executive authority to launch military actions is not limited to periods of heightened national security or moments of crisis. In 1999 President Clinton commenced air strikes over the former Yugoslavia in a NATO-backed campaign to prevent the Serbian army from committing human rights abuses or genocide against ethnic minorities in Kosovo. Clinton operated with the support of the United Nations (UN), but without Congress. Despite pending impeachment charges and a lawsuit filed by Republican members claiming that President Clinton's military actions violated the War Powers Act, a Republican-led Congress continued to provide funds to carry out the military operation. In the succeeding administration, President George W. Bush reacted to sweeping Republican losses in the 2006 midterm election and a Democratic "mandate" to end the ongoing war in Iraq by directing a troop surge in the region, which the Democratic majority in Congress continued to fund through a series of supplemental spending bills. Repeating the precedent, in 2011 President Barack Obama ordered US air strikes over Libya to enforce a no-fly zone in support of the rebel movement to oust Libyan dictator Muammar Gaddafi. Obama acted in conjunction with UN security forces, but without consulting Congress—and he did so after historic Democratic losses in the 2010 midterm elections, in the midst of two major wars, and while the nation suffered a severe fiscal crisis. Even in these extreme circumstances, Congress has persistently refused to use its spending power to challenge an opposing administration and terminate an unpopular mission.

While a long tradition of scholarship mourns Congress's institutional weakness, recent work challenges the view that legislators' refusal to draw the purse strings renders Congress impotent in military affairs. These scholars point out that legislative majorities facing a president of the opposing party regularly criticize executive military commitments and heighten the political costs of the president's military actions.[2] Presidents also anticipate a firestorm of legislative dissent during periods of divided government and often modify their military goals to avoid the negative publicity.[3]

However, while some members do mount sustained opposition to executive war policies, the opposition party rarely unites against the president's military actions. Rather, members of Congress opposing the president's party tend to splinter on measures that would limit war funding or end military operations, while maintaining greater unity on symbolic matters such as criticizing the president's handling of the war. The literature does not address why some members aligned against the president's party thwart the attempts of their own partisan allies to withdraw war funding and end a military conflict. Instead, most research assumes that legislators uniformly refuse to use the purse to limit military operations because members lack technical intelligence expertise, seek to avoid responsibility, and fear being branded as disloyal to the president, the troops, or the nation.[4]

In addition to Congress's institutional disadvantages, these fears may also be compounded by a more fundamental imbalance: To impose a meaningful funding restriction, members must draw down the defense budget—a politically difficult act for legislators representing areas that rely on a war economy for job security and growth. To examine economic reliance and legislators' support for war systematically, the chapter draws on the original database of nationwide locations of defense contractors introduced in chapters 5 and 6 and examines the influence of local defense dependence on members' support for a selection of military actions and wars. The analysis suggests that legislators representing constituencies that are disproportionately reliant on the defense funding they receive are more predisposed to support war and war spending than their partisan colleagues. Although members of Congress have always been reluctant to limit appropriations in order to curtail an ongoing military venture, economic dependence on a military economy exacerbates the political obstacles that legislative coalitions must surmount.

The analysis proceeds as follows: The next section elaborates on the theory of economic reliance introduced in previous chapters. Local economic imperatives not only influence legislators' political priorities, but also reinforce some members' ideological commitments to American military supremacy and interventionism. The second section discusses the research design and modeling techniques. The third section introduces new evidence suggesting that local economic reliance shapes legislators' support for war and war spending. Case studies documenting interbranch conflict in various military operations complement individual-level analysis of members' support for specific wars. The case studies illustrate how patterns of ongoing defense spending weaken Congress's collective ability to use its spending power to challenge executive military actions. Large defense budgets provide executives with ample resources to initiate and carry out military actions independently—despite low public approval of specific wars and strong legislative majorities opposing the president's party. The final section introduces additional empirical models estimating the extent to which economic reliance influences members' support for controversial wars and war funding.

RELIANT RESIDENTS AND RED-HUNTERS

Since the Vietnam War, congresses have regularly authorized open-ended military actions and failed to end unpopular wars, even during periods of heightened public opposition and divided government. While most scholarship suggests that legislators' partisan commitments, ideological beliefs, or deferential posture shape their military and foreign policy decisions, these explanations cannot fully explain why some members prioritize spending that undermines their party's efforts to force the president's hand and curtail a specific military action.[5] On its face, these patterns of legislative behavior seem to belie deepening divisions between the political parties and defy Congress's well-known eagerness to claim credit for policies that please their voters.[6]

However, just as local economic reliance contributes to legislative support for defense procurement spending, economic imperatives may also strengthen political support for military action and war. Although Congress can maintain large defense budgets in the absence of major shooting wars, US warfare (or the perpetual threat of warfare) serves as an underlying justification for military growth. Wartime expansion not only fuels the defense establishment, but also elevates its political importance. In fact, ongoing US military activity almost always stimulates increased demand for weapons, hardware, and equipment, and promotes additional spending beyond the baseline defense budget. Accordingly, members of Congress representing constituencies that are disproportionately reliant on the defense spending they receive and members who are ideologically committed to American military hegemony have shared interests in military buildups and interventionism.

Regulatory economist Bruce Yandle famously introduced the phrase "bootleggers and Baptists" to describe an unusual political alliance that forms for mutual benefit.[7] While the bootleggers and Baptists found common cause in support of the early twentieth-century prohibition movement, economically reliant residents and red-hunters also formed a durable political coalition in support of large defense budgets and an aggressive American military posture since the onset of the Cold War. While deep-seated moral and religious convictions moved Baptist prohibitionists, bootleggers enjoyed the inflated profits from alcohol sales on the black market. Similarly, while red-hunters (or in contemporary parlance, defense hawks) support American military hegemony in order to keep the world safe from villains and zealots, economically reliant residents depend on defense spending to support local jobs and revenue. Just as Baptists provide moral justification for the bootleggers' business, red-hunters also provide political cover for the residents that rely most heavily on employment and revenue from local weapons suppliers. Like their bootlegger counterparts, economically reliant residents are much less visible but no less vital to policymaking.

However, unlike the bootleggers and Baptists—an unlikely coalition united by independently held, overlapping interests—economic reliance may not only add to the red-hunters' political coalition, but also shape and reinforce some members' pro-military views. While local interests and ideologies are not simply reducible, economic circumstances may strengthen elite views in areas where salient political values overlap with widely shared local interests.[8] In fact, evidence presented in the previous chapters indicates that congressional defense hawks are overrepresented in areas that rely most heavily on local defense industries and underrepresented in districts with more diverse economies and cross-cutting political interests.

Although legislators may support defense programs for a variety of reasons, they ultimately have allegiances to their voters—at least to the extent that they value their jobs. Like leading members of the defense establishment who build careers on identifying and extinguishing national security threats, legislators representing areas that rely most heavily on military spending also have much to gain from US power projection and a great deal to lose from a peace dividend. People belonging to organizations, institutions, or communities with a large stake in US military dominance are predisposed to embrace worldviews that see American military muscle as a foreign policy virtue. While political elites may self-select into these settings, their environment also promotes and reinforces militaristic views.

To be clear, the notion that economic interests shape members' war policies does not mean that the United States goes to war in order to prop up major defense industries or subsidize economically vulnerable areas. Rather, the theory suggests that the existence of a military economy and widespread local reliance on continued military spending make it easier to go to war and may reinforce belief systems favoring US hegemony and military interventionism.

CASE STUDIES AND MODELING TECHNIQUES

To examine legislative support for US military actions and war systematically, I located a selection of roll-call votes taken in the US House of Representatives on the authorization for war, troop withdrawal initiatives and supplemental war spending measures from 1993 to 2007, extracted from *CQ Weekly* and GovTrack.us. I selected two high-profile, politically divisive votes for war and continued war spending in Iraq in 2002 and 2007 (respectively), in addition to several minor military interventions that took place in the 1990s. To help verify that the model is capturing economic reliance on war spending, as opposed to a conservative orientation present in more rural areas, I also included a vote regarding gay soldiers in the military as a control case. Unfortunately, I am unable to measure economic reliance during earlier periods, so I cannot extend the time series to include the

Cold War era. However, in-depth case studies of interbranch conflict over the Vietnam War and minor military actions in the 1980s help illustrate how patterns of ongoing military spending consistently weaken Congress's ability to curb the president's military actions. The analysis focuses on military actions and wars that sparked interbranch conflict and excludes military operations characterized by sustained legislative-executive cooperation.[9] The statistical models capture periods under a Democratic and a Republican president, with nearly every permutation of unified and divided government. A prowar vote (including pro–war spending and antispending restrictions) is coded "1," and an antiwar vote is coded "0." (Tables 7.1 and 7.2 include more detailed information on each roll-call vote.)

To capture disproportionate economic reliance, I used the measures introduced in chapters 5 and 6. I employed my original database consisting of the nationwide locations of leading US defense contractors in 1995 and 2006, including Lockheed Martin, Boeing Company, Raytheon, Northrop Grumman, General Dynamics, SAIC, TRW Inc., and Alliant Techsystems, transformed to each congressional district. I also applied the inverse of the population density for each congressional district, where higher values indicate lower density.[10] The interaction term, *low density*facilities*, gauges the influence of a large defense-sector presence in a more sparsely populated area, or greater economic reliance on the military economy.

In addition, the models include the control variables employed in chapter 5, which are updated through 2007 (the 110th Congress). These variables include the military population in each district, the number of military bases per district, a dummy variable signifying whether a member belongs to a defense committee, campaign contributions from the defense industry given to each congressional member, and a standard political science measurement for ideology, Poole and Rosenthal's DW-NOMINATE scores.[11] Finally, instead of applying a measure capturing the military population or base presence in 2007, I include a variable signifying the number of Iraq war deaths in a district. Iraq War fatalities consists of the number of soldiers from the congressional district who were killed between March 21, 2003, and May 9, 2007, one day before the McGovern bill proposing a troop withdrawal came to a floor vote.[12]

The analysis employs a dummy measurement as the dependent variable, capturing either a prowar or antiwar vote. Therefore, I used logistic regression, which maximizes the likelihood of a observing a prowar vote. Given the difficulties parsing the effect of an interaction term, I also report the effects of defense facilities and low density when these variables are set to high and low values.[13]

I am unable to include fixed effects that account for all time-invariant characteristics because data limitations preclude a time-series analysis. Therefore, I cannot rule out the possibility that a president will only use force when he or she knows that Congress will agree. However, the models account for the principal factors that prominent scholarship suggests will lead members of Congress to mount sustained opposition to the president's military actions, including periods of divided government, polarized parties, unpopular wars, and statistical controls for members' ideologies. Defense committee members also have more access to intelligence information than other members, offering a reasonable control for legislators' expertise on defense issues. In short, the analysis provides the most rigorous test of economic reliance possible given current data availabilities. Qualitative evidence of legislative opposition to the military engagements under study strengthens the statistical findings even more. It would be difficult to argue that the president could predict sustained congressional support for the military ventures in the dataset if he or she could not make the same calculation for any military operation that an administration prioritizes.

ECONOMIC RELIANCE AND CONGRESS'S BLANK-CHECK POLICY

Historical case studies document periods of legislative opposition to military engagements and highlight prominent congressional efforts to curb unpopular missions. Quantitative analyses examine individual legislators' support for several specific military actions and wars that members opposing the president's party sought to limit or prevent. Taken together, the analysis highlights important structural barriers that contribute to Congress's persistent failure to use its spending power to curtail an armed conflict, despite unpopular wars, divided government, polarized parties, and congressional reforms. The first prominent attempt to force the president's hand occurred in response to the military debacle in Vietnam.[14]

Vietnam (1964–1973)

In August 1964 Congress passed the Gulf of Tonkin Resolution authorizing the president to use military force in Southeast Asia in retaliation for attacks against US naval forces off the Vietnam coast. (Evidence later called the circumstances of the attacks into question, although Congress had already accepted the administration's account of the events.) The resolution passed unanimously in the House and with only two opposing votes in the Senate. Most Americans saw the war as a key element in the fight against communism and supported the mission. However, as the war dragged on, public opposition mounted, the initiation of a draft lottery sparked massive protests, and Congress expressed increasing concern over protracted US military involvement.

Growing legislative disagreement with the war, however, failed to resonate in Congress's war spending decisions. In 1967 both chambers voted almost unanimously to approve the Johnson administration's annual defense bill—the single-largest annual appropriation that Congress had ever passed.[15] An amendment proposed by the antiwar senator Wayne Morse (D-OR) to cut annual defense appropriations by 10 percent fell on deaf ears, garnering only five votes in favor, despite a provision allowing the secretary of defense to make necessary budget transfers.[16]

While the constitutional framers envisioned Congress's control over revenue as a potent source of influence over military affairs, Sen. Frank Church (D-ID) depicted Congress's spending power as a useless policy instrument in an age of standing armies and permanent military mobilization, lamenting that "the power to maintain armies and control the purse [are] meaningless when the president . . . has assumed the right to send our armed forces into action whenever he deems it in the national interest."[17] Lacking the votes to impose meaningful restrictions on war funding, antiwar coalitions in Congress held hearings and issued nonbinding resolutions. Rather than scale back military operations, in 1968 the Johnson administration capitalized on an overstock of congressionally appropriated resources to repel the Tet Offensive.

Richard Nixon was elected to office in 1968 with a campaign pledge to end the war that had destroyed Johnson's presidency and restore "peace with honor." Nixon's policy of Vietnamization sought to equip the South Vietnamese to handle the war on their own and eliminate the need for US ground forces. However, Nixon could not withdraw US troops too abruptly without harming the mission and abandoning his right-wing base. Despite the administration's goal of troop withdrawal, US troop count reached a peak of 542,000, and Americans killed in action averaged 1,200 a month. Further, educational deferments were lifted in 1967 and 1968, which exposed middle-class families to the draft and increased the scale of public involvement. Antiwar Democrats in Congress intensified their opposition, but still lacked the votes to cut off war spending.

Unlike President Johnson, whose craft, cunning, and browbeating had helped him carry out the war without alienating Congress, Nixon's relations with the Democratic Congress are most gently characterized as hostile.[18] He openly defied Congress's resolutions, referring to their tactics as an "obstruction and a nuisance."[19] Even as Nixon began a course of gradual US troop withdrawal in 1970, his administration accelerated an air war without notifying Congress or the American public. Nixon's unauthorized bombing campaign in neighboring regions of Cambodia and Laos was limited only in the sense that he did it in secret rather than openly flout Congress.

As the bombing intensified and knowledge of the campaign leaked, many members proposed measures to cut off appropriations for military operations in Southeast Asia, but these initiatives were ultimately rejected or so weakened by amendments that they were almost entirely symbolic.[20] Instead of eliminating military spending, Congress continued to pass legislation instructing the president to end the war while appropriating funds to carry it out. For instance, a 1971 resolution sponsored by Senate Majority Leader Mike Mansfield (D-MT) expressed US policy to end all military operations in Indochina "at the earliest practicable date" with one breath, while Congress approved a defense appropriations bill stripped clean of any timetables or spending restrictions with the next.[21] Even Congress's formal legislative repeal of the Gulf of Tonkin Resolution in January 1971 was so inconsequential that Nixon signed it into law, citing his authority as commander-in-chief to end the war at the pace that he thought best. Senator William Fulbright (D-AR) aptly characterized Congress's impossible predicament when he exclaimed, "What can we do? We passed the Church-Cooper Amendment [restricting funding for US ground troops], but we gave them money for Cambodia anyway."[22]

Congress did not muster the votes to enact a spending restriction until 1973, after President Nixon escalated the bombing raid in Cambodia in support of the Lon Nol government. Evidence of President Nixon's involvement in the Watergate cover-up, complete US troop withdrawal from Vietnam (which nullified the administration's earlier justification for the bombing), and clear public disapproval of the air strikes provided the tipping point in which both chambers of Congress voted to restrict the president's use of war funds.[23] However, unlike earlier periods of history, Congress could not simply withhold funding for military operations; instead, they had to pass legislation denying the president use of existing military appropriations to carry out his actions.

To intensify the air strikes without notifying Congress or requesting new resources, the administration relied on the Pentagon's transfer authority—a routine measure allowing agencies to shift money between accounts and meet budget shortfalls. By using existing resources already appropriated for other purposes, executives sidestep even the most limited dependence on Congress and force legislators to take the positive action of passing legislation in order to provide an effective check.

On May 10, 1973, the House deleted nearly $500 million in transfer authority for the Department of Defense and passed an amendment to a supplemental spending bill to prohibit the use of any funds therein for military operations in Cambodia.[24] When the bill reached the Senate, an amendment proposed by Sen. Thomas Eagleton (D-MO) closed an existing loophole and prohibited the administration from using *any* available funding for the bombing in Cambodia. On June 26, 1973, the supplemental appropriations act with the Eagleton Amendment had passed both chambers with bipartisan support, emerged from House-Senate conference, received final approval on the floor of the House and Senate, and reached the president's desk for his signature. Nixon vetoed the amendment and the House failed to override by a vote of 241 to 173, just shy of the necessary two-thirds.[25]

Ultimately, a revised version of the amendment attached to a crucial measure to extend the federal debt ceiling forced Nixon to compromise. At the behest of White House Counsel and Secretary of Defense Melvin Laird, Senator Fulbright brokered a deal set on the president's terms.[26] Nixon agreed not to veto the amendment, but at the enormous cost of allowing him to continue bombing Cambodia for another forty-five days—a time period in which the United States had previously dropped approximately 75,000 tons of bombs on Cambodia and Laos.[27]

Despite unprecedented legislative assertion and the president's concession, many supporters of the compromise admitted that it was a defeat— or at best, a necessary evil to muster support within their ranks. Senator Church conceded that to insist on an immediate end to the bombing would be nothing more than "a futile debate, flouting our impotence and allowing this war in Cambodia to continue indefinitely."[28] Senator Mark Hatfield, an outspoken critic of the Vietnam War and sponsor of several failed amendments to eliminate war funding, voted for the compromise but described it as "an emasculation of congressional power" that "contributes to the erosion of the power of the Federal purse." Others characterized the vote as "political blackmail," forcing Congress to "[declare] war on Cambodia until August" and as "the only way out of a nearly impossible situation."[29]

The exchange between antiwar senators Fulbright and Eagleton in the floor debate over the compromise measure characterizes the pervasive sense of legislative impotence in the face of an executive armed with resources, a funding stream and institutional mechanisms to employ them:

EAGLETON: I want to inquire as to what this resolution includes. . . .
Does it permit continued bombing between now and August 15?

FULBRIGHT: I do not regard him as having the right to this. He has the power to do it. . . .

EAGLETON: . . . Will we with the adoption of this resolution permit the bombing of Cambodia for the next 45 days?

FULBRIGHT: Until August 15.

EAGLETON: Would it permit the bombing of Laos?

FULBRIGHT: It would not prevent it.

EAGLETON: Would it permit the bombing of North and South Vietnam until August 15?

FULBRIGHT: I do not think it is legal or constitutional. But whether it is right to do it or not, [the president] has done it. He has the power to do it because under our system there is not any easy way to stop him. . . . I do not want my statement taken to mean that I approve of it. . . . He can do it. He has done it. Do I make myself clear?[30]

Perpetual military mobilization skews the institutional playing field heavily in favor of the executive. As Nixon's actions illustrate, presidents can exploit executive control over ongoing defense funds to wage war and direct military actions at their discretion. Moreover, preemptive executive initiative can reverse the onus placed on Congress by requiring positive legislative action to *stop* military actions rather than to start them. For most of the nation's history, Congress could exercise its spending power by simply withholding funds, which requires that it do nothing. To provide an effective check, Congress now faces the added burden of passing legislation, which is then subject to a presidential veto. To prevent independent executive military actions altogether, the obstacles are even greater: Congress has to withhold funds far enough in advance and in sufficiently detailed language to close potential loopholes and prevent the president from reappropriating other lines of the budget.

Limited Military Interventions (1981–2000)

The deployment of violence often has unintended consequences. In 1963 President Kennedy sent 17,000 military advisers to South Vietnam and directed the Central Intelligence Agency (CIA) to sponsor a coup overthrowing the South Vietnamese autocrat Ngo Dinh Diem, unleashing chaos and instability that paved the path to years of brutal warfare. During the 1980s, President Reagan's National Security Council instructed the CIA to arm and train some of the same Afghan rebels that later harbored the Al-Qaida terrorist network responsible for the attacks of September 11, 2001, and who fought against US forces in decade-long war of counter-insurgency.[31] In

2002 George W. Bush's war cabinet expected a cheap and easy Iraq intervention and ended up unleashing a $3-trillion war a decade later.

The 1973 War Powers Resolution enacted in the wake of Vietnam was meant to prevent creeping wars where the deployment of forces gradually drifts toward full-scale war or nation-building enterprises. Passed over President Nixon's veto, the resolution requires presidents to notify Congress of troop deployments "in every possible instance." It also requires either congressional authorization or an automatic troop withdrawal after sixty days when presidents report that hostilities are "imminent." The resolution has been criticized on a host of counts: it not only implicitly suggests that the president can independently deploy troops and direct their activities for sixty days, but also the language invites the executive to exploit various loopholes in its reporting requirements.[32] Subsequently, presidents have continued to introduce US armed forces into hostilities without consulting Congress or obtaining legislative authorization. In fact, only one president ever activated the sixty-day clock, when President Ford ordered armed forces to retrieve a US vessel seized by Cambodia in 1975, and by the time he reported the action it was already nearly over.[33] While scholars have pointed to "faulty draftsmanship" as a basis for presidential discretion in reporting requirements, questionable wording simply reinforces the lack of congressional inclination to impose stronger language and absence of resources with which to back it up.[34]

To the extent that the Vietnam War inspired any inclination to scale back US military interventions, that consideration faded away by the end of the 1970s. For the next two decades, the use of force became more frequent and less contentious. Even as the Soviet threat subsided and disappeared, the Pentagon promoted new rationales for continued military readiness and the projection of US force. Rather than constraining independent executive actions, presidents have construed the War Powers Resolution as affirmative authorization to commit military forces for up to sixty days without permission. When limited wars unexpectedly escalate or extend beyond two months, presidents have already side-stepped language that would have activated the deadline. Presidents' persistent refusal to recognize statutory limitations leaves Congress with several unsavory choices: Given sufficient notification of the president's military action, Congress can activate the War Powers Resolution and support the mission. In other cases, however, Congress might not be able respond to the president's military actions until the mission is over—a default mechanism that was meant to end military operations, but instead operates as tacit endorsement. Finally, the majority party may attempt to enforce a withdrawal deadline. However,

Congress has repeatedly failed to restrict war funding and lacks alternative mechanisms to end a military conflict on its own terms.

Qualified Legislative Support: Lebanon (1982–1984),
Grenada (1983), Panama (1989)

President Reagan first tested the limitations of the War Powers Resolution on August 21, 1982, when he sent US marines to Lebanon to drive out the Palestine Liberation Organization (PLO) and support the sovereignty of the Lebanese regime, a Christian government that maintained friendly relations with Israel. He notified Congress but refused to recognize any limitations on the scope and duration of the operation. The PLO withdrew on August 30, but the assassination of Lebanese president Bashir Gemayel on September 14 and the massacre of hundreds of Palestinian refugees prompted Reagan to organize another multinational force (MNF) with Italy and France. Their mission was to support the new Lebanese government, counter Soviet forces allied to the opposing side, and promote stability in the region.

In June 1983, after eight months of legislative silence, Congress passed the Lebanon Emergency Assistance Act providing emergency funds for the mission while prohibiting its expansion.[35] President Reagan signed the bill into law, but issued a signing statement declaring that the language does not prevent him from expanding US military activity in Lebanon without legislative authorization should circumstances require it.[36] By September US marines had been stationed in Lebanon for a year under periodic fire from factions in the 1975 Lebanese Civil War. The president did not report hostilities pursuant to the War Powers Resolution, so Congress activated the provision for him. Both houses passed a joint resolution determining that the sixty-day deadline became operational on August 29, 1983, and authorizing the military action for another eighteen months.[37]

When suicide bombers hit the US and French barracks in Beirut, killing 241 American servicemen and 58 French soldiers on October 21, Congress put pressure on the administration to withdraw US forces. Although legislators voiced increasing opposition to the mission, Congress did not withdraw funds or reduce the eighteen-month timetable. Despite legislative criticism, Reagan insisted that the mission would continue. Several months later, Syrian forces entered the fray, an American crewman was held captive, and the Lebanese prime minister and his cabinet resigned. Faced with Lebanon's descent into chaos and the threat of increased public opposition to US involvement should conditions continue to deteriorate, President Reagan ordered US marines to withdraw from the region on February 26, 1984—well short of Congress's eighteen-month timeline.

Sustained legislative opposition may have made it more difficult for Reagan to stay the course and forced to him to risk alienating Congress in doing so.[38] However, while Congress could claim credit for putting pressure on the president to redeploy US forces in advance of their withdrawal date, none of their actions required that Reagan end the mission when he did. Instead, Reagan's military actions set a precedent that presidents can deploy troops overseas without consulting Congress in advance, circumvent the two-month deadline in the War Powers Resolution, and face only the restraint of public opinion as a mission escalates and US casualties mount.

On October 25, 1983, four days after the Beirut suicide bombing, Reagan repeated the precedent. With forces still embroiled in Lebanon, approximately 7,000 US armed forces invaded Grenada to put down a left-wing revolutionary government that had seized power in a violent coup. Reagan reported the action to Congress but failed to trigger the sixty-day withdrawal date. Although Congress immediately voted to activate the deadline, the mission was over by December 15, and the Marxist regime was successfully deposed.[39]

Since Lebanon and Grenada, presidents have interpreted the War Powers Act as affirmative authorization to employ military force for at least sixty days without permission. Moreover, with a massive display of force or precision-guided weaponry, a mission might be over before Congress even has time to respond. In December 1989 President George H. W. Bush deployed 14,000 military forces to Panama to apprehend Gen. Manuel Noriega—a former US ally and CIA informant known for drug trafficking and eluding US pressure to abrogate power. Congress was in recess and did not react to the operation until February, when the House passed a nonbinding resolution expressing sadness over the loss of soldiers' lives and commending President Bush's efforts to conclude the mission in a timely fashion.[40] By that time, the operation was virtually over.

Heightened Legislative Opposition: Somalia (1992–1994), Haiti (1994–1996), Bosnia (1995–2004), Kosovo (1999)

Legislative majorities regularly appropriate emergency funding necessary to carry out an ongoing military mission, regardless of whether Congress can muster the votes to authorize the use of force. In the decade following the Cold War, President George H. W. Bush introduced US forces in Somalia to provide humanitarian relief, and President Clinton repeated the formulation in Haiti, Bosnia, and Kosovo. Both presidents operated in conjunction with the United Nations but without Congress. Even after the Republican Party swept the 1994 midterm elections, congressional majorities passed nonbinding resolutions expressing opposition to Clinton's military actions, but lacked the votes to withdraw war spending. Instead, they continued to appropriate funds in emergency supplemental measures and through the normal budget process.

On December 8, 1992, President Bush sent US forces to Somalia to assist UN forces in response to the humanitarian crisis in the region. The Senate and House passed a joint resolution authorizing the action in February and May of 1993, respectively, but they failed to reconcile in conference.[41] In June 1993 the UN linked the death of twenty-four peacekeeping soldiers to Mohamed Aidid, the leader of a violent Somali faction. In response, the UN launched an effort to capture Aidid and destroy his militia. Two months later, a landmine linked to Aidid's forces killed four US soldiers. The relief mission began to entrench US soldiers in a conflict among rival Somali warlords, and Congress put pressure on the administration to end US involvement.

However, absent any legally binding action from Congress, an elite US combat team stormed Aidid's compound on October 3, 1993. The Battle of Mogadishu resulted in the loss of eighteen American lives, eighty-four Americans wounded, and another taken hostage by Aidid's forces, who displayed the captured pilot on television cameras and dragged the body of a dead US soldier through the streets of Mogadishu. Four days later, on October 7, the administration summoned congressional leaders for a meeting, and President Clinton announced a March 31, 1994, withdrawal date to the American people that same evening.[42] Many accounts of these events suggest that Congress forced President Clinton to accept a March 31, 1994, pullout date by attaching it to a defense appropriations bill or by using their agenda control to pressure the president to set a withdrawal date.[43] However, the Defense Appropriations bill with the amendment prohibiting funding for operations in Somalia after March 31 did not pass until two weeks after Clinton had already announced his withdrawal policy.[44] Statements by congressional leaders after the meeting on October 7 also suggest a lack of consensus within their own delegation, and legislators regularly referred to the decision as "the president's policy."[45]

While legislative opposition to continued US involvement in Somalia may have encouraged the president to set a withdrawal date, historical records suggest that Congress was not the decisive factor in the March 31 decision. Both chambers lacked the votes to cut off funds and force a deadline, and legislators split along party lines on a series of votes upholding the president's policy to end the conflict.[46]

Following an ignominious withdrawal from Somalia, President Clinton capitalized on uninterrupted military funding and deployed over 20,000 troops in Haiti in September 1994 in a UN-backed mission to reinstate the democratically elected president Jean-Bertrand Aristide, who had been overthrown in a coup. Clinton reported the action to Congress after the troops had landed but evaded the sixty-day deadline implemented in the 1973 War Powers Act, claiming that infrequent outbursts of violence do not constitute "hostilities" and therefore do not trigger a withdrawal date. Congress immediately passed a series of nonbinding resolutions expressing support for the US armed forces while calling for "an orderly withdrawal of US forces as soon as possible," along with symbolic legislation chiding Clinton with reminders that "[the] President should have sought congressional approval before the deployment of troops."[47] Yet, despite legislation calling for an immediate withdrawal, Congress rejected proposals to prohibit the use of funding for the military operation.[48] Given a slate of resources to support the mission, Clinton maintained forces in Haiti in combat, peacekeeping, and nation-building capacities until April 1996.

With troops still stationed in Haiti, President Clinton sent 20,000 combat troops to Bosnia without congressional approval in December 1995 as part of a NATO-led peacekeeping force. Despite some members' opposition to ongoing air strikes in the region and a Senate measure prohibiting the unauthorized deployment of US combat troops, both chambers failed to agree to legislation that would have prohibited the use of existing funds for deployment of ground troops.[49] Instead, they favored nonbinding resolutions expressing opposition to the president's policy.[50] Subsequent measures to limit funding, invoke the War Powers Resolution, and bring troops home did not succeed, despite strong Republican majorities opposed to Clinton's war policies.[51]

Foreshadowing the Democrats' tactics to end the war in Iraq a decade later, in 1997 Republican majorities agreed to a timetable to end military actions in Bosnia which they inserted in the FY1998 Defense Appropriations bill and enforced with a June 30, 1998, funding cutoff.[52] However, President Clinton issued a line-item veto eliminating the funding proscription. Rather than withhold funding—which is not subject to a veto—the Republicans resorted to symbolic language expressing the sense that US troops should exit Bosnia by June 1998.[53] When this deadline appeared increasingly unrealistic, Congress downgraded its language to encourage the president to withdraw US forces "within a reasonable period of time."[54]

In response, Clinton rescinded his previous timeline for US withdrawal from Bosnia and escalated military operations against Serbia. In 1999 Clinton committed US forces in an air war over the former Yugoslavia to prevent ethnic cleansing and genocide against the Albanian population in Kosovo. The president's action led Republican members of Congress to file a suit in federal district court arguing that the president was violating the War Powers Resolution by introducing military forces without congressional authorization, which the court dismissed for lack of standing.[55] Although the Republican-controlled Congress introduced a series of bills aiming to limit or cut off funds for Kosovo operations and the continuing air war against Serbia, most measures failed by narrow margins. Instead, Congress passed an emergency supplemental appropriations bill in FY1999 providing billions of dollars for the existing Kosovo operations.[56] As long as congresses continue to appropriate defense funding that presidents can use to initiate and carry out a military operation, they reverse the constitutional threshold and require veto-proof majorities in both chambers to *stop* military operations rather than start them.

To examine individual members' incentives to fund these military actions systematically, table 7.1 displays the influence of economic reliance on legislators' support for military operations in Somalia, Haiti, Bosnia, and Kosovo and supplemental military spending recouping the DoD for these expenses. Since most congressional Democrats united behind President Clinton's military operations, and Republican members had a partisan basis to oppose these actions, the GOP caucus is analyzed separately. In addition to the four models examining members' support for military actions and supplemental spending, table 7.1 also includes a control case on the "don't ask don't tell" (DADT) policy with regard to gays in the military taken in 1993 (model 5).[57] Ideology is expected to influence members' support for DADT, but economic reliance should have no effect.

The results in table 7.1 are mixed. Legislators with more economically reliant constituencies are no more likely to oppose a deadline for troop withdrawal from Somalia (model 1) or support continued funding for military operations in Kosovo (model 4) than other members.[58] The absence of a consistent economic interest is not especially surprising considering the relatively minor character of military operations at stake and the comparatively low levels of spending necessary to sustain them. Instead, legislative support for military action in Somalia and Kosovo is characterized by strong Democratic partisan unity and corresponds with more ideologically liberal voting patterns ($p < .001$).

Although economic reliance does not directly influence members' support for these minor military ventures, local defense dependence (*low density*facilities*) is associated with increased legislative support for supple-

Table 7.1. Influence of economic reliance on US House members' support for minor military interventions

Independent variable	Coefficients				
	Model 1: Somalia withdrawal deadline, 1993	Model 2: Delete DoD funds replacing money spent on humanitarian operations, 1994	Model 3: Republicans only, 1994	Model 4: Retain funding for operations in Kosovo, reject spending deadline, 1999	Model 5 (control case): Delete provision codifying Don't Ask Don't Tell, 1993
Low density*facilities[a] (economic reliance)	-.007 (.008)	.00804*† (.00498)	.0313* (.0141)	.0274 (.0234)	.009 (.014)
Low density[a]	.002 (.03)	.00172 (.00558)	-.103*† (.0551)	-.260 (.269)	.020 (.021)
Defense facilities	1.47 (1.57)	-1.452 (.946)	-5.93* (2.73)	-.004 (.047)	-1.83 (2.77)
Military bases	.026 (.160)	.063 (.124)	.103 (.214)	-.010 (.141)	.039 (.254)
Military population[a]	-.013 (.032)	-.0002 (.0236)	-.0214 (.0415)	-.011 (.024)	.022 (.057)
Defense committee	-.004 (.509)	.462 (.379)	2.01* (.812)	.131 (.395)	.237 (.523)

	Roth (R-WI) Amendment to S.J. Res 45	Frank-Burton Amendment to H.R. 3759	Frank (D-MA)–Burton (R-IN) Amendment to H.R. 3759	Skelton (D-MO) Amendment to H.R. 1141	Meehan (D-MA) Amendment to H.R. 2401
Defense contribution[a]	.009 (.010)	.038** (.014)	.003 (.017)	.033** (.012)	-.004 (.010)
Ideology (conservative)	-7.73*** (.807)	.234 (.308)	-3.37* (1.59)	-4.23*** (.397)	11.92*** (1.38)
Ideology (South)	—	1.48*** (.298)	1.73** (.655)	—	6.67*** (.695)
N	N = 421	N = 415	N = 172	N = 425	N = 429
	Prob > χ^2 = 0.00	Prob > χ^2 = 0.00	Prob > χ^2 = 0.00	Prob > χ^2 = 0.00	Prob > χ^2 = 0.00
	McFadden's R^2 = .56	McFadden's R^2 = .16	McFadden's R^2 = .17	McFadden's R^2 = .39	McFadden's R^2 = .70
	127–299 (failed)	158–260 (failed)		270–155 (adopted)	169–264 (failed)
	3–251 (Dem)	92–154 (Dem)		193–13 (Dem)	158–101 (Dem)
	124–48 (GOP)	66–106 (GOP)	66–106 (GOP)	77–142 (GOP)	11–163 (GOP)

Note: All entries are logit coefficients. Standard errors are in parentheses. The dependent variable is a roll-call vote on spending for minor US military operations, the use of supplemental war spending for military operations or policy regarding gays in the military taken in the House of Representatives. Votes favoring war and war spending are coded "1"; votes opposing war or war spending are coded "0." Votes supporting 'Don't Ask Don't Tell' with regard to gays in the military are coded "1"; votes opposing the policy are coded "0."

[a] In thousands

*** $p < .001$; ** $p < .01$; * $p < .05$ (two-tailed test), † (one-tailed test) mental military spending that recovers expenses for these operations ($p <$ .05, one-tailed test, model 2). The finding is even more pronounced among Republican members ($p < .05$, model 3).

The Frank-Burton Amendment examined in models 2 and 3 proposed to delete $1.2 billion that was tacked onto a 1994 earthquake relief bill to refund money that the Defense Department already spent on humanitarian operations in Somalia, Haiti, Bosnia, and the Iraq "no-fly" zone.[59] The amendment came to a floor vote seven weeks prior to the March 1994 Somalia withdrawal date, and as US involvement in Haiti and Bosnia loomed on the horizon. While Congress struggled to end military operations in Somalia in October 1993, President Clinton reported that US ships had begun to enforce a UN embargo against Haiti. Meanwhile, US forces had been conducting humanitarian operations to aid victims of genocide in Bosnia since 1992, and Congress began to seek ways to prevent the deployment of US ground troops beyond peacekeeping capacities.[60] In February 1994 Rep. Barney Frank (D-MA) and Rep. Dan Burton (R-IN) offered an amendment to help prevent the administration from pursuing unauthorized military ventures and to force "the Department [of Defense] to live within its budget."[61]

On the House floor, Representative Frank pointed out that the peacekeeping operations were known in advance and paid for out the normal defense budget. In a largely uncontested account, he argued that the funding request had "nothing particularly to do with any agreements about peacekeeping" and was simply a back-door channel to "give additional funds to the Pentagon."[62] An impassioned exchange on the House floor between Frank and opponents Norm Dicks (D-WA) and Randy ("Duke") Cunningham (R-CA)—both representatives of districts with outsized defense-sector dependence—characterizes the stakes of the vote:

> DICKS: We have been cutting defense spending since 1985, and . . . it
> is time to stop. . . . The gentleman from Massachusetts [Mr. Frank]
> wants us to eat out of the budget of the services, where [the]
> funding there for these peacekeeping operations [is] very minimal.
> He wants us to take it out of their hide, and they just simply cannot
> take it out of their hide any further.
>
> FRANK: The gentleman from Washington [Mr. Dicks] says we are
> asking them to eat these contingencies. These [peacekeeping
> missions] were part of the budget request last year. . . . [The
> Defense Department] decided . . . that they did not get enough. So

they [the administration] use this opportunity to get more. . . .
They are seizing an opportunity. They saw the train going. They
jumped on. . . .

CUNNINGHAM: The military did not ask to go to Somalia. It did not ask
to go to Haiti, but is has expenses. Historically, these expenses are
passed on to DoD. . . . [Ongoing defense] cuts are putting us below
a hollow force. I agree with the gentleman from Massachusetts [Mr.
Frank] that it should not be funded in this way. However, if we do
not, the military . . . will not get it in the future.

FRANK: I want to reiterate that this has nothing to do with ending
operations in Bosnia [and various parts of the world]. The
administration's letter does not say that. It says we will continue in
Bosnia, but we would then not be able to do other things. . . . The
gentleman from Washington [Mr. Dicks] says do not cut. This is not
a cut. This is an effort to prevent an add-on.[63]

Although bill sponsors Barney Frank and Dan Burton warned of setting
the "precedent that the military budget is simply for maintenance, and that
any time the military has to be called into action, no matter how small . . .
they will get extra money," this provided an ironic selling point for members
of Congress with constituencies that are invested in military spending, but
have no direct stake in minor humanitarian operations. Blocs of Republican
and Democratic legislators overrepresenting more economically reliant areas overwhelmingly rejected the funding cut, cementing its defeat ($p < .05$,
model 2). Legislative interests in exploiting US military activity as justification to extend the defense budget is also corroborated by the finding
that members of Congress with a higher campaign contribution from the
defense sector were more likely to oppose the Frank-Burton measure than
other members, all else equal ($p < .01$, model 2).

The model isolating Republican voting patterns echoes and amplifies
these results. Republicans with more economically reliant constituencies
were more likely to oppose Frank-Burton and press for supplemental military funding than other Republicans representing less economically vulnerable areas ($p < .05$, model 3).[64] At the same time, more liberal (or moderate) Republicans were also more likely to oppose the amendment and
press for additional DoD funding than their more conservative Republican
colleagues ($p < .05$, model 3), perhaps because they favored freeing up additional funds for peacekeeping operations and felt a weaker allegiance to
principles of fiscal austerity.[65]

As expected, economic reliance has no statistically meaningful effect on legislators' support for the 1993 "don't ask don't tell" policy with respect to gays in the military (model 5). Rather, members split along partisan and ideological lines. These results indicate that economic reliance is not simply a proxy for members' ideologically conservative leanings, lending additional support for the validity of the measure.

Although economic reliance does not influence members' direct support for minor military operations, such as Somalia (model 1) and Kosovo (model 4), Congress's broader patterns of defense spending provide presidents with adequate resources to pursue these actions independently. Moreover, evidence suggests that legislators representing more defense-dependent areas support supplemental DoD spending to recoup unforeseen expenses more than their colleagues and fellow partisans (models 2 and 3)—even though these funds contribute to the president's ability to carry out unauthorized military actions.[66] As long as Congress continues to appropriate defense resources, executives can circumvent their historical dependence on the legislature for additional funding to sustain a mission.

Iraq 2003–

After thirty years of covert actions and limited military operations, the terrorist attacks of September 11, 2001, propelled a US war on terrorism. With US troops ensconced in Afghanistan in retaliation for the attacks of 9/11, the George W. Bush administration began to stoke popular support for regime change in Iraq. The administration built a case for US invasion based on suspicions that Iraq harbored weapons of mass destruction and an alleged connection between Iraq and the 9/11 hijackers, capitalizing on public hatred and distrust of Iraqi dictator Saddam Hussein dating back to the 1990 Gulf War. In a closed congressional session, US intelligence officials informed senators that Saddam Hussein's unstable regime possessed chemical and biological weapons capable of a lethal attack against the Eastern Seaboard of the United States.[67] Although there were vigorous disputes within the intelligence communities as to whether these reports were accurate, the CIA backed the findings and Congress lacked the resources to disprove them. On October 11–12, 2002, Congress passed legislation authorizing the executive use of military force in the region by a vote of 296–133 in the House and 77–23 in the Senate, in compliance with the president's request. While nearly all Republicans voted in favor of executive authorization, many House Democrats also broke rank with their party and voted in favor of war authorization.[68]

Table 7.2 displays the effect of economic reliance on US House members' support for the Authorization for Use of Military Force Iraq in 2002 (model 1).[69] Democratic voting patterns are also analyzed separately because Democrats splintered over the measure, dividing by a vote of 81–127 (model 2).

Although economic reliance has no statistically meaningful effect on legislative support for the AUMF among all House members (model 1), Democrats representing more economically reliant areas (*low density facilities*) were more likely to support the authorization for the Iraq War than other Democrats who represent constituencies that have a lower stake in a war economy ($p < .05$, one-tailed test, model 2). Controlling for members' more conservative leanings, the House Democrats who broke rank with their party and voted in favor of war authorization overrepresented lawmakers from more economically reliant areas. The finding is particularly striking given that Democrats representing more sparsely populated areas were *less* likely to support the war than their more urban counterparts, all else equal ($p < .05$, model 3).[70]

Given sweeping legislative authorization, President Bush launched military operations in Iraq on March 19, 2003. Although earlier reports that Iraq harbored weapons of mass destruction proved to be false and spawned congressional allegations of forged nuclear intelligence, and statements linking Iraq and Al-Qaida were entirely baseless, US troops were already deeply entrenched in a ground war.[71] As the war dragged on, the unexpected duration and complexity of the mission quickly became a political liability for the Republican Party—particularly congressional Republicans representing states and districts that shouldered disproportionate military fatalities.[72]

In 2006 the Democratic Party swept the midterm elections and dealt a blow to the Bush administration's handling of the Iraq War. Public debate shifted discussion toward the need for an exit strategy, and Democratic majorities in both Houses looked to capitalize on the public's antiwar sentiment. However, the Democratic Congress continued to support the president's requests for annual supplemental spending necessary to carry out the war, despite rising US death tolls, soaring financial costs, and legislative charges of corruption and mismanagement.[73]

In 2006 Congress approved $67.5 billion in emergency funding to prosecute the concurrent wars in Iraq and Afghanistan in the 2007 fiscal year, in addition to $50 billion in bridge funding to cover the gap between the beginning of the fiscal year and the passage of the appropriation bill. For FY2008, Congress appropriated $162 billion to cover war costs, plus $70 billion in bridge funding.[74] For the first time in the nation's history, none of these expenses included a single dollar in the Pentagon's annual

Table 7.2. *Influence of economic reliance on US House members' support for war*

Independent variables	Coefficients				
	Model 1: Authorization for use of force in Iraq, 2002	Model 2: Democrats only, 2002	Model 3 (condensed model): Democrats only, 2002	Model 4: Withdrawal of US forces from Iraq, 2007	Model 5: Democrats only, 2007
Low density* facilities [economic reliance]	.054 (.036)	.079*† (.046)	—	.060*† (.035)	.133* (.064)
Low density	-.255 (.197)	-.401*† (.241)	-.254* (.123)	.049 (.062)	-.050 (.096)
Defense facilities	-.079 (.097)	-.376* (.147)	-.009 (.070)	-.094 (.086)	-.166 (.126)
Military bases	-.260 (.203)	-.106 (.233)	-.189 (.211)	—	—
Military population[a]	.024 (.042)	-.016 (.049)	-.007 (.040)	—	—
Iraq military fatalities	—	—	—	.019 (.026)	.081*† (.043)

	(1)	(2)	(3)	(4)	(5)
Defense Committee	-.447	-.925	-.878	.092	-.992
	(.492)	(.662)	(.649)	(.559)	(.809)
Defense contribution[a]	.015	.012	.010	-.0006	.003
	(.012)	(.013)	(.012)	(.004)	(.005)
Ideology (conservative)	6.31***	20.06***	19.38***	10.49***	34.34***
	(.828)	(2.97)	(2.86)	(1.63)	(5.98)
	N = 429	N = 208	N = 208	N = 424	N = 227
	Prob > χ^2 = 0.00	Prob > χ^2 = 0.00	Prob > χ^2 = 0.00	Prob > χ^2 = 0.00	Prob > χ^2 = 0.00
	McFadden's R^2 = .52	McFadden's R^2 = .49	McFadden's R^2 = .41	McFadden's R^2 = .70	McFadden's R^2 = .70
	H.J. Res 114	H.J. Res 114	H.J. Res 114	H.R. 2237	H.R. 2237 Dem:
	296–133 (adopted)	Dem: 81–127	Dem: 81–127	171–255 (failed)	169–59
	81–127 (Dem)			169–59 (Dem)	
	215–6 (GOP)			2–196 (GOP)	

Note: All entries are logit coefficients. Standard errors are in parentheses. The dependent variable is a roll-call vote on the authorization for war or war funding restrictions taken in the House of Representatives. Votes favoring war and war spending are coded "1"; votes opposing war and war spending are coded "0."

[a] In thousands

***p < .001; **p < .01; *p < .05 (two-tailed test), † (one-tailed test) operating budget, which reached $471 billion for baseline DoD activities in the 2008 fiscal year.

Rather than factor expected war costs in the annual defense budget, President Bush relied on emergency supplemental requests—money that comes in addition to funds from annual budgets. Supplemental funding is typically reserved for emergencies that were not factored into the budget, such as costs incurred from natural disasters, the initial stages of major wars, and unforeseen changes in military strategies. Administrations and congresses have historically used the normal appropriations process to fund wars as soon as they could factor in cost projections—usually by the second or third year.[75] Shifting war costs into emergency spending bills obfuscates the actual expense of the conflict by removing these costs from transparent budgeting processes. It also raises the upper limit on war spending and frees space in the annual defense budget for additional programs that might otherwise be cut.[76]

Congress not only went along with Bush's emergency war funding scheme but also authorized unprecedented levels of military funding within the annual budget process.[77] To avoid withholding funds, Congress held hearings, conducted investigations exposing executive mismanagement, issued critical media statements, and passed nonbinding resolutions to convince the president to change course in Iraq. For example, a February 16, 2007, nonbinding resolution expressed Congress's disapproval of the president's plan to send an additional 21,500 troops to Iraq as part of the strategy known as the "surge."[78] While the measure passed the House with 229 Democrats and 2 Republicans in favor, the Senate fell short of the sixty votes necessary to invoke cloture and failed to pass the resolution. In similar attempts to influence the conduct of the war short of direct spending cuts, Congress passed amendments to war funding legislation to try to force President Bush to accept a timetable. By April 2007 both houses passed the president's emergency supplemental funding request along with an amendment requiring an end to combat operations in Iraq by March 31, 2008. However, President Bush vetoed the bill and Congress failed to override. Having lost every prior attempt to limit the president, Democrats inserted provisions for over $100 billion in emergency funds for domestic programs that their members favored while authorizing $162 billion in unrestricted war funds.

While the outspoken antiwar representative Dennis Kucinich (D-OH) sought to eliminate funding for military operations in Iraq, Democratic leaders from several of the nation's most defense-dependent districts—including House Armed Services chairman Ike Skelton (D-MO), House Appropriations Defense Subcommittee chairman John Murtha (D-PA), and House Majority Leader Steny Hoyer (D-MD)—rejected this strategy.[79] In a less drastic measure, Rep. Jim McGovern (D-MA) introduced legislation requiring the removal of US troops from Iraq within ninety days. The bill prohibited the president from using any appropriated funding for combat operations in the region after the complete withdrawal of US forces.[80] Although not as forceful as withholding funds by refusing to pass Bush's spending request, the bill did leave money for the safe withdrawal of troops, allowing members to dodge a major political liability. Nonetheless, the legislation failed by a vote of 171–255.

As displayed in table 7.2, while the Republican Party united in opposition to the bill (with only two members defecting from the party line), a voting bloc consisting largely of Democratic members from more economically reliant districts tipped the scale in favor of continued war spending (models 4 and 5). Economic reliance is associated with increased congressional opposition to US troop withdrawal in 2007, despite spiraling expenses, rising US death tolls, and strong antiwar sentiment ($p < .05$, one-tailed test, model 4). The finding is even more pronounced among Democrats ($p < .05$, model 5).

As expected, more ideologically conservative members were also more likely to support the Iraq War in 2002 and 2007, both among all House members and in the Democratic caucus ($p < .001$). Controlling for ideology, however, economic reliance consistently shapes and reinforces Democrat members' support for the war. All else equal, an increase in economic reliance corresponds with greater Democratic endorsement of a contentious war affiliated with a Republican administration. Heightened economic vulnerability on a war economy may sway members who lack a partisan basis to support the war and would otherwise have a partisan incentive to oppose it.

In addition to the effect of economic reliance, higher Iraq War fatalities also correspond with legislative support for continued US involvement in the war ($p < .05$, one-tailed test, model 5). While the number of military deaths in a district has no discernible effect among all House members (model 4), a higher number Iraq War deaths in Democratically held districts is associated with increased Democratic opposition to US troop withdrawal in 2007 (model 5). The counterintuitive finding might be explained by evidence that Republicans were badly blamed for military fatalities resulting from the Iraq War in the 2006 midterm election, but Democrats were not.[81] Democratic legislators may have a stronger interest in ensuring that soldiers from their districts did not die in vain, while their Republican colleagues united in continuing support of the war even though they bore the responsibility for the fallout.

The passage of the timetable amendment that President Bush vetoed in the spring of 2007 represents the peak of Congress's opposition to the war in Iraq. By refusing to withhold funds for the war, Congress was ultimately subject to a presidential veto it could not override. Over the next year, attempts to pass withdrawal legislation repeatedly failed, while Congress continued to pass supplemental appropriation bills to fund the war. It took the 2008 election of President Barack Obama, who ran opposed to the war, and a price tag estimated to exceed $3 trillion in accumulated war costs to begin a policy of gradual US troop withdrawal.[82]

ECONOMIC RELIANCE AND LEGISLATIVE SUPPORT FOR WAR

Tables 7.1 and 7.2 demonstrate a positive relationship at statistically meaningful levels between local economic reliance and legislative support for the Iraq War and for supplemental military spending compensating the DoD for expenses associated with minor military operations. The influence of local defense dependence is only consistent among members of the political party opposing the administration, who have a partisan motivation to oppose the president's military policies. However, the logit coefficients do not exhibit the magnitude of influence that economic reliance has on members' support for war and war spending. To gauge the extent of the influence, table 7.3 displays the predicted probabilities and estimated differences of Republicans' support for 1994 supplemental military spending (column 1), Democrats' support for the 2002 Authorization for Use of Military Force (AUMF) in Iraq (column 2), and Democrats' opposition to Iraq troop withdrawals in 2007 (column 3) when population density and defense facilities are set at high and low values.

The first three rows show the predicted probability of a prowar or pro–war spending vote when a district changes from an area with no economic reliance (zero defense facilities and medium density) to high economic reliance (a rural district with ten or more defense facilities). The second three rows document the predicted probability of a prowar vote when the number of defense facilities in a district changes from zero facilities (5th percentile) to more than ten facilities (95th percentile), given an equal population density. The last three rows capture legislative support for war or war spending when population density moves from a highly urban setting (5th percentile) to a very rural setting (95th percentile), given an equal number of defense facilities. The model holds all other variables constant at their respective mean values.

Table 7.3. *Estimated influence of economic reliance on Republican and Democratic House members' support for supplemental military spending and war*

	Supplemental war spending, 1994 (Republicans only)	Authorization for use of military force, 2002 (Democrats only)	Opposition to withdrawal from Iraq, 2007 (Democrats only)
Change in economic reliance			
Medium density, no defense facilities (5th percentile)	.61 (.06)***	.28 (.06)***	.043 (.024)*†
Rural, >10 facilities[a] (95th percentile)	.91 (.07)***	.72 (.29)*	.926 (.218)***
Difference	.30 (.10)**	.44 (.25)*†	.88 (.23)***
Percent change	33%**	61%*†	95%***
Change in defense facilities			
Medium density, no facilities (5th percentile)	.61 (.06)***	.28 (.06)***	.043 (.024)*†
Medium density, >10 facilities[a] (95th percentile)	.84 (.10)***	.42 (.18)*	.227 (22.5)
Difference	.23 (.13)*†	.14 (.21)	.184 (.23)
Percent change	27%*†	33%	81%
Change in Density (Urban to Rural)[b]			
Urban, 2.5 facilities (5th percentile)	.71 (.06)***	.40 (.08)***	.033 (.021)
Rural, 2.5 facilities (95th percentile)	.67 (.05)***	.22 (.09)*	.281 (.165)*†
Difference	–.04 (.07)	–.18 (.14)	.248 (.16)
Percent change	–6%	–45%	88%

Note: Table 7.3 entries are calculated by the author from the logit analysis in tables 7.1 and 7.2 using CLARIFY. The dependent variable is legislators' support for war and war spending measures (0 = antiwar, 1 = prowar). Entries are predicted values and estimated changes in predicted values. The standard errors of the predictions are in parentheses. All control variables are held constant at their sample means.

[a] Defense facilities is set to its 95th percentile for each respective model (ranging from 11 to 13).

[b] Change in population density denotes the value of low density set to its 5th and 95th percentile, respectively.

*** $p < .001$; ** $p < .01$; * $p < .05$ (two-tailed test), † (one-tailed test)

As the theory of economic reliance suggests, a large defense-sector presence in a rural district yields high levels of congressional support for war and war spending. Controlling for ideology and other factors, Republicans from rural districts with a large defense-sector presence were 33 percent more likely to support the 1994 supplemental spending measure recouping DoD expenses for operations in Somalia, Haiti, Bosnia, and the Iraq no-fly zone than Republicans from areas with average population density and no defense facilities ($p < .01$). At the same time, Democrats representing rural constituencies with large concentrations of defense industries were 61 percent more likely support the contentious 2002 authorization for the use of force in Iraq ($p < .05$, one-tailed test) and 95 percent more likely to oppose US withdrawal in 2007 ($p < .001$) than Democrats with no conceivable economic stake in a war economy. Democrats and Republicans with the most economically reliant constituencies are estimated to support these particular war and war spending initiatives between 72 and 92 percent of the time, even while other members of their political party railed against these military actions ($p < .05$). Economic reliance adds considerable fuel to partisan, ideological, and institutional pressures encouraging members to support continued war funding.

The table also isolates the effect of an increasing number of defense facilities in a district and the effect of population density. First, given an average population density, members representing districts that have the largest defense-sector capacity support war and war spending at greater rates than members from districts with no defense facilities. However, the difference is not nearly as pronounced as the change in economic reliance and does not reach statistically meaningful levels across all three votes.

Second, in 1994 and 2002, members from more rural areas appear to be *less* likely to support war spending and war than members from densely populated urban areas, given an average number of defense facilities. However, these results are ultimately inconclusive since the differences do not reach statistically meaningful levels. The influence of a large sector presence in a rural area is particularly notable considering that neither defense facilities nor low population density has a consistent influence on congressional support for war policies independently of one another.

However, it is also important to note that the effect of economic reliance is not as consistent when explaining members' support for war and war spending as when estimating members' support for the weapons expenditures examined in chapter 5 or defense committee membership and the distribution of defense assignments analyzed in chapter 6. While the results presented in earlier chapters are more robust to alternative specifi-

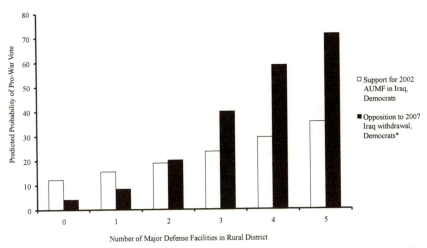

Figure 7.1. *Estimated influence of economic reliance on House Democrats' support for the Iraq war, 2002 and 2007.*

*Estimates for more than five defense facilities are not statistically significant at the .05 or .10 level. The figure displays predicted probabilities calculated by the author from the logit analysis in table 7.2 using CLARIFY. The figure exhibits a change in the number of defense facilities in a district when low density is set to its 95th percentile (very rural). All control variables are held constant at their sample means.

cations, the number of defense facilities in a district only has a consistent effect on members' support for war and war spending in rural and semirural areas.[83]

To account for this factor, figure 7.1 displays predicted probabilities of observing Democratic support for the Iraq War in 2002 and 2007 as the number of defense facilities increases from zero to five within a sparsely populated area, controlling for other possible influences.[84] As the figure shows, an increasing number of defense facilities in a rural area exhibits a positive, linear influence on Democratic House members' support for the Iraq War in 2002, changing from about a 12 percent probability of observing Democratic support for the war in rural areas with no defense facilities to approximately 35 percent in rural areas with five defense facilities. Economic reliance yields an even more pronounced effect on Democratic legislators' support for continued US involvement in 2007, after the war exceeded its expected scope and duration. The probability of observing Democratic opposition to the measure requiring US troop withdrawal changes from roughly 4 percent in rural areas with no defense facilities to 70 percent in rural areas with five defense facilities.

Figure 7.2 documents the effects of economic reliance on Democratic members' support for the AUMF in 2002 and Republicans' support for sup-

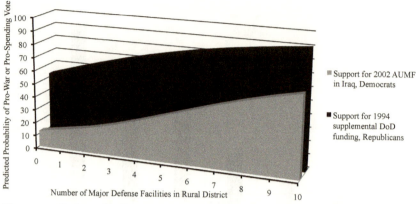

Figure 7.2. *Estimated influence of economic reliance on House members' support for supplemental military spending and war, 1994, 2002.*

The figure displays predicted probabilities calculated by the author from the logit analysis in tables 7.1 and 7.2 using CLARIFY. The figure exhibits a change in the number of defense facilities in a district when low density is set to its 95th percentile (very rural). All control variables are held constant at their sample means.

plemental war spending in 1994. The graph displays the predicted probabilities of observing a prowar (or pro–war spending) vote as the number of defense facilities increases from zero to ten, while controlling for other factors that might influence legislative preferences.

All else equal, heightened economic reliance in rural areas yields consistent, positive support for war and war spending among Democrats and Republicans (respectively). However, while Democratic and Republican voting patterns follow parallel trends, the two parties begin from drastically different baselines: Republican support for 1994 supplemental war spending hits a low point of 52 percent in rural areas with no defense facilities and approaches 90 percent support in rural areas with ten defense facilities (38% difference). By contrast, Democrats show greater overall opposition to the AUMF, with a probability of 12 percent support in rural areas with no defense facilities reaching about 62 percent in rural areas with 10 defense facilities (50% difference).

While members belonging to the president's party support executive military policy almost uniformly, the opposing party often splits its votes on measures restricting war funding. These results suggest that economic reliance in more rural districts promotes considerable support for war and war spending among members of Congress opposing the president's party, adding to existing pressures to support the troops, uphold the mission, and defer to executive intelligence assessments. These findings do not suggest that the United States goes to war in order to maintain a military economy or bolster defense industry sales. Rather, the analysis illustrates a far more nuanced interplay between ideology and interest: the existence of a military economy and widespread reliance on continued war spending make it easier to prioritize military solutions to foreign policy problems and strengthen political coalitions supporting US hegemony and aggressive military interventionism.

SHARED INTERESTS AND CONCENTRATED POWER

While national security goals and commitment to US troops are legitimate concerns for *all* members of Congress, these goals do not lead all legislators to uniformly defer to executive military policy. Rather, members' priorities are filtered through both partisan and constituency lenses. While members of Congress opposing the president's party have shared incentives to criticize ongoing military actions and aggressively draw attention to executive missteps, these members invariably split ranks on votes that would curb the president's war funding. Economic dependence on a war economy helps explain why some members opposing the president's party authorize open-ended military actions and continue to support unpopular wars, even during periods of heightened public opposition and divided government. Legislators representing constituencies that rely most heavily on a military economy are more likely to appeal to national security and troop safety as a reason to uphold a mission, even while their partisan allies cite the same goals as justification to end an armed conflict. Local economic dependence does not directly influence members' support for minor military actions, perhaps because these actions do not typically have a considerable influence on the military budget. However, local reliance on the defense sector does encourage members to press for more military spending to recoup expenses that these operations incur. These legislative strategies promote spending beyond the baseline military budget, which ironically gives the executive a freer hand and invites more unauthorized military actions.

Moreover, post–World War II congresses have also reacted to military hostilities and wars that began either without their permission or without full access to intelligence information. In this context, many members may find it difficult to refuse additional funding for soldiers on the front lines in conflicts that do not directly influence most Americans and may benefit many of them. Congresses have also maintained a defense establishment extensive enough to permit executives to employ existing resources and initiate military hostilities at their discretion. Although individual legislators may still mount serious challenges to executive military actions, the political environment is stacked against such efforts becoming an effective check on presidential war powers. As the next chapter will show, presidents exploit these circumstances by structuring institutions to control the military technologies that Congress appropriates, conceal intelligence information, and consolidate their authority over the national security agenda.

Executive Independence in Military Affairs

Those who are to conduct a war cannot in the nature of things, be proper or safe judges, whether a war ought to be commenced, continued, or concluded. —James Madison (1793)

When I moved those forces [into the Persian Gulf] I didn't have to ask Senator Kennedy or some liberal Democrat whether we were going to do it. We just did it. —George H. W. Bush (quoted in Dowd 1992)

On August 2, 1990, President George H. W. Bush denounced the Iraqi invasion of Kuwait as an act of intolerable aggression. Four days later, Secretary of Defense Dick Cheney publicized the US commitment that the president had made to defend Saudi Arabia in the event of an attack by Iraq. The administration claimed that the president did not need congressional approval before taking military action. Bush cited his constitutional authority, stating, "I have the right, as commander-in-chief, to fulfill my responsibilities, and I'm going to safeguard those executive powers."[1] On August 8 the president initiated a troop deployment without consulting Congress, positioning 200,000 US soldiers along the Saudi-Kuwait border. On December 3, 1990, Secretary of Defense Dick Cheney testified before the Armed Services Committee that "I do not believe the President requires any additional authorization from the Congress before committing US forces to achieve our objectives in the Gulf."[2] Fifty-four legislators responded by filing a suit in federal court to prohibit the president from using force without congressional authorization. (The court dismissed the suit as premature.) The president later gave in to pressure from advisors to persuade members of Congress to endorse his military agenda.

When President Bush requested approval for the use of force in the Gulf in a letter to Congress on January 8, 1991, many members extolled the restoration of their proper constitutional authority. Senator Sam Nunn (D-GA) rose to "commend President Bush for recognizing Congress's constitutional role." House Foreign Affairs Committee Chairman Dante Fascell (D-FL) marveled that "[the president] acknowledged the principle! . . . This is very important. By specific language, Congress authorized the war!" House minority leader Robert Michel (R-IL) remarked that "the Constitution, the American people, and the cause of freedom have been well served."[3] However, despite this display of congressional exuberance, the president never acknowledged that statutory authorization was constitutionally required to commit troops in military engagements. Rather, in a press conference on January 9—one day after the president requested approval from Congress—Bush said: "I don't think I need [a congressional resolution]. . . . I feel I have the authority to fully implement the United Nations Resolution [678]."[4] Even as the Soviet threat receded, the president retained sufficient resources to go to war regardless of whether or not Congress endorsed the action. Furnished with troops, funding, and equipment, Bush maintained that the administration had the right to defy any restrictions that Congress might impose.[5]

The Gulf War scenario fits historical patterns dating back to the end of World War II. For the first time in the nation's history, presidents have not only exercised military force without explicit authorization from Congress, but have also claimed the constitutional authority to act independently in military affairs.[6] A heightened national security environment cannot fully account for the shift. While imminent security threats certainly contribute to the president's authority as commander-in-chief, they cannot explain George H. W. Bush's rhetoric or Bill Clinton's independent military actions in Iraq, Haiti, Bosnia, and Kosovo, which occurred during a period of reduced threat. Further, increased executive ambition, heightened legislative compliance, and judicial tolerance may be symptoms of weak checks and balances, but they do not explain what caused these asymmetries in the first place.

Executive independence in military affairs is not only a response to the national security climate, but also an unintended consequence of the nation's transformation to the largest military economy in the world. This argument builds from evidence introduced in the previous chapters suggesting that local economic reliance on weapons suppliers encourages a critical subset of Congress members to prioritize uninterrupted defense investments, including funding for major wars. These members face weak opposition because US power projection promotes overlapping political and economic interests, while policies shield most Americans from the immediate costs of large defense buildups and military interventions. Instead, the public sacrifices necessary to go to war or maintain large defense budgets have shifted onto a minority of volunteer soldiers, future generations of taxpayers, and foreign nations where US wars take place. In this context, American military hegemony is widely viewed as a moral and existential imperative, while appearing "soft" on defense is a serious political liability.

This chapter will argue that, as the underlying incentives driving congressional defense spending shifted, presidents exploited their access to funding, equipment, and technology to fortify their authority over the military. While members of Congress prioritize the growth of defense resources and find it politically difficult to withdraw war spending, presidents also work to monopolize the military resources that Congress appropriates. A new incentive structure rewards key members of Congress who expand the pool of defense resources, while increasing the president's ability to exercise force at his or her own discretion. This arrangement promotes the short-term interests of Congress members and their voters, while empowering presidents to consolidate their authority over national security policy.

The analysis proceeds as follows: part I reviews structural arguments suggesting that the executive office equips all presidents with the energy to initiate military and foreign policy. However, as the second section shows, post–World War II presidents benefit from far more extensive access to defense resources than their predecessors. Emboldened by these developments, they structure executive institutions to control available military technologies, insulate intelligence information, and carry out their national security policies with few restraints. The final section examines new presidential strategies that reduce effective congressional oversight, including the increasing classification of executive communications and the privatization of multiple aspects of military activity.

EXECUTIVE AMBITION

In 1788 Alexander Hamilton crafted an argument in support of a single executive equipped with the energy and flexibility required for effective governance.[7] Although there are relatively few executive powers listed in Article II of the US Constitution, Hamilton expected that the structure of the executive branch would encourage presidents to take initiative to carry out the prerogatives of the office. While these views were by no means universal, the framers did adopt a system that enables a sole executive leader to govern within the bounds set by a (presumably) jealous Congress.[8]

Consequently, although Article I gives Congress almost all of the enumerated powers over foreign affairs, and the powers allotted to the president are few in number and vaguely defined, both proponents and critics of contemporary executive war powers recognize that the president is ideally structured to initiate foreign policy.[9] As early as 1793, George Washington issued a unilateral neutrality proclamation to keep the nation out of war against Britain on behalf of France. In response, Hamilton advanced a structural argument in support of the action, as "the text and structure of the Constitution make the President the sole organ of intercourse between the United States and foreign nations."[10] During Andrew Jackson's administration, French traveler Alexis de Tocqueville contrasted the president's domestic weakness with his extensive authority over international affairs, pointing out that "a negotiation can scarcely be opened and followed fruitfully except by one man."[11] In fact, presidents are uniquely equipped to initiate policy efficiently, flexibly, and (if necessary) secretly on behalf of a broad, national constituency. The structural view of presidential authority suggests that the Constitution assigns powers to a legislature that is unsuited to exercise them; this shortcoming led to the "flow of power from Congress to the presidency."[12]

Modern presidents have also developed resources that allow them to initiate and carry out their policies. First, presidents are uniquely situated as national party leaders—a distinction that grants them considerable leverage in setting the national party agenda and determining its priorities.[13] Second, presidents can engage in autonomous policy innovation, issuing directives such as executive orders, executive agreements, presidential signing statements, proclamations, and memoranda. In 1947 the establishment of a national security and intelligence community prompted the development of national security directives (NSDs)—unpublished notifications used to direct foreign, military, and intelligence policy. These presidential directives all carry the force of law without formal congressional endorsement. Although the majority of NSDs remain classified, a database of declassified documents reveals presidents' extensive use of NSDs to unilaterally direct national security policy. Presidents have relied on classified national security directives to issue policy toward "rogue" nations such as Egypt and Syria (Kennedy, NSD 105), direct war strategies in Vietnam (Nixon, NSD 24) and Cambodia (Nixon, NSD 29), circumvent congressional restrictions on foreign arms sales (Reagan, NSD 17) and implement a Persian Gulf security framework (Bush I, NSD 26, 45).[14] The use of NSD's shields information from the public, sidesteps congressional consultation and, according to one expert, "[poses] particular challenges to Congress and the courts to effectively constrain the president's unilateral powers."[15]

The political construction of presidential authority is consistent with the energy and vigor that Hamilton eulogized, and which Terry Moe and Scott

Wilson have characterized by a "drive for leadership that almost always motivates [presidents] to promote the power of their institution."[16] However, a purely structural view cannot account for the dramatic growth of the executive office over the course of American political development. After all, President Millard Fillmore (1850–53), who is widely credited for opening Japan to outside trade and opposing foreign intervention in Hawaii, occupied the same office as Harry Truman (1945–53)—who a century later made the unilateral decision to drop an atomic bomb on Japan and launch full-scale war in Korea. Since the Truman administration, presidents have made far more extensive uses of their resources than their predecessors and have amassed unprecedented levels of authority. As the next section shows, modern executives are particularly emboldened in military affairs because they can take advantage of the defense resources that Congress appropriates.

CONGRESSIONAL DEFENSE SPENDING AND EXECUTIVE USE OF FORCE

Until the mid-twentieth century, members of Congress safeguarded their control over the military by increasing defense spending in preparation for specific wars and dismantling the military following the termination of conflict. However, since World War II, Congress has continued to provide a persistent baseline of funding, regardless whether or not the nation was engaged in a war. When legislators continually maintain levels of defense spending, they free the president to set the national security agenda and exercise his powers as commander-in-chief. Most critically, executives no longer rely on emergency funds from Congress to mobilize an army or purchase military equipment. The practical need to consult Congress for a declaration of war is obsolete because legislators continue to prioritize ongoing defense funding available at any time. Presidents take advantage of these new circumstances by structuring executive institutions to leverage congressionally appropriated resources at their own discretion.

Although a permanent weapons arsenal frees executives from traditional constraints on their authority, increasing funding beyond the baseline weapons budget also has diminishing returns for the president's military authority. Rather, presidents must weigh geopolitical, strategic, and fiscal matters when they set their policy priorities and submit budget requests. By contrast, legislators representing constituencies that are disproportionately dependent on local weapons suppliers are overrepresented on defense committees, and they are among the most consistent legislative advocates for military and war spending. These legislators' priorities help explain why President Jimmy Carter's decision to cancel the notoriously expensive and poor-performing B-1 bomber in 1977 was not enough to kill the program, and why Congress did not cancel a single major weapon platform after the Cold War—despite pressure from presidents George H. W. Bush and Bill Clinton to reduce military spending and direct attention to the nation's nonmilitary needs. As chapter 5 discussed in detail, pressure from influential members of Congress kept most weapons platforms alive. Even after the terrorist attacks of September 11, 2001, President George W. Bush was unable to redirect funding for stealth technology to less expensive programs that would more effectively advance the nation's military goals in Iraq and Afghanistan.[17]

Since the policymakers directly in charge of defense spending typically have the most at stake in promoting defense-sector growth and resisting major cutbacks, a substantial baseline of funds should cushion the procurement budget, regardless of a nuclear deterrent, periodic troop withdrawals, and periods of relative peace. At the same time, however, presidents, DoD personnel, and members of Congress must publicly justify defense budget levels based on intelligence assessments and strategic considerations. Variations in military strategy, the cessation of major wars, and domestic agenda-setting should also result in budgetary fluctuations, with increased defense spending occurring during major wars and soft declines in periods of reduced conflict.

To examine these assessments, figure 8.1 displays national weapons outlays from 1962 to 2011. Procurement outlays represent money appropriated by Congress and spent by DoD on contracted weapons programs. These expenditures provide one important gauge of resources available to executives, who rely on available military technology in order to exercise military force independently. Although troop strength was historically an important factor as well, advances in military technology—including the development of cruise missiles and unmanned aerial vehicles (UAVs)—allow presidents to attack enemy targets without large troop deployments. Further, as elaborated in the next section, presidents also rely on covert operatives, special operations forces, and private military and security companies (PMSCs) to conduct military actions, placing less emphasis on troop strength. While troop count is subject to congressional reductions at any time, weapons supplies build up over time regardless of whether Congress authorizes further production. These budget levels gauge the extent to which congresses have provided spending that allow presidents to direct military affairs independently. (The numbers are adjusted to constant 2006 dollars.)

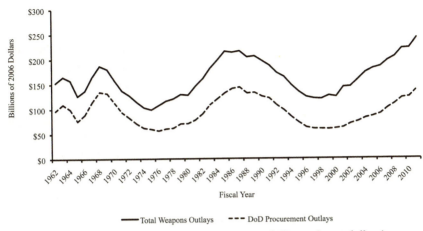

$300

$250

$200

$150

$100

$50

$0

Billions of 2006 Dollars

1962 1964 1966 1968 1970 1972 1974 1976 1978 1980 1982 1984 1986 1988 1990 1992 1994 1996 1998 2000 2002 2004 2006 2008 2010

Fiscal Year

——— Total Weapons Outlays   - - - DoD Procurement Outlays

Figure 8.1. *Weapons spending outlays, 1962–2011 (in billions of 2006 dollars).*
Total weapons outlays include expenditures for DoD procurements and research and development (R&D),
Department of Energy (DoE) atomic energy and weapons activity, and DoE national security. Total DoD
procurement outlays include procurements and R&D.
Sources: The raw (unadjusted) numbers were drawn from Office of Management and Budget, "Historical
Tables, Budget of the United States Government: Outlays for Discretionary Programs," US Government
Printing Office, Washington, DC (http://www.whitehouse.gov/omb/budget/Historicals). For a more
detailed breakdown of national security spending by function and subfunction, refer to http://www
.truthandpolitics.org/budget-numbers-intro.php. Inflation conversion factors are the average of OMB
and CBO inflation estimates for each year compiled by Sahr (2009).

As expected, weapons outlays follow cyclical trends. However, spending
levels do not directly track major military engagements. Instead, these patterns are sensitive to a variety of political factors. Most strikingly, despite
periods of threat reductions, backlash to unpopular wars, and domestic priorities, Congress and DoD have maintained a baseline of nearly $100 billion
in annual weapons outlays (approximately $50 billion in DoD procurements
alone). Given this budget cushion, it is not surprising that executives enjoy
considerable resources and flexibility to pursue their policy goals.

As shown above, weapons expenditures hit a low ebb at the immediate
onset of formal US entrance in the Vietnam War in 1965 ($126 billion in
weapons outlays and $75 billion in DoD procurements). Although Congress
was solidly behind Lyndon Johnson's Vietnam policy—the 1964 Tonkin Gulf
Resolution passed both houses with only two votes in opposition—Johnson
did not require any additional weapons buildup in order to initiate war the
following year. When the Tonkin resolution was repealed in 1971, President
Richard Nixon cited his constitutional power as commander-in-chief as sufficient authority to end the war at his own pace. While Congress voiced
opposition with soft reductions in weapons spending levels, no constitu-

tional confrontation arose because Congress kept appropriating the money necessary to fight the war.

The weapons budget reached a $100-billion nadir in the 1975 fiscal year, in the immediate aftermath of the Vietnam War, Watergate, and the resignation of President Nixon. Still, despite the absence of a major military engagement, procurement outlays increased systematically in the mid- to late 1970s until surpassing $200 billion in 1985. Former Pentagon acquisition chief Jacques Gansler documents a number of problems brought on by these spending policies, including a rate of only 50 percent utilized equipment and hundreds of billions of dollars in pending procurement claims.[18] Accordingly, the post-Vietnam growth in procurement spending, combined with the decline in military activity, helped catalyze a 90 percent increase in foreign military sales and defense industry dependence on international arms exports.

In addition to the substantial baseline of funds that expenditures provide, the weapons budget also peaked in absence of a major troop deployment. Weapons outlays during the Reagan buildup of the 1980s exceeded expenditures during the Vietnam War and rivaled military spending levels during the wars in Iraq and Afghanistan, until spending surpassed 1980s levels in the 2009–10 fiscal years. Reagan's political success in achieving a $216-billion arms buildup suggests that presidential leadership can help spur increased spending levels without a major military engagement. However, it is also evident that the "Reagan buildup" actually began under Carter, and began to decline *before* the fall of the Soviet Union. While weapons outlays receded in the 1990s, after the Cold War was over, Congress still spent more on weapons in FY1996 than it did to counter Soviet expansion during the Nixon administration in FY1975 (by a factor of 30%, in inflation-adjusted dollars). Even in a period of defense reduction, these spending levels effectively allowed Clinton to deploy 20,000 troops in Bosnia, overthrow a coup in Haiti, and direct an air war in Kosovo, despite opposition from Republican majorities in Congress. Meanwhile, Clinton's efforts to contain Saddam Hussein in the 1990s included employing US aircraft to penetrate Iraqi airspace on a daily basis and extending tens of thousands of weapons to attack Iraqi targets. The president operated with minimal oversight and few Americans were directly affected.

Spending remained above $120 billion in the late 1990s and increased when George W. Bush took office. Weapons outlays trended upward during the "war on terrorism," exceeded 1980s spending levels at the end of the George W. Bush administration, and continued to increase steadily under President Barack Obama's stewardship. As discussed in chapter 7, weapons

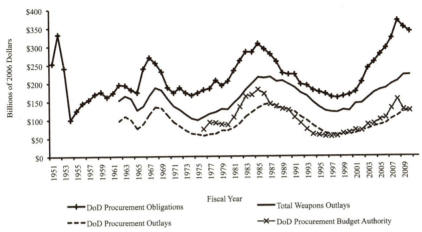

Figure 8.2. *Weapons procurement spending, 1951–2010 (in billions of 2006 dollars).*

Sources: Total weapons outlays and DoD procurement outlays are drawn from figure 8.1. Procurement obligations are extracted from US Department of Defense, Statistical Information Analysis Division, Procurement Summary, FY1951–2006, US Department of Defense, Washington, DC (http://siadapp. dmdc.osd.mil/procurement/historical_reports/trends/PROTREND/PROCHIST/ACTIONS2006.pdf); OMB Watch, "Federal Contracts of the Department of Defense, FY2007–2010" (http://www. fedspending.org).

spending outlays during George W. Bush's presidency do not include hundreds of billions of dollars in war funds, which were systematically tucked into emergency supplemental spending bills. These unparalleled spending levels allowed the Bush administration to continue to prosecute the war in Iraq, despite protests from the Democratic majority in Congress. The continued growth in weapons spending also enabled President Obama's use of hundreds of missiles and unmanned drones in unauthorized air strikes in Libya in 2011.

Figure 8.2 juxtaposes weapons outlays (above) with defense procurement budgetary authorizations (FY1976–2010) and contract obligations (FY1951–2010), adjusted to constant 2006 dollars. Authorizations, obligations, and outlays comprise different stages of the budget process. Congress grants executive agencies authority to spend up to a certain level, which allows DoD to enter into legally binding agreements with contractors or suppliers. These contract obligations are the dollars the agency legally commits to spending to acquire goods and services. The obligations due result in budget outlays or payments made from the federal treasury. One scholar aptly compares budget authority to putting money in a checking account and budget outlays to writing a check.[19] Extending the analogy, entering into contract obligations is like making purchases with a credit card and promising payment at a later date.

Perhaps most stunningly, DoD procurement obligations dwarf the legal budgetary authorization that Congress sets and the outlays that Congress appropriates for weapons programs. In fact, since 1950, procurement obligations have not dipped below $100 billion, and funding has not fallen below a $150-billion baseline since the brief drawdown following the Korean War (relative to a $50-billion baseline in DoD procurement outlays). Weapons obligations typically fluctuated between $150 billion and $300 billion per year, and peaked at more than $360 billion in 2008 (relative to $110 billion in 2008 procurement outlays). While this could reflect DoD contract obligations that Congress later cancels or refuses to fund, it also means that DoD is contracting approximately two-thirds of weapons purchases beyond its procurement budget. These unauthorized funds also reflect contracts obligated for future years and dollars that go straight into the national debt.

DoD procurement obligations peaked during the Bay of Pigs (1961), Tet Offensive buildup (1967–68), in the heat of the Iran-Contra scandal (1985), and in the context of the Iraq War "surge" (2008); sharp increases in Congress's procurement outlays echoed these trends, peaking in 1962, 1968, 1987 and 2009–11, at a one- to two-year lag. However, DoD obligations track Congress's budget authorizations more closely. Despite the considerable discrepancy between levels of authorized and unauthorized funds, authorizations and obligations follow almost identical patterns, peaking and ebbing in coinciding years. DoD personnel may systematically contract a certain point beyond the budget authority that Congress sets, pending either program cancellation or future payment. The finding is also consistent with political economist Robert Higgs's projections that defense-related expenditures roll over into deficit spending from year to year.[20]

It is also clear that Congress has relinquished its traditional role in mobilizing and demobilizing the military. Procurement obligations during and after the Korean War still loosely resemble historical wartime spending policies, as procurement obligations reached nearly $350 billion at the height of the Korean War in 1952 and immediately fell below $100 billion in 1954, the year after the war ended. No war since Korea has required such a massive spending buildup or motivated a 70 percent reduction in procurement spending immediately following the end of the conflict. Instead, members of Congress have provided hundreds of billions of dollars annually to purchase military technology and improve weapons capabilities, regardless of whether the nation was engaged in a war. Presidents, in turn, have leveraged these resources to carry out their military policies regardless of whether or not Congress has endorsed the decision. Congressional defense spending policies led the legendary senator Patrick P. Moynihan to conclude, "The great armed force [created to fight the Cold War is] now at the president's disposal for any diversion he may wish, no matter what it costs."[21]

EXECUTIVE SECRECY AND MILITARY PRIVATIZATION

The development of a permanent weapons arsenal gave rise to several executive strategies that further insulate the president's authority from legislative control, restrict information from public scrutiny, and afford presidents greater flexibility to set the national security agenda. First, presidents have systematically relied on executive secrecy, including covert military operations and heightened document classification levels. These tactics remove executive actors from official legal channels, exacerbate information gaps between the executive branch and Congress, and weaken legislative capacity to monitor. Second, and more recently, presidents have sought to privatize multiple aspects of military activity, including the use of contractors to handle the military's logistical activities and outsourcing to private companies to provide security and conduct other military operations. Employing private contractors in combat zones makes oversight more difficult and creates new opportunities for presidents to circumvent statutory limitations on their authority.

In the 1940s the executive branch created numerous organizations involved in intelligence analysis, propaganda dissemination, espionage, and guerrilla warfare. These entities were structured "within the executive branch almost entirely at presidential initiative."[22] In fact, Congress did not formally authorize these agencies until the director of Central Intelligence requested assistance from Congress in order to strengthen his position relative to his competitors in the FBI, War Department, and State Department. In response, Congress passed the 1947 National Security Act (NSA). The NSA established a new National Security Council (NSC) as a White House forum for national security decisions. The act also created the office of Secretary of Defense to unify the military departments and made the air force a separate service.

While the 1947 act formally secured the Central Intelligence Agency (CIA) within the intelligence bureaucracy, it did not authorize covert operations overseas; rather, it instructed the CIA to evaluate and disseminate intelligence, and to perform "other functions and duties related to intelligence affecting the national security." However, the NSC immediately passed a number of classified directives authorizing the CIA to engage in covert, paramilitary operations and other "black" activities, including influencing the 1948 Italian elections (NSC-4-A, NSC-10-2). In response to these events, Congress passed the CIA Act of 1949, which exempts the agency from disclosing its "organization, functions, officials, titles, salaries, or numbers of personnel employed."

While presidents have had access to a small secret service fund since the earliest years of the republic, they had nothing even approximating covert armies capable of infiltrating foreign nations or an annual "black" budget with which to fund clandestine operations. Presidents did not submit many receipts for undocumented expenses in these earlier periods.[23] However, in 1949, Congress authorized a classified black budget subject only to approval by a small armed services subcommittee, which provides the CIA with untraceable funds to raise its own armies and conduct classified operations overseas. The Pentagon's black budget consists of classified funds for intelligence gathering, covert operations, military research, and weapons programs hidden in the Pentagon's overall budget. It includes spending by the CIA, the Defense Intelligence Agency (DIA), the National Security Agency (NSA), and military research and development. Although it is difficult to calculate, estimates suggest that the budget may hit nearly $60 billion a year.[24]

In the 1950s and early 1960s, Congress allowed intelligence agencies wide latitude to take the offensive against the Soviet Union. Under the leadership of CIA director Allen Dulles, the agency infiltrated, destabilized, and overthrew left-leaning and nationalist regimes that maintained friendly relations with the Soviet Union (or refused to align with the United States) using clandestine tactics, without congressional notification or public awareness of its actions.[25] Congress did not develop institutional mechanisms to oversee intelligence activity until 1975, when the Senate Church Committee and House Pike Committee formed to monitor intelligence information and covert actions. The trigger for congressional participation occurred in response to CIA-sponsored domestic wiretapping,[26] President Nixon's Watergate break-ins, US withdrawal from the unpopular war in Vietnam, and the CIA's active role in the overthrow of Salvador Allende, a popularly elected Chilean leader. The Church Committee investigated and reported on FBI- and CIA-sponsored domestic surveillance activity, covert actions abroad, and US counterintelligence.

During the congressional reform movement, Congress passed the 1980 Intelligence Oversight Act requiring "timely" notice of covert military or intelligence activities overseas to permanent select standing committees. However, only two years after the passage of the 1980 act, one of the most ambitious congressional attempts at curtailing a large-scale covert action program effectively drove the mission even further underground. In 1982 a Democratic Congress passed a series of amendments aimed at limiting the Reagan administration's support for the Nicaraguan Contras—right-wing militants guilty of murder, rape, arson, and scores of human rights abuses in a guerrilla war to topple the leftist Sandinista government. Collectively known as the Boland Amendments (named after Rep. Edward Patrick Boland [D-MA], their prime sponsor), the legislation expressly prohibited all US military and covert assistance to the Contras. Despite the broad, inclusive wording in the prohibitory legislation that Congress passed, the NSC secretly employed CIA operatives in Nicaragua while seeking finances for the Contras from private parties and friendly governments, including illicit weapons transactions with Iran.[27] While breaking news of these events spurred congressional investigations and uncovered evidence of illegal activities, executive defiance of oversight laws is hardly exceptional. In fact, a 1993 report by the Intelligence Oversight Board suggests a broader trend of noncompliance among CIA and NSC leadership with respect to congressional notification and other requirements pursuant to the 1980 act.[28]

While the creation of a national security and intelligence apparatus makes it easier for the executive branch to operate in secrecy, opportunity alone does not reveal the extent to which presidents or agency directors have used their ability to withhold information and operate outside of traditional legal channels. Of course, the obvious challenge to conducting such a study is that information on executive secrecy is, by definition, unavailable. However, analyzing the level of classified material reported in each fiscal year provides a preliminary gauge of undisclosed executive communications.

Figure 8.3 includes data on annual document classification levels from FY1980 to FY2008.[29] Organizations reporting include the CIA, DoD, State Department, Department of Justice (DoJ), NSC, Federal Emergency Management Agency (FEMA), Department of Energy (DoE), and Treasury. However, the CIA, DoD, and State Department account typically account for almost all of the reported document classifications (approximately 99%).

As displayed in figure 8.3, document classification levels tend to follow predictable patterns in light of geopolitical factors and national security policies. Classification activity peaked during the Iran-Contra scandal in FY1985 (15,120,298 documents) and again in FY2006–2008 during the escalation of the Iraq war and NSA warrantless surveillance controversy (20,556,445 documents). Also not surprisingly, classification levels dropped considerably throughout the 1990s, in a period of reduced conflict. In fact, in 1994, President Clinton issued Executive Order 12937, which declassified a number of records dating back to the 1970s within the National Archives.

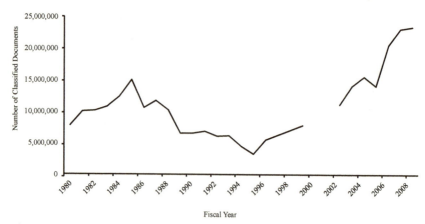

Figure 8.3. *Executive classification activity, 1980–2008.*

Figures for FY2001 and 2002 are characterized as unreliable due to temporary changes in departmental reporting techniques. FY2009–2011 are substantially higher than previous years on account of "revised reporting requirements" attributed to an increasing volume of electronic communication. These figures are all excluded from the analysis. FY1980–1984 are reported as estimated outcomes.

Source: National Archives and Records Administration, Information Security Oversight Office (http://www.archives.gov/isoo/reports/).

The following year, in FY1995, classified materials fell to the lowest point on record (3,579,505). Nonetheless, classification activity increased systematically during the late 1990s, more than doubling in volume by FY1999 (8,038,592). On November 1, 2001, President Bush issued EO 13222, reclassifying a number of documents and setting new restrictions on access to presidential records. In 2003 the George W. Bush administration initiated the war in Iraq—which later spawned probes regarding forged nuclear intelligence—and classification levels nearly quadrupled from the FY1995 volume (14,228,020). However, despite the considerable variation in levels of disclosure over this time period, the executive branch has systematically classified millions of documents annually—at least tens of thousands of documents per day—regardless of whether the US armed forces are engaged in major operation requiring authorized military secrecy.

Figure 8.4 compares the rate of annual classification activity and annual military contract obligations (drawn from figures 8.2 and 8.3). It is immediately evident that levels of military capabilities and executive secrecy follow roughly equivalent trends from year to year. Each peaked in FY1985, softly receded in the late 1980s and early 1990s, and shot back up toward 1980s levels at the turn of the twenty-first century (classification activity surpassed 1980s levels in FY2004). Despite the arresting similarity of these patterns, however, one must interpret these results cautiously. These figures

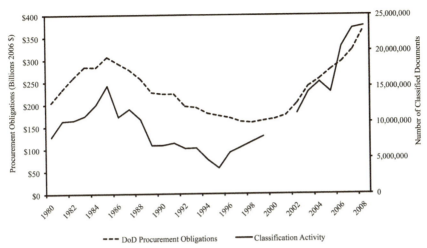

Figure 8.4. *Military capability and executive secrecy.*

Information drawn from figures 8.2 and 8.3.

alone do not provide evidence that military capability and executive secrecy are directly related. Rather, each factor is also shaped by geopolitical events and US policy responses (such as the US-Soviet arms race in the 1980s, military de-escalation in the 1990s, and heightened national security after the attacks of September 11, 2001). However, the results do suggest that military capability may be a necessary (if insufficient) factor for increased covert activity, as available defense assets and the potential to use force make it easier for executives to operate independently. It is also possible that the executive agenda can influence military capability and classification activity as two components of the same strategy. Despite the lack of causal evidence, the finding is important given the strong indication that weapons spending obligations and government secrecy are at least indirectly related.

Systematic nondisclosure within the national security and intelligence communities and the proliferation of hidden, untraceable funds have allowed presidents to direct covert military operations without explicit approval from Congress, subject only to the availability of military technology. After the Vietnam War, with overt military tactics severely discredited, the Pentagon increased "black" activities, extending well beyond the strategies pursued by CIA of the 1950s and 1960s. In fact, as President Obama's State Department legal advisor Harold Koh remarked in 1990, presidents have strategically transferred power away from larger, more accountable bureaucratic institutions, such as the DoD and State Department, to smaller, covert entities capable of swift, flexible action—such as the NSC and CIA.[30]

In the 1990s and early 2000s the CIA ceased to enjoy even the approximation of a monopoly over covert action. An array of special operations forces and elite units—Navy SEALs, Army Rangers, Green Berets, Delta Force, and 160th Aviation Regiment—performed missions ranging from clandestine reconnaissance and counterterrorism to hostage rescue and psychological operations (PSYOPS). While the Navy SEAL Team Six gained prominence for killing Osama bin Laden in 2011, most of what happens in the world of special operations lies beyond the radar of the American public. Although the use of elite forces provides many military and intelligence benefits, they also provide new opportunities for presidents to expand their power. In 2008 investigative journalist Seymour Hersh reported that the George W. Bush administration secretly used CIA and Joint Special Operations Command (JSOC) forces to destabilize the Ahmadinejad regime in Iran. In doing so, the president deliberately circumvented congressional reporting requirements enacted to cover CIA, but not JSOC, activities.[31] President Obama also relied on both JSOC forces and private security contractors to carry out hundreds of drone strikes targeted at suspected terrorists. Unlike uniformed soldiers, JSOC forces operate in coordination with the White House, but outside of the military chain of command and without congressional oversight.[32]

The emphasis on maximum efficiency in modern warfare extends from the use of covert action to the recent push for military privatization. The genesis of private security contractors traces back to the early careers of Donald Rumsfeld, Dick Cheney, and Paul Wolfowitz in the 1970s, and the strategy was circulated in think tanks such as Project for a New American Century. As discussed in chapter 4, President Clinton first embraced privatization during the Balkans conflict and 1999 Kosovo war. Clinton authorized the Virginia-based military consulting firm Military Professional Resources Incorporated to train the Croatian military in its secessionist war against Serb-dominated Yugoslavia. However, the privatization agenda (later part of the Rumsfeld Doctrine) reached its climax under the George W. Bush administration.

The widespread use of contractors in modern warfare and the transformation of the Pentagon bureaucracy "to behave less like bureaucrats and more like venture capitalists" also affected the internal restructuring of the Pentagon.[33] Historically, civilian defense agencies have decreased in size during periods of reduced conflict and increased during prolonged military engagements. However, as the Rumsfeld Doctrine was put into practice, many of bureaucratic agencies that have traditionally managed military and security functions were systematically downsized, despite ongoing military commitments in Afghanistan and Iraq.[34] Executive reliance on military outsourcing is important because private firms operate with fewer restrictions than bureaucratic agencies, and they free up executives by minimizing viable congressional oversight.

The extensive use of private military and security companies (PMSCs) in US war zones drew heightened media attention after four armed security contractors hired by Blackwater USA (rebranded twice, first as Xe and then Academi) were ambushed and killed, and their corpses were dragged through the streets of Fallujah, Iraq, in 2004. The company generated increased scrutiny following reports that contractors had shot and killed unarmed civilians and overbilled the US government. However, while PMSCs are clearly less accountable to Congress, they also offer new opportunities for presidents to evade traditional limits on their authority. Representative Jan Schakowsky (D-IL) reflected on the "disturbing" and "enormous" consequences of companies like private security company Blackwater USA (Academi) for executive war power:

> [Blackwater] empowers . . . the Bush administration—if they can engage in this kind of private war-making or a private army, then what do they even need [Congress] for? They can operate in a totally separate arena and engage in conflicts all over the world, and it seems like they don't much need to consult with us about it.[35]

PMSCs fundamentally change the constitutional balance. Unlike uniformed troops, Congress does not legally need to authorize—or even know about—the deployment of private contractors apart from any statutory restrictions that legislators might enact. Even if Congress does pass laws limiting the use of PMSCs in US war zones, presidents can sidestep legislation limiting the use of military contractors by drawing on third-party nationals instead.[36] Moreover, it is not clear whether Congress always wants control over contractors, given the low levels of public knowledge about their role in combat zones. PMSCs receive less media coverage than uniformed soldiers, which reduces transparency regarding war casualties and troop morale.[37] In addition, contractor numbers and fatalities are not included in DoD military records, deflating official casualty statistics and limiting the negative risk on public opinion.

The private sector makes it easier to initiate and prolong wars without a draft or more extensive recruitment efforts and undermines mechanisms of democratic control over the military. For most of the nation's history, the need for Congress to mobilize troops and raise taxes in order to prosecute wars created major obstacles to any military interventions that an administration might seek to undertake. Domestic opposition to wars resulted in fewer people volunteering to serve in the armed forces, deflating troop size or requiring a military draft. However, contractors reduce pressures to recruit military volunteers, which shrinks US troops counts and lessens internal resistance from Congress and the American public. In addition, a private-sector option allows presidents to circumvent statutory limitations governing the deployment of uniformed soldiers and weakens Congress's oversight capabilities.

CONCLUSION: THE MAGINOT LINE

Although Congress periodically attempts to strengthen its oversight mechanisms through internal restructuring and statutory reforms, members also continue to appropriate hundreds of billions of dollars annually in weapons spending. Much like the Maginot Line—a concrete fortification designed by the French to keep German troops out in the run-up to World War II—congressional reforms typically avert direct confrontation with the president but invariably fail to achieve their stated purpose. In the French case, the Germans avoided direct assault on the line, instead invading France by moving through Belgium and the Netherlands. Similarly, executives can draw on appropriated defense resources, intelligence agents, special operations forces, and private security contractors to circumvent any restrictions on the use of military force that Congress might impose.

Ongoing defense spending advances legislators' institutional ambitions, while furnishing presidents with historically unparalleled resources to implement their national security policies. When an administration of the opposing party oversteps its bounds, legislative majorities may find partisan incentives to check the executive branch. However, despite statutory reforms and periods of heightened oversight, an ongoing weapons arsenal consistently frees presidents from traditional constraints on their war powers. Given continued streams of funding, equipment, and technology, presidents work to insulate available defense assets and use them to carry out their policies. Presidents have devised mechanisms to shield executive communications, employ intelligence agents and elite forces covertly, and draw on private security contractors to perform traditional military functions. These developments undermine Congress's control over the military and weaken its capacity to monitor.

Conclusion: The
Warfare State

Now that I have shown how legislators' interests in promoting large defense budgets encourage more independent executive military actions and weaken Congress's ability to challenge the president's national security agenda, it is appropriate to return to the broader focus presented in the introduction. The book began by questioning why a nation founded on a severe distrust of standing armies and centralized power embraced consolidated executive authority over the most powerful military in history. While the constitutional framers relied on institutional checks and competing interests to limit power, structural barriers failed to prevent military capacity from concentrating in the executive branch. However, the political system has not degenerated into the despotic alternative the Constitution's opponents feared either. Both supporters and opponents of the proposed Constitution miscalculated because neither side foresaw the crucial role that defense spending would play in the health of local economies across the nation, or the extent to which these expenditures could be maintained by shielding most Americans from the direct costs of large military budgets and wars.

For most of the nation's history, the nation had no armaments industry, and presidents could not conduct major wars without obtaining funding and support from Congress. In 1939 the United States maintained the world's sixteenth-largest army—behind the former Yugoslavia, Romania, Turkey, and Poland—and had no formal military alliances. In 1944, at the peak of World War II production, 16 million men had enlisted in the armed services and an additional 10 million workers were employed in war-related industries, out of a total a labor force of 56 million. While geopolitical threats provided an initial catalyst for an arms industry, my analysis shows that the transformation to a permanent war economy is also rooted in the expansive geography of World War II military mobilization. New research presented here demonstrates that defense facilities spread out into more rural and semirural areas outside of large cities for full-scale war production. Consequently, the growth of defense infrastructure throughout regions and localities without a diverse industrial base disproportionately affected migration patterns and local development, creating excessive dependencies in these areas. Although no one deliberately set out to create long-term structural reliance on a war economy, this became an uncoordinated result of a national military mobilization strategy where multiple actors pursued their own immediate goals.

After World War II, large percentages of the workforce were either employed in defense industries or in the armed forces, and local economic reliance on defense jobs promoted continued political support for military spending. These new economic imperatives coincided with the emerging dominance of a political ideology that views American military supremacy as a moral force for good. Just as large defense budgets help meet local, regional, and national economic goals, they also help secure overlapping political interests, such as advancing the national security, policing the international sphere, or protecting US economic interests abroad. As economic goals and political ideologies coincided, the historical sacrifices necessary to maintain large defense buildups and go to war gradually shifted onto a small percentage of uniformed soldiers who volunteer to fight, future generations of taxpayers who will fund American military expeditions, and foreign populations where US wars and military strikes take place.

Overlapping political and economic interests in defense-sector expansion also weaken Congress's ability to limit executive independence in military affairs. Large defense budgets furnish presidents with unprecedented capacity to exercise their military policies independently, and they make it more difficult for Congress to mount effective opposition. However, presidents never needed to co-opt power by dissolving Congress or obstructing democratic processes. Rather, since World War II, legislators have given presidents heightened control over a permanent military establishment because defense spending and the projection of military force advance widely shared economic and political interests, regardless of costs borne elsewhere. As long as political majorities are not directly affected by defense buildups or military actions overseas, policymakers can pursue these strategies with minimal opposition.

My analysis draws on powerful accounts of executive usurpation in matters of war and defense that Louis Fisher and other excellent scholars have documented. However, I argue that existing diagnoses of this power imbalance provide only a partial explanation. Heightened executive ambition, legislative atrophy, and expansive interpretations of the president's constitutional war powers are all symptomatic of a new underlying incentive structure that earlier scholars have missed. Previous scholarship has overlooked the connection between legislators' interests in defense-sector growth and expansive executive authority over the military, because these accounts do not consider how local economic reliance on defense spending shapes the political development of the nation's military apparatus. In contrast, my emphasis on the broad historical picture led me to consider how a nation so resistant to centralized military force became the largest military economy in the world, and why the constitution's structural safeguards failed to prevent the consolidation of power over such an extraordinary establishment of state violence.

The evidence indicates that large defense budgets have become an integral component of nation's economic and foreign policy apparatus, which can be maintained without directly infringing on most Americans' livelihoods or their pocketbooks. In this new climate, Congress has relinquished its strict budgetary control over the military and provided presidents with resources necessary to exercise their powers as commander-in-chief. The framers' use of institutions to compartmentalize interests, structure competition, and neutralize private vice has generated policies favoring the short-term, mutual benefits of voters, officeholders, and defense industries—regardless of the long-term consequences or the costs to nonvoting populations. This evidence suggests a flaw in the modern reliance on institutional checks and competing interests as principal mechanisms for limiting power and promoting the public good.

WHY INSTITUTIONAL REMEDIES FAILED

In the late eighteenth century, James Madison advanced a seminal argument for structural restraints on military aggrandizement and warfare. Railing against an antiquated, if not naïve, reliance on collective action and goodwill to promote peace and avoid war, Madison argued that institutions can redirect the self-interest of leaders and citizens. From Julius Caesar's Roman army to eighteenth-century European monarchies, the allurements of war and ability to avoid personal sacrifice allowed rulers to reap the benefits of warfare while imposing heavy burdens on the general public. However, monarchies and dictatorships plagued with perpetual war or military despotism lacked institutional safeguards preventing political power from concentrating and checking private vice. Specifically, these failed regimes lacked mechanisms that divide military powers between separate governing departments and institute a measure of popular control over rulers.

To shift historical incentives, Madison favored a representative government equipped with institutional checks and balances. He reasoned that a legislature vested with the power to declare war, raise armies, and tax and spend would be less likely to build large peacetime armies and initiate unpopular military ventures if members must appeal to the public for re-election. Further, a system of separated powers would ensure that the legislature must raise troops and appropriate resources in order for the president to exercise force or employ coercion. The institutional design ultimately hinges on officeholders' ambitions to safeguard their powers and citizens' limited readiness to sacrifice.

Guided by this new science of politics, the US Constitution grants a single executive broad authority to command the armed forces, but with the understanding that Congress controls the resources necessary to initiate military actions. Congress possesses plenary authority to raise armies and the power to declare war, though legislators' willingness to mobilize the military depends largely on the popular appeal of their actions. In short, institutional structures work to ensure that the appropriation of defense resources reflect the immediate interests of the voters, who were expected to bear the burdens traditionally associated with permanent armies and warfare.

As chapter 2 illustrates, late eighteenth-century congresses largely adhered to the framers' expectations. The nascent republic inherited deficient procurement infrastructure, a tiny naval force, disorganized state militias, and severe fiscal constraints, including limits on federal borrowing. As a result, early administrations and congresses relied heavily on imported weapons and called upon state militias and large volunteer contingents in preparation for war. Military mobilization also drained public revenue, requiring higher taxes and domestic spending reductions during wartime. Defense appropriations could not persist without broad public willingness to pay for it.

In the nineteenth and early twentieth centuries, the emergence of domestic markets for weapons procurements and the ability to print money and accrue debt made it easier for Congress to periodically increase military spending without provoking opposition from voters. At the same time, more flexible armies (facilitated by a new legislative strategy of decreasing regiments rather than eliminating entire units) and heightened investments in defense resources allowed presidents to use available troops and equipment without permission from Congress. For instance, in 1846 James Polk drew upon more expansible army contingents and demonstrated a willingness to move existing forces in a manner that precipitated war, seeking legislative approval only after military hostilities appeared inevitable. In the early twentieth century, presidents Roosevelt, Taft, and Wilson took advantage of the modern naval resources procured during industrialization and heightened congressional interest in regional expansion by stationing forces abroad and issuing limited military engagements independently.

Like their post–World War II counterparts, nineteenth- and early twentieth-century presidents eagerly capitalized on periodic congressional investments in defense resources. However, patterns of military demobilization limited earlier presidents' capacity to wage wars and sustain military interventions independently—despite episodic increases in the president's authority over the military. As the constitutional framers had anticipated, a permanent military establishment was considered unnecessarily costly and politically disadvantageous. Consequently, presidents consistently relied on Congress to raise troops and supply funds to go to war.

After World War II, the incentives shaping members' defense-spending decisions changed dramatically. The ascent of Nazi Germany and Japan's attack at Pearl Harbor motivated Congress to create large armies and to fund a geographically extensive weapons arsenal. However, as chapter 3 shows, the expansion of defense infrastructure into suburbs, towns, and agrarian regions that lacked diverse industrial economies generated pervasive dependence on the defense sector to sustain employment and revenue. Local economic imperatives created new legislative incentives to procure ongoing defense resources, rather than demobilizing as had occurred after previous wars.

When World War II ended, the American economy was still poised for war production. Despite a sizable retrenchment in 1945, the United States retained an immense military establishment by any historical standard. Many locations retained defense infrastructure that had been established during the war, and US troops kept up a strong overseas presence. As a result, President Truman was able to call upon existing forces and draw on remaining weapons in order to independently engage troops in Korea in 1950. Although President Eisenhower criticized imprudent military spending when he took office in 1953, new research presented in chapter 4 demonstrates that defense dollars continued to spread into increasing numbers of regions and localities in every decade through the George W. Bush administration, regardless of the geopolitical climate or the size of the overall procurement budget. Further, modest increments of defense dollars systematically extended to more economically reliant areas with less developed infrastructure, including the formerly agrarian South and Southwest, more sparsely populated areas on the outskirts of large cities, and, most recently, plains, desert and mountain regions.

Evidence introduced in chapter 4 also shows that policymakers worked to finance military mobilization and conduct wars in ways that makes it easier to sustain popular approval. The 1973 all-volunteer force transformed military service from an obligation tied to citizenship to a voluntary act. Subsequently, the use of military and security contractors reduced the need for a large volunteer contingent and contributed to lower US troop counts during major wars. Meanwhile, increased reliance on federal borrowing and deficit spending also circumvented the historical need to raise taxes and adjust domestic spending priorities in order to fund troops and supply military equipment. Finally, the development of more sophisticated military technologies contributed to an ability to fight wars far removed from US soil, minimizing disruption to domestic life. Unmanned aerial vehicles (UAVS), or drone technologies, have made it possible to engage in overseas conflicts without even deploying US troops or placing American lives at risk.

The ability to obviate or reduce public sacrifices in wartime undermines the system of checks and balances that the Constitution's framers envisioned. Rather than imposing the sacrifices on political majorities with electoral power over governing officials, policymakers can promote initiatives that reduce the immediate costs of war for most Americans. The broad extension of defense benefits and the shifting of war costs make it easier for elected officials to perpetuate military spending and exercise force abroad without fear of electoral reprisal.

OVERLAPPING INCENTIVES AND CONCENTRATED POWER

Despite the broad dispersion of defense benefits, members of Congress do not typically support weapons programs based solely on the potential for constituency gain. Rather, legislative support for weapons spending varies based on the relative importance of the defense sector for a local economy. Specifically, more economically homogenous, rural constituencies typically experience greater dependence on the major defense companies in their district than densely populated urban areas. Members of Congress representing constituencies that are disproportionately reliant on the defense funds that they receive work especially hard to promote more military spending, regardless of whether these funds are needed for national security. Even after the fall of the Soviet Union, when the United States faced no serious national adversaries, Congress defeated nearly every proposal for a specific defense cut that came to a floor vote. After the attacks of September 11, 2001, in a period of asymmetrical warfare and no comparable US military rivals, Congress spent almost as much on the military as the rest of the world combined. As the analyses in chapters 5 and 6 show, legislators representing more economically reliant areas take a special interest in continued defense spending and join committees with jurisdiction over the military budget.

Local economic reliance on defense dollars helps explain why some members not only supply presidents with resources necessary to initiate hostilities, but also break rank with their partisan allies and support major wars associated with a president of the opposing party. As the analysis in chapter 7 suggests, members representing areas that rely most heavily on a war economy are more predisposed to support war and war spending, even while their fellow partisans criticize these military operations. Rather than simply acquiescing to the president's war policies out of fear, weakness, or deference, many members gain politically by supplying the resources that allow presidents act. Given the potential benefits of military buildups and wars and deferred costs for a majority of Americans, there is rarely strong incentive for legislators to restrict war funding in order to prevent the president from carrying out his policies.

Just as Congress has provided hundreds of billions of dollars in annual weapons spending available for mobilization at any time, presidents have structured institutions to leverage congressionally appropriated resources at their own discretion. As chapter 8 documents, presidents have structured executive agencies to implement their foreign policy decisions and pursued strategies that shield information from Congress, weakening congressional oversight capabilities. Despite episodes of statutory reform and heightened oversight activity, patterns of ongoing defense spending contribute to the president's ability to direct the national security agenda independently.

Taken cumulatively, my analysis suggests that the constitutional framers' reliance on institutional mechanisms and competing interests as a means to disperse power and limit war ultimately fell short of their professed aims. The constructive use of popular and institutional checks failed to prevent resources and authority from concentrating in the executive department. Rather, an institutional structure premised on competing interests has generated a system that maximizes short-term benefits of officeholders, voters, and defense industries, while empowering presidents to achieve their ends militarily. Policies have also shifted most of the costs of war onto political minorities, future generations of Americans and foreign nations where US wars take place. Institutional checks and competing interests do not reliably limit power or promote the public good.

Appendixes

Note: Appendixes not appearing in print can be found online at http://www.press.uchicago.edu/sites/thorpe.

3.1 US military aircraft conversion for war production, 1940, 1944, 1950 (online)

3.2 US automobile conversion for war production, 1944, 1950 (online)

3.3 Government-owned, company-operated war production facilities, 1944, 1950 (online)

3.4 Population change in cities and towns with defense infrastructure, 1940–1950 (online)

5.1 Descriptive statistics (online)

5.2 House roll-call votes (online)

5.3 Influence of economic reliance on US House members' support for defense expenditures in the 103rd–105th Congresses (1993–98)

5.4 Influence of economic reliance on Democratic and Republican House members' support for defense expenditures in the 103rd–105th congresses (1993–98)

5.5 Influence of economic reliance on Democratic and Republican House members' support for defense expenditures by vote type, 103rd–105th congresses (1993–98, pooled)

6.1 Descriptive statistics (online)

6.2 Economically reliant districts (online)

6.3 Influence of economic reliance on congressional Defense Committee membership in the 106th–109th Congresses (1999–2005)

6.4 Influence of economic reliance and Defense Committee membership on defense subcontract locations in the 106th and 109th Congresses

Appendix 5.3. *Influence of economic reliance on US House members' support for defense expenditures in the 103rd–105th Congresses*

Independent variable	Coefficients			
	103rd Congress (1993–94)	104th Congress (1995–96)	105th Congress (1997–98)	103rd Congress (Condensed)
Low density* facilities[a] (economic reliance)	.00114*	.00148**	.000907*†	—
	(.000534)	(.000458)	(.000498)	
Low density[a]	.00183**	.00202***	.00168**	.00219***
	(.000611)	(.000527)	(.000572)	(.000590)
Defense facilities	-.201*	-.265**	-.162	.017**
	(.102)	(.087)	(.095)	(.005)
Military population[a]	.00329*	.00170	.00356*	.00338*
	(.00159)	(.00135)	(.00145)	(.00159)
Defense Committee	.097**	.046	.037	.098**
	(.037)	(.031)	(.053)	(.037)

	(1)	(2)	(3)	(4)
Defense contribution[a]	.00288***	.00232***	.00275**	.00287***
	(.000625)	(.000641)	(.000794)	(.000627)
Party (1 = Republican)	.436***	.399***	.337***	.437***
	(.026)	(.022)	(.024)	(.025)
	N = 434	N = 434	N = 435	N = 434
	Prob > F = 0.00	Prob > F = 0.00	Prob > F = 0.00	Prob > F = 0.00
	R^2 = .52	R^2 = .59	R^2 = .46	R^2 = .46
	Adj. R^2 = .51	Adj. R^2 = .58	Adj. R^2 = .45	Adj. R^2 = .45

Note: All entries are OLS coefficients. Standard errors are in parentheses. The dependent variable indicates the average roll call vote on controversial weapons expenditures, defense procurement cuts, and arms sale policies per district in the House of Representatives for each separate congressional term (scaled from 0 to 1). Votes favoring increased defense expenditures, opposing defense cuts and relaxing arms sale restrictions are coded "1"; votes opposing defense expenditures, favoring cuts, and tightening arms sale restrictions are coded "0."

[a] In thousands

*** $p < .001$; ** $p < .01$; * $p < .05$ (two-tailed test), † (one-tailed test)

Appendix 5.4. *Influence of economic reliance on Democratic and Republican House members' support for defense expenditures in the 103rd–105th Congresses*

Coefficients

Independent variable	103rd Congress (1993–94)		104th Congress (1995–96)		105th Congress (1997–98)	
	Democrats	Republicans	Democrats	Republicans	Democrats	Republicans
Low density* facilities[a] (economic reliance)	.00141* (.000742)	.00201* (.00113)	.00218** (.000695)	.00113 (.000767)	-.0000184 (.000650)	.00277* (.00372)
Low density[a]	.000270 (.000589)	-.00924*† (.00495)	.000524 (.000510)	-.000955 (.00303)	.000483 (.000620)	-.00372 (.00454)
Defense facilities	-.247*† (.141)	-.384*† (.219)	-.391** (.132)	-.206 (.148)	.018 (.123)	-.528* (.237)
Military population[a]	.00231 (.00168)	.00498 (.00295)	.00301* (.00155)	-.00106 (.00198)	.00352*† (.00190)	.00191 (.00205)
Defense Committee	.074*† (.043)	.143** (.054)	.071*† (.041)	.027 (.038)	.143 (.094)	.015 (.057)

Defense contribution[a]	.00290*** (.000658)	-.0000661 (.00119)	.00321** (.000912)	.00140 (.000761)	.00296* (.00147)	.00175* (.000851)
Ideology (conservative)	.689*** (.089)	.438** (.129)	.632*** (.090)	.239** (.083)	.668*** (.106)	.042 (.085)
	N = 258	N = 176	N = 200	N = 234	N = 207	N = 228
	Prob > F = 0.00	Prob > F = 0.00	Prob > F = 0.00	Prob > F = 0.00	Prob > F = 0.00	Prob > F = 0.00
	R^2 = .47	R^2 = .16	R^2 = .54	R^2 = .11	R^2 = .34	R^2 = .09
	Adj R^2 = .45	Adj R^2 = .12	Adj. R^2 = .52	Adj. R^2 = .09	Adj R^2 = .32	Adj R^2 = .06

Note: All entries are OLS coefficients. Standard errors are in parentheses. The dependent variable indicates the average roll call vote on controversial weapons expenditures, defense procurement cuts, and arms sale policies analyzed separately for Democratic (column 1) and Republican (column 2) members of the US House in each separate congressional term (scaled from 0 to 1). Votes favoring increased defense expenditures, opposing defense cuts and relaxing arms sale restrictions are coded "1"; votes opposing defense spending in these three types of bills are coded "0."

[a] In thousands

***p < .001; **p < .01; *p < .05 (two-tailed test), † (one-tailed test)

Appendix 5-5. *Influence of economic reliance on Democratic and Republican House members' support for defense expenditures by vote type, 103rd–105th Congresses (1993–98, pooled)*

Coefficients

Independent variable	Controversial Weapons		Defense Cuts		Arms Sales	
	Democrats	Republicans	Democrats	Republicans	Democrats	Republicans
Low density* facilities[a] *(economic reliance)*	.000861* (.000387)	.00154** (.000597)	.00166*** (.000430)	.00254*** (.000601)	.00131*** (.000390)	.000412 (.000529)
Low density[a]	.000543*† (.000324)	-.00363 (.000241)	.00153*** (.000360)	-.00481* (.00243)	.000570*† (.000326)	.00171 (.000214)
Defense facilities	-.133*† (.073)	-.285* (.116)	-.295*** (.082)	-.477*** (.116)	-.227** (.074)	-.072 (.102)
Military population[a]	.00259** (.000962)	.00155 (.000137)	.00391*** (.00107)	.000997 (.00138)	.000299 (.000970)	-.00255* (.00122)

	(1)	(2)	(3)	(4)	(5)	(6)
Defense Committee	.056*	.064*	.034	.063*	.013	.020
	(.028)	(.028)	(.031)	(.028)	(.028)	(.025)
Defense contribution[a]	.00263***	.00120*	.00223***	.00114*	.00238***	.00168***
	(.000487)	(.000539)	(.000542)	(.000543)	(.000491)	(.000478)
Ideology (conservative)	.688***	.188***	.763***	.172**	.495***	.057
	(.053)	(.058)	(.059)	(.058)	(.053)	(.051)
	$N = 666$	$N = 639$	$N = 666$	$N = 639$	$N = 666$	$N = 639$
	Prob > F = 0.00	Prob > F = 0.00	Prob > F = 0.00	Prob > F = 0.00	Prob > F = 0.00	Prob > F = 0.00
	$R^2 = .48$	$R^2 = .10$	$R^2 = .46$	$R^2 = .11$	$R^2 = .34$	$R^2 = .06$
	Adj $R^2 = .47$	Adj $R^2 = .09$	Adj $R^2 = .46$	Adj $R^2 = .10$	Adj $R^2 = .33$	Adj $R^2 = .05$

Note: All entries are OLS coefficients. Standard errors are in parentheses. The dependent variable indicates the average roll-call vote on controversial weapons expenditures, defense cuts, and arms sale policies (respectively) for Democratic and Republican members of the US House pooled across the 103rd, 104th, and 105th congresses (scaled from 0 to 1). Votes favoring increased defense expenditures, opposing defense cuts and relaxing arms sale restrictions are coded "1"; votes opposing defense spending in these three types of bills are coded "0."

[a] In thousands ***$p < .001$; **$p < .01$; *$p < .05$ (two-tailed test), † (one-tailed test)

Appendix 6.3. *Influence of economic reliance on congressional Defense Committee membership in the 106th–109th Congresses (1999–2005)*

Independent variable	Coefficients			109th Congress	
	106th Congress	107th Congress	108th Congress	Model A	Model B
Population density* facilities[a] *(economic reliance)*	-.012 (.0060)* [-0.06]	-.00743 (.0056) [-0.04]	-.0001 (.0057) [-0.0009]	-.000211 (.0056) [-0.0018]	-.000284 (.0056) [-0.0024]
Defense facilities	.31 (.05)*** [0.16]	.24 (.05)*** [0.12]	.25 (.05)*** [0.16]	.28 (.05)*** [0.17]	.28 (.05)*** [0.17]
Population density[a]	-.0251 (.021) [-0.07]	-.022 (.019) [-0.07]	-.039 (.022) [-0.14]	-.031 (.021) [-0.11]	-.032 (.021) [-0.11]
Headquarters	-1.10 (.56)* [-0.04]	-.88 (.52) [-0.03]	-.23 (.53) [-0.01]	-.43 (.55) [-0.02]	-.42 (.55) [-0.02]
Gunbelt	.04 (.28) [0.003]	.49 (.29) [0.03]	-.04 (.26) [-0.003]	-.16 (.27) [-0.01]	-.16 (.27) [-0.01]
Ideology (conservative)	.14 (.31) [0.009]	-.007 (.30) [-0.0005]	-.055 (.27) [-0.005]	.009 (.275) [0.0007]	-.16 (.01) [-0.01]
Party (Republican)	—	—	—	—	-.05 (.27) [-0.004]
	N = 435	N = 435	N = 435	N = 435	N = 435
	McFadden's R^2 = .15	McFadden's R^2 = .13	McFadden's R^2 = .13	McFadden's R^2 = .15	McFadden's R^2 = .15
	Count R^2 = .81	Count R^2 = .81	Count R^2 = .76	Count R^2 = .79	Count R^2 = .78
	Prob > χ^2 = 0.00	Prob > χ^2 = 0.00	Prob > χ^2 = 0.00	Prob > χ^2 = 0.00	Prob > χ^2 = 0.00

Note: Appendix 6.3 displays logit coefficients. Standard errors are in parentheses. Changes in predicted probabilities from ±½ standard deviation around the mean are in brackets. The dependent variable indicates a defense committee assignment (coded "1" for defense committee and "0" for no defense committee).

[a] Coefficients in thousands people/square mile

*** p < .001; ** p < .01; * p < .05 (two-tailed test)

Appendix 6.4. *Influence of economic reliance and Defense Committee membership on defense subcontract locations in the 106th and 109th Congresses*

Independent variable	106th Congress	109th Congress
Population density* facilities[a]	.0005 (.004)	−.0027 (.003)
	[0.06]	[−0.34]
Defense facilities (economic reliance)	.21 (.03)***	.22 (.03)***
	[2.51]	[1.96]
Population density[a]	−.01 (.006)*	−.02 (.008)*
	[−0.72]	[−1.02]
Defense Committee	.54 (.20)**	.70 (.17)***
	[0.70]	[0.66]
Defense Committee leadership	−.06 (.56)	.02 (.53)
	[−0.02]	[0.005]
Headquarters	.34 (.27)	.58 (.26)*
	[0.30]	[0.41]
Defense contribution[b]	.01 (.006)*†	.005 (.002)*
	[.56]	[.45]
Gunbelt	.55 (.15)***	.55 (.15)***
	[0.86]	[0.63]
Party (Republican)	.01 (.15)	−.09 (.14)
	[0.02]	[−0.11]
	$N = 435$	$N = 435$
	PseudoR^2 = .08	PseudoR^2 = .11
	Prob $> F = 0.00$	Prob $> F = 0.00$

Note: Appendix 6.4 displays negative binomial regression coefficients. Standard errors are in parentheses. Changes in predicted rates from ±1/2 standard deviation around the mean are in brackets. The dependent variable indicates the principal location in which defense procurement projects are built. The data were extracted from the Federal Procurement Data System and transformed to the district level for the years 1999, 2000, and 2005.
[a] Coefficients in thousand people/sq mi
[b] Coefficients in thousands of dollars
***$p < .001$; **$p < .01$; *$p < .05$ (two-tailed test); †(one-tailed test)

Notes

CHAPTER I

1. Defense contracting exceeded $219 billion allocated for defense procurements and research and development in the 2010 fiscal year. This figure does not include expenditures for the 3.2 million civilian and military Department of Defense employees, funding for military bases, nuclear weaponry, or supplemental funding for the wars in Iraq and Afghanistan. Nor does it include billions of dollars of annual weapons sales to foreign nations. (Also see Higgs 1990, xviii; Gholz and Sapolsky 1999–2000 for estimated figures on defense employment.)

2. Mayer 1990, 218–31; 1991; Rundquist 1978, 42. While Kenneth Mayer (1990, 1991) utilized specified subcontracting data to assess the overall dispersion of program benefits, the data presented here afford a more refined analysis of the distribution of subcontracts in more economically vulnerable districts.

3. See Ackerman 2010, Cooper 2002, Corwin 1957, Howell 2003, Lewis 2008, Maddow 2012, Mills 1956, Pfiffner 2008, Rudalevige 2005, and Schlesinger 2004 [1973] on the increase in presidential power. See Farrier 2010; Fisher 2000, 2004; Koh 1988, 1990; Mann and Ornstein 2006; and Silverstein 1997 on the constitutional "imbalance" of war powers and congressional decline post–World War II.

4. Quoting Schlesinger 2004 [1973]; also see Rudalevige 2005.

5. A line is a privately held or managed facility that builds a particular weapon platform. The failure to eliminate a production line means that the same factories still manufacture the same aircraft, ships, and armored vehicles and their various replacements (Gholz and Sapolsky 1999–2000, 5). See chapter 5 for more detailed analysis.

6. The State Department budget was $51 billion in the 2010 fiscal year, during a period of reconstruction and stabilization in Iraq, compared to $683 billion allocated to the Department of Defense.

7. For example, see Rumerman n.d.

8. According to Lasswell's 1941 account, a garrison state is controlled by military elite, relies on compulsory labor service, and stamps out political opposition, rival parties, and democratic institutions. See Friedberg 2000 on domestic constraints on Cold War military expansion that prevented this outcome.

Regarding opportunity costs, presidents are particularly sensitive to fiscal concerns and budgetary tradeoffs. Following Eisenhower, many presidents have championed efforts to reduce defense budgets and fought to eliminate expensive weapons programs, especially during periods of reduced threat and a changing geopolitical environment. See chapters 5 and 8 for further elaboration.

9. Most notably, see Madison, "Federalist No. 51," in Rossiter 2003. (All "Federalist" essays are drawn from Rossiter 2003 unless otherwise noted.)

10. Madison, "Federalist No. 48" and "Federalist No. 58."

11. Under art. I, § 9, "No money shall be drawn from the Treasury, but in the Consequence of Appropriations made by law."

12. Hamilton, "Federalist No. 69." See US Const., art. I, § 8, cl. 11–13.

13. Following Moe and Wilson (1994), this characterization of presidential power refers to the institutional authority of the president and his or her relation to the office—not to the types

of foreign policies that a president might pursue. Also see Corwin 1957; Hamilton, "Federalist No. 70"; Howell 2003, 2005; Moe and Howell 1999; Moe and Wilson 1994; Whittington and Carpenter 2003.

14. On "energy," see Hamilton, "Federalist No. 70." On a "history of aggrandizement" see Corwin 1957; also see Schlesinger 2004 [1973].

15. See Arnold 1990, Farrier 2010, Fiorina 1989, and Mayhew 1974 on members' electoral incentives. Also see Cox and McCubbins 2005 and Lee 2009 on partisan behavior in Congress.

16. Quoting Mayhew 1974, 126.

17. Koh 1988, 1990; Olson 1971; Silverstein 1997. While party leadership does impose some control over member behavior, party leaders are still notoriously weak compared to their executive counterparts. Moreover, congressional structures reinforce this weakness by promoting leadership strategies that allow individual members to serve the interests of their constituencies (Moe and Wilson 1994, 25).

18. Madison, "Federalist No. 51."

19. Defense employment provided more than 9 million jobs during this period if uniformed soldiers and DoD personnel are included (Higgs 1990, xviii).

20. The data collection and methodology for figures 1.4 and 1.5 is elaborated in chapter 4.

21. In 2010 US military spending accounted for 43% of the total global defense investment and exceeded that of its nearest rival, China, sixfold. See Stockholm International Peace Research Institute, "Background Paper on SIPRI Military Expenditure Data, 2010," April 11, 2011 (accessed at http://www.sipri.org/research/armaments/milex/factsheet2010).

22. For example, see Adams 1981, Cavanaugh 1999, Higgs 2006, Kotz 1988, Kurth 1972, Ledbetter 2011, Markusen et al. 1991, Melman 1974, Twight 1990, and Wheeler 2004. Also see Eugene Jarecki's critically acclaimed 2005 documentary, *Why We Fight*.

23. For example, Gordon Adams's (1981) important study on military contracting documents the flow of personnel and money between defense firms and military contractors, executive defense bureaus, and key members of Congress. Also see Freeman (1955) for a classic account of reciprocal executive bureau-legislative committee relations, and Stein and Bickers (1995) for a more nuanced analysis of policy subsystems.

24. Cavanaugh 1999; Kotz 1988.

25. Gansler 1980; Higgs 1990, xxvi–xxviii; Markusen et al. 1991; Patillo 1998.

26. Quoting Ledbetter 2011, 210.

27. For statistical studies casting doubt on the thesis, see Bernstein and Anthony 1974; Cobb 1976; Goss 1972; Lindsay 1991; Mayer 1991; Ray 1981a; Rundquist 1973, 1978; Rundquist and Griffith 1976; also see Mayer 1990; Rundquist and Carsey 2002 for evidence of political influences in defense contracting.

28. On nuclear weapons development see Bernstein and Anthony 1974; on space-based missiles see Lindsay 1991; on foreign policy see Cobb 1974, Ray 1981a.

29. Mayer 1991; Ray 1980, 1981b; Rundquist 1973, 1978; Rundquist and Griffith 1976; but see Rundquist and Carsey 2002.

30. Since World War II, presidents have requested legislative authorization on four occasions—the Vietnam War in 1964, the first Gulf war in 1991, the Afghanistan War in 2001, and the Iraq War of 2003. An authorization of war shields presidents from potential fallout by creating a sense of shared responsibility with Congress for the outcome. In each case of legislative authorization, the president has contended that he does not need legislative support, but expressed gratitude for Congress' broad grant of authority. Congress has not issued a single declaration of war during this period.

31. For several exemplary accounts, see Friedberg 2000; Skocpol 1992; Skowronek 1982; Whittington and Carpenter 2003.

32. See Mills (1956) on symbiotic interests and concentrated authority among the "power elite"; Bacevich (2010) on the host of beneficiaries of the national security establishment, including defense contractors, corporations, large banks, universities and mainstream Congress members belonging to both political parties, who perpetuate the "Washington rules" of US global dominance; and Maddow 2012 on the increasing privatization of war and growth of executive military capabilities.

33. Quoting Mann and Ornstein 2006 ("broken" legislative branch). On checks and balances, see Farrier 2010; Fisher 2004; Koh 1988, 1990; Silverstein 1997. Quoting Ackerman 2010 ("decline of the American republic").

34. For example, see Howell and Pevehouse 2007, Kriner 2010, Levinson and Pildes 2006, and Schickler and Kriner 2012.

35. Kriner 2010.

CHAPTER 2

1. Hamilton, quoted in Sofaer 1976, 103.

2. Schlesinger 2004 [1973], 33–34

3. Letters of May 14 and May 31, 1780, in Fitzpatrick 1931–44, vol. 18.

4. See Sofaer 1976, 23; Wood 2003, 70–74, for a more detailed analysis.

5. Letter to Alexander Hamilton, Newburgh, March 4, 1783, in Fitzpatrick 1931–44, vol. 26.

6. "In less time and with much less [expense] than has been incurred, the War might have been brought to the same happy conclusion, if the resources of the Continent could have been properly drawn forth" (Circular to the States, Headquarters, Newburgh, June 8, 1783, in Fitzpatrick 1931–44, vol. 26).

7. Ibid.

8. In June 1783 unpaid soldiers marched to Philadelphia and protested before Independence Hall. Lacking authority to interfere, Congress was forced to temporarily relocate. When confronted with Shay's Rebellion in 1787, Congress faced requests for assistance to contain the armed uprising, but again lacked the institutional authority to do so.

9. Just prior to the Constitutional Convention, James Madison summed up these concerns in "Vices of the Political System of the United States," pointing to the Confederacy's inability to control internal violence and the unchecked control of state legislatures, which proved destructive to creditors: "Paper money, installments of debt, occlusion of Courts, making property a legal tender . . . affect the Creditor State, in the same manner they do its own citizens who are relatively creditors toward other citizens" (Madison 1787; also see Sofaer 1976, 24; Wood 1998, 409–13).

10. Hamilton, "Federalist No. 15."

11. See Edling 2003, 81.

12. Following Maier (2010), I will borrow the term "Federalists," but avoid using the label "Anti-Federalists" and instead reference the opponents of the proposed constitution.

13. Hamilton, "Federalist No. 23" (emphasis in original).

14. US Const. art. I, § 8, cl. 11–16 (delegating power to declare war; raise and support armies; provide and maintain a navy; regulate land and naval forces; call forth the militia; and provide for organizing, arming, and disciplining the militia). Congress's power to appropriate funds are also delegated in art. I, § 8, cl. 1, 2, and 5 (empowering Congress to lay and collect taxes, duties, imposts, and excises; borrow money on the credit of the United States; and to coin money and regulate its value).

15. "There can be no limitation of that authority which is to provide for the defense and protection of the community, in any matter essential to its efficacy that is, in any matter essential to the *formation, direction,* or *support* of the *national forces*" (Hamilton, "Federalist No. 23," emphasis in original).

16. Though Hamilton expressed doubts as to whether large peacetime armies would be necessary, his line of argument maintained that Congress should retain the authority to appropriate whatever force is necessary to prevent internal uprisings or foreign invasions (Hamilton, "Federalist No. 24"; also see Madison, "Federalist No. 37").

17. "How could a readiness for war in time of peace be safely prohibited, unless we could prohibit, in like manner, the preparations and establishments of every hostile nation? The means of security can only be regulated by the means and the danger of attack. . . . It is in vain to oppose constitutional barriers to the impulse of self-preservation" (Madison, "Federalist No. 41").

18. Brutus, Essay VIII–X; Centinel, Letter I; Agrippa, Essay V; Impartial Examiner, Essay I. (The Anti-Federalist essays are drawn from Storing [1985], unless otherwise noted.)

19. "The far greater part of the different nations, who have fallen from the glorious state of liberty, owe their ruin to standing armies" (The Impartial Examiner, February 20, 1788). In Essay VIII, Brutus quoted an argument from *Cobbett's Parliamentary History of England* delivered in the House of Commons in favor or reducing Great Britain's army: "The nations around us, sir, are already enslaved, and have been enslaved . . . by their standing armies they have lost their liberties; it is indeed impossible that the liberties of the people in any country can be preserved where a numerous standing army is kept up."

20. "Are we so much better than the people of other ages and other countries, that the same allurements of power and greatness, which led them aside from their duty, will have no influence upon men in our country? Such an idea, is wild and extravagant. Had we indulged such a delusion, enough has appeared in a little time past, to convince the most credulous, that the passion for pomp, power and greatness, works as powerfully in the hearts of many of our better sort, as it ever did in any country under heaven" (Brutus, Essay X, 1788).

21. "The soldiery, who are generally composed of the dregs of the people, when disbanded, or unfit for military service . . . become extremely burthensome" (The Impartial Examiner, February 20, 1788).

22. Quoted in Brutus, Essay X. The constitution's opponents commonly expressed concerns that, like Julius Caesar's Roman army, unlimited legislative discretion over military appropriations would lead Congress to dismantle state militias and create a large standing army "to deprive [the] citizens of freedom and reduce them to slavery" (quoting Luther Martin, in Ferrand 1911, vol. 3, chap. 158, "Luther Martin: Genuine Information").

23. Patrick Henry also echoed this view during the Virginia convention: "Have we the means of resisting disciplined armies, when our only defence, the militia, is put in the hands of Congress?" Speech at the Virginia Ratifying Convention, June 5, 1788.

24. Hamilton, "Federalist No. 25" (emphasis added).

25. Quoting Madison, "Federalist No. 51."

26. "The legislature are not *at liberty* to vest in the executive department permanent funds for the support of an army if they were even incautious enough to be willing to repose in it so improper a confidence" (Hamilton, "Federalist No. 26").

27. Hamilton, "Federalist No. 70." "The President shall be Commander in Chief of the Army and Navy of the United States, and of the Militia of the several States, when called into the actual Service of the United States" (US Const. art. II, § 2, cl. 1).

28. Hamilton, "Federalist No. 74."

29. Iredell, in Elliot 1836, vol. 4, Debates in the Convention of the State of North Carolina, on the Adoption of the Federal Constitution.

30. Pinckney, in Elliot 1836, vol. 5, Debates in the Federal Convention of 1787.

31. Iredell, in Elliot 1836, vol. 4; also see Hamilton, "Federalist No. 69."

32. Mason, in Elliot 1836, vol. 3, Debates in the Convention in the Commonwealth of Virginia, on the Adoption of the Federal Constitution.

33. Wilson's opposition to granting the House sole authority to initiate revenue measures reflect his understanding of the importance of the spending power: "War, Commerce, and Revenue were the great objects of the [federal] Government. All of them are connected with money. The restriction in favor of the [House of Representatives] would exclude the Senate from originating any important bills whatever." Edmund Randolph's response—that the means of war ought to remain with the less corruptible House—demonstrates similar awareness that appropriations would be drawn upon to influence military policy (Elliot 1836, vol. 5).

34. Sofaer 1976, 35.

35. Mason, in Elliot 1836, vol 5.

36. Hamilton, "Federalist No. 26."

37. Madison also employed the logic of legislative dependence on the people to win support for unlimited legislative authority over military resources: "[Ought] not suspicion herself to blush, in pretending that the representatives of the United States, elected *freely* by the *whole body* of the people, every *second year*, cannot be safely [entrusted] with the discretion over such appropriations, expressly limited to the short period of *two years*?" (Madison, "Federalist No. 41").

38. Edling 2003; Kohn 1975; Mahon and Danyish 1972; Sofaer 1976.

39. Stofft 1989, 115.

40. 1 Stat. 547, 552, 554–56, 558–61, 565–66, 569–70, 572–73, 574–75, 578–80, 611 (1798). All statutory references are drawn from Library of Congress, Statutes-at-Large, 1789–1875, vols. 1–18; http://memory.loc.gov/ammem/amlaw/lwsllink.html.

41. An Act to suspend the commercial intercourse between the United States and France, and the dependencies thereof, 1 Stat. 565, § 1 (1798).

42. *Little v Barreme* 6 US 170 (1804).

43. Quoting Edling 2003, 141; also see Mahon and Danyish 1972.

44. "The real alternative before us is whether to abandon the Mediterranean or to keep up a cruise in it. . . . But this Congress must decide" (Jefferson 1801). On March 3, 1801, one day before Jefferson's presidency, Congress passed legislation authorizing six frigates to be "kept in constant service in time of peace . . . [and] officered and manned as the President of the United States may direct" (An Act providing for a naval peace establishment, and for other purposes, 2 Stat. 110–11, § 2 (1801)).

45. An Act to protect the commerce and seamen of the United States against the Barbary powers, 2 Stat. 291–92, § 1, 3 (1804).

46. Jefferson had so few resources on hand that he purchased small amounts of ammunition without appropriation and obtained congressional approval after the fact. Congress later upheld the actions with the Embargo Act, a series of laws regulating American shippers and their vessels (An Act laying an embargo on all ships and vessels in the ports and harbors of the United States, 2 Stat. 451–52 (1807); replaced by Act of January 9, 1808, 2 Stat. 553; Act of March 12 1808, 2 Stat. 473; Act of April 25, 1808, 2 Stat. 499–502; Act of March 1, 1809, 2 Stat. 528–33).

47. However, Congress did organize volunteer corps and authorize modest increases in the size of the navy (Act of February 6, 1812, 2 Stat. 676).

48. Smith 1977, 25–29; Wilentz 2005, 157.

49. Sofaer 1976, 273.

50. Quoting Wilentz 2005, 164.

51. Congress authorized military experiments with torpedoes (Act of March 30, 1810, 2 Stat. 569), instructed the president to build certain gun barges "without delay" (Act of July 5 1813, 3 Stat. 3), and attached restrictions to the completion of fortifications of certain forts and harbors (Act of Feb. 10, 1809, 2 Stat. 516). After the war with Britain ended, Congress also suspended appropriations for several fortifications despite executive opposition.

52. Sofaer 1976, 269; also see Hormats 2007, 53.

53. The destruction was retaliation for the burning of York (Toronto) by American forces the previous year.

54. An Act fixing the military peace establishment of the United States, 3 Stat. 224 (1815).

55. However, prohibitive capitalization costs, increasingly rigorous production standards, frequent model changes, and uncertainty of further patronage contributed to growing contractor attrition rates throughout the 1830 and 1840s (see Smith 1977, 29).

56. Congress reduced troop size by nearly one-third, from 12,500 to 8,500 personnel. Though still small by comparative standards, the troop count was considerably higher than the 3,000 personnel army prior to the War of 1812 (Stofft 1989, 166).

57. Fisher 2004, 39.

58. In a statement to Congress, Jackson explicitly deferred to the legislature's authority to declare war: "It will almost always be considered consistent with the spirit of the Constitution, and most safe, that [the power of recognizing the independence of Texas] should be exercised, when probably leading to war, with a previous understanding with that [legislative] body by whom war alone can be declared, and by whom all the provisions for sustaining its perils must be furnished" (quoted in Fisher 2004, 39).

59. Mahon and Danyish 1972, 23.

60. Quoting Stofft 1989, 180.

61. See Congressional Research Service Report for Congress, "Instances of U.S. Force Abroad: 1787–2004," October 5, 2005, prepared by Richard Grimmett, Congressional Research Service, Washington, DC (http://www.au.af.mil/au/awc/awcgate/crs/rl30172.htm).

62. Quoting Schlesinger 2004 [1973], 50.

63. Military spending increased from $804 million in 1861 to $14.2 billion in 1865 (in constant 2006 dollars).

64. The income tax was gradually phased out after the passage of the Legal Tender Act of 1862. Subsequently, federal spending ballooned from less than 2% of GPD to in early 1861 to 25% of GDP by the spring of 1865 (Hormats 2007, 83).

65. Quoting Smith 1977, 39. Defense appropriations fell from over $14 billion in 1865 to less than $1 billion in 1871 (in constant 2006 dollars).

66. The United States successfully seized the Hawaiian territory in 1898.

67. The United States supplied roughly half of Cuban imports and received nearly 90% of Cuban exports (cited in Fisher 2004, 52).

68. 55 Cong. Rec., 2d sess., March 25, 1898.

69. William McKinley, War Message 1898, in Richardson 2004. McKinley's message to Congress suggested that Spain was the perpetrator. Subsequent studies conclude that the blast came from the interior of the ship, suggesting that Spain did not cause the incident.

70. Mahon and Danyish 1972, 35; Stofft 1989, 322.

71. Despite the need for military personnel, the conflict with Spain did not lead to a notable increase in the regular army. Instead, Congress passed an act calling for a volunteer army consisting of regiments raised and officered by the states within organized militia units. Subsequently, McKinley called forth 125,000 military volunteers to support the US naval blockade. US Department of State Timeline of US Diplomatic History, 1866–1898, accessed at http://www.state.gov/r/pa/ho/time/gp/90609.htm.

72. Stofft 1989, 344.

73. See Beaver 1977, 76.

74. Theodore Roosevelt, Fourth Annual Message to Congress, December 6, 1904, from the John Woolley and Gerhard Peters, American Presidency Project, Document Archive, 1999–2013, University of California Santa Barbara, accessed at http://www.presidency.ucsb.edu/ws/ (hereafter American Presidency Project).

75. "The experience of over a half century has shown Colombia to be utterly incapable of keeping order on the isthmus. . . . We, in effect, policed the isthmus in the interest of its inhabitants and for our own national needs, and for the good of the entire civilized world" (Roosevelt, Third Annual Message to Congress, December 7, 1903).

76. Fisher 2004, 61.

77. See Fisher 2004, 66. (The Central Intelligence Agency engaged in covert operations in Guatemala in 1954 and Cuba in 1961.)

78. Quoting Beaver 1977, 80; also see Skowronek 1982.

CHAPTER 3

1. According to Goldsmith's (1946, 70) estimate, in 1944 the United States produced 40% of the world's munitions output.

2. US Bureau of the Census, *Historical Statistics of the United States, Colonial Times to 1957* (Washington, DC: US Government Printing Office, 1960), 70.

3. US Bureau of the Census, *Statistical Abstract of the United States: Historical Statistics*, No. HS-29. Employment Status of the Civilian Population, 1929–2002 (Washington, DC: US Government Printing Office, DC, 2003).

4. See Pierson 2000, 2004.

5. Arthur 1994, chap. 4.

6. External economies of scale are achieved when an industry's scope of operation expands and decreases costs for a company working within that industry.

7. Kennedy 1999, 617.

8. See Beaver 1977; Smith 1977.

9. Adams and Adams 1972, 284.

10. Kennedy 1999, 626–27.

11. Friedberg 2000, 85.

12. The database draws from Cunningham's (1951) landmark study on the aircraft industry and consists of locations where aircraft industries converted their facilities for defense production in 1940, expanded military production at the peak of wartime output in 1944, and retained their facilities at the onset of the 1950 Korean War. Areas where automobile industries converted their facilities for defense activity and government-owned company-operated facilities are also included.

13. Quoting Hooks and McQueen 2010.

14. Franklin D. Roosevelt, "Message to Congress on Appropriations for National Defense. Address before a Joint Session of Congress," May 16, 1940, 76th Cong., 3rd sess., in Papers of

Franklin Delano Roosevelt, American Presidency Project (http://www.presidency.ucsb.edu/ws/index.php?pid=15954&st=&st1=).

15. Cunningham 1951, 76.

16. Ibid., 109.

17. Ibid., 115.

18. US Bureau of the Census, *Historical Statistics* (see note 3).

19. According to Aircraft Industries Association of American, Inc., the federal government financed 91.8% of the entire facilities expansion program from 1940 to 1944, while only 8.2% was privately funded ("Aviation Facts and Figures 1945," cited in Cunningham 1951, 116).

20. US Executive Office, National Resources Planning Board (NPRB), *Industrial Location and National Resources* (Washington, DC: Government Printing Office, 1941), 1.

21. Despite the nominal control of civilian agencies, the Army and Navy departments oversaw most subsidized private investments and federal lending decisions (Hooks 1993, 48–49).

22. Cunningham 1951, 128.

23. See Downs 1973, 18.

24. Ibid.

25. US Bureau of the Census, *US Census of Population: 1950*, vol. 1, *Number of Inhabitants: Introduction* (Washington, DC: US Government Printing Office, 1952), xxii.

26. Smith 1959, 72.

27. See Gansler 1980 for a more detailed analysis of the defense industry.

28. Burnett and Scherer 1990; Gansler 1980.

29. For example, in the first 2008 presidential debate, presidential candidate John McCain admonished the cost-plus incentives that characterize defense contracting. Transcript, "First Presidential Debate: Election 2008," September 26, 2008, *New York Times*, accessed at http://elections.nytimes.com/2008/president/debates/transcripts/first-presidential-debate.html.

30. OMB Watch, Federal Contracts of the Department of Defense, FY2000–2012 (including contracts subject to full and open competition with at least two bidders), http://www.fedspending.org/ (updated January 10, 2012). The Government Accountability Office also found that the preponderance of DoD prime contract dollars were awarded on a noncompetitive basis every year from 1977-1994 (US GAO Report, "Defense Industry: Trends in DoD Spending, Industrial Productivity, and Competition." Report to Congressional Requesters, US Government Accountability Office, Washington, DC, GAO-PEMD-97-3, January 1997).

31. For an alternative metric, see Patillo (1998), utilizing Fortune 500 rank, sales and number of employees, in 1967, 1989.

32. Gholz 2000.

33. Gholz and Sapolsky 1999–2000.

34. Gansler 1980, 26.

CHAPTER 4

1. Grose and Oppenheimer 2007; Karol and Miguel 2007; Kriner and Shen 2007; Mueller 2005 on US troop fatalities and a "democratic brake" on military ventures; see Gelpi, Feaver, and Reifler 2005/6 on the expectation of military success and public support for war.

2. The dataset includes defense contract allocations (the number and dollar amount) at the city, county and state level in FY1966, FY1976, FY1986, FY1996, and FY2006.

3. See Bryan, Minton, and Sartre 2007; Ciccone and Hall 1996; Jacobs 1969; Lucas 2001.

4. By contrast, some rural areas that benefit from greater natural resources do experience economic transformation along with rapid population growth. The relationship between

economic vitality and increased residency suggests that some areas do gradually urbanize by developing more attractive markets. US Economic Research Service, "Measuring Rurality," US Department of Agriculture, Washington, DC, accessed at http://151.121.68.30/Briefing/Rurality/ (last updated November 7, 2008).

5. Beale 1993, 1996; Carlson 1995.

6. Variables in the CS-Index include employment, population, net personal income, residence adjustment, and proprietors' income by county (see Mack, Grubesic, and Kessler 2007). (The authors include two indices, with and without an infrastructure variable capturing mileage for highways and railways. Since economic reliance captures local employment and income characteristics, I use the index without the infrastructure variables.)

7. While measuring population density per county offers less precision than a smaller unit of analysis such as FIPS places or zip codes, it is also easier to visualize county-level data alongside defense contract distributions in cities in towns. Further, counties are less subject to boundary changes, offer more accessible information, and represent more stable units over time than FIPS places.

8. There are several notable exceptions to this trend, which I discuss at greater length in chapter 8.

9. Schulman 1991, 135–74.

10. Defense dollars and population density are sorted with jenks natural breaks. Figures illustrating decennial defense distributions in the 1970s, 1980s and 1990s (not shown here) are available upon request.

11. See Fordham 2007; Zelizer 2009.

12. However, several areas attracted new defense investments after the war. For instance, the government purchased a missile development site, Cape Canaveral, Florida, in 1949. The Boeing Company acquired Piasecki Helicopter Company in Ridley Park, Pennsylvania, in 1960; and Northrop Grumman expanded its operations into Rolling Meadows, Illinois, in 1966. Defense industries also flocked to areas with large military bases and airfields, such as Colorado Springs and Denver.

13. Zelizer 2009.

14. Quoted in Schulman 1991, 135.

15. Trubowitz 1998; Zelizer 2009.

16. Markusen et al. 1991; also see Hooks and Bloomquist 1992.

17. See Higgs 2006, 176–85.

18. Fordham 2007.

19. Trubowitz 1998, 171.

20. See Higgs 2006.

21. Champagne et al. 2009, 188.

22. Markusen et al. 1991, 62–68.

23. Schulman 1991; Wright 1986.

24. Schulman 1991; Trubowitz 1998; Zelizer 2009.

25. Madison 1792.

26. Machiavelli 1998, chapters 12–14.

27. Also see Avant 2010.

28. DoD employed 145,000 uniformed personnel in Iraq and Afghanistan and 155,000 contractors in March 2011 (see Congressional Research Service Report for Congress, "Department of Defense Contractors in Afghanistan and Iraq: Background and Analysis," prepared by Moshe Schwartz and Joyprada Swain, May 13, 2011, Congressional Research Service, Washington, DC).

29. Congressional Budget Office, "Contractor Support of U.S. Operations in Iraq," Congressional Budget Office, Washington, DC, August 12, 2008.

30. Mueller 1973, 2005; Kriner and Shen 2010.

31. Gelpi, Feaver, and Reifler 2005/6.

32. Kriner and Shen 2010.

33. Gimpel and Althaus 2009; Mueller 2005.

34. Hormats 2007.

35. In real (2008) dollars, the debt increased from $2.3 trillion in FY1980 to $7.2 trillion in FY1995, or 313% (see fig. 4.5a).

36. Bureau of Economic Analysis, National Economic Accounts: Current-dollar and "Real" GDP, in constant 2005 dollars (accessed at http://www.bea.gov/national/).

CHAPTER 5

1. Center for Defense Information (CDI), "Weapons the Pentagon Doesn't Want," Video Transcript, December 27, 1992, accessed at http://www.cdi.org/adm/615/.

2. See Adams 1981; Cavanagh 1990; Higgs 2006; Kotz 1988; Ledbetter 2011; Project on Government Oversight, National Security Investigations: Wasteful Spending Reports, http://www.pogo.org/investigations/national-security/wasteful-defense-spending.html; Twight (on congressional resistance to military base closures); Wheeler 2004. Also see Eugene Jarecki's 2005 award-winning documentary, *Why We Fight*.

3. Cavanaugh 1999; Kotz 1988; Thompson 2007; Whittle 2010.

4. For example, see Project on Government Oversight Reports on the FA-22 Fighter Aircraft (accessed at http://www.pogo.org/investigations/national-security/fa-22.html) and the Joint Strike Fighter Aircraft (accessed at http://www.pogo.org/investigations/national-security/joint-strike-fighter.html). Also see Higgs 2006.

5. For example, see Bernstein and Anthony 1974; Cobb 1976; Fleisher 1985; Goss 1972; Lindsay 1991; Ray 1981a.

6. See Adler and Lapinski 1997; Cobb 1976; Fleisher 1985; Lindsay 1991; Mayer 1991; Ray 1981a.

7. Carol Goss (1972) does employ data estimating private plant employment in 1968, but notes that the figures are limited to locations with prime defense contracts exceeding $10,000 and "distinctly inferior to [existing data] on military and civilian employment at military installations" (217).

8. "Congressmen will still fight—and fight hard—for a defense project with *direct implications* for their districts, but may allow the 'world' view, as opposed to their 'constituency' view, to determine their positions on more general national security measures" (quoting Ray 1981a, 444).

9. Fleisher (1985, 209) acknowledges that California received over 60% of B-1 dollars during the time period examined, thus minimizing the importance of program benefits in other states. "Looking at the behavior of [California's] liberal Senators, Cranston and Tunney, one finds that they were constant supporters of the B-1. All other liberals from high benefit states can be considered as not crossing that minimum threshold [of economic importance]. That is, the amount of benefits that the state received was not so great as to reduce the Senators' options."

10. Bailey and Brady 1998.

11. For example, an atmosphere of perpetual military buildup and permanent crisis creates large opportunities to prescribe and enforce a global order beneficial to US interests, including international political stability, trade, credit and access to oil. Meanwhile, wars also promote

the professional careers of many executive and military officials, while channeling continued military spending across politically important regions and localities.

12. Trubowitz 1998.

13. Aldrich and Rohde 2000.

14. The votes are pooled across all three congressional terms in order to increase the number of cases examined.

15. For example, see Bender and Robinson 1997; George H. W. Bush 1992, Address before a Joint Session of Congress on the State of the Union; Center for Defense Information (CDI) Transcript 1992; Congressional Research Service Report, "V-22 Osprey Tilt-Rotor Aircraft," prepared by Christopher Bolkcom, August 4, 2005, Congressional Research Service, Washington, DC (http://www.dtic.mil/dtic/tr/fulltext/u2/a477901.pdf); Congressional Research Service Report, "V-22 Osprey Tilt-Rotor Aircraft," prepared by Christopher Bolkcom, January 2, 2009, Congressional Research Service, Washington DC (http://crs.wikileaks-press.org/RL31384.pdf); Federation of American Scientists, "SSN-21 Seawolf-Class," Military Analysis Network. n.d. (accessed at http://www.fas.org/man/dod-101/sys/ship/ssn-21.htm); USGAO, "B-2 Bomber: Cost and Operational Issues," report to Congressional Committees, GAO-NSIAD 97-18, August 1997; USGAO, "Defense Acquisitions: Recent F-22 Production Cost Estimates Exceeded Congressional Limitations," report for the Chairman, Subcommittee on National Security, Veterans Affairs and International Relations, Committee on Government Reform, House of Representatives, GAO-NSIAD 00-178, August 2000; USGAO, "DoD Acquisitions: Contracting for Better Outcomes," testimony before the Subcommittee on Defense, Committee on Appropriations, House of Representatives, GAO-06-800T, September 2006, US Government Accountability Office, Washington, DC.

16. A bill to expand NATO (HR3564, July 23, 1996) is included because the measure effectively grants greater access for US arms sales abroad.

17. US Bureau of Labor Statistics (various years), "Occupational Employment Statistics," National Industry-Specific Occupational Employment and Wage Statistics: Aerospace Products and Parts Manufacturing, US Department of Labor, Washington, DC.

18. Lockheed Martin and Boeing Company manufacture the F-22 fighter plane; Northrop Grumman Corp, TRW Inc. and Boeing produce the B-2 bomber; Alliant Techsystems manufactures the Trident D5 missile. The Boeing Airborne Laser, Lockheed Martin Aegis Ballistic Missile Defense, Northrop Grumman Kinetic Energy Interceptor (KEI), and Raytheon Integrated Defense all contribute crucial aspects to the ballistic missile defense (BMD) program. In FY1995, Boeing, Lockheed Martin, Raytheon, and TRW Inc. (a subsidiary of Northrop Grumman Corp.) ranked as the top four major BMD contractors. Alliant Techsystems served as the largest Pentagon supplier of ammunition and cluster bombs.

19. These reports are located at the Security and Exchange Commission, EDGAR Database Archive, "Company 10K Reports," FY1995 (http://www.sec.gov/edgar.shtml). Given the lack of annual defense-sector data, the analysis employs a snapshot of defense industry locations in FY1995 for the entire time period under study.

20. Locations of Boeing, Lockheed Martin, Raytheon and TRW from Center for Media and Democracy, http://www.sourcewatch.org (accessed April 15, 2006).

21. US Bureau of Census, *Congressional District Atlas: 103rd Congress* (Washington, DC: US Government Printing Office). When a city location cut across multiple congressional districts, I included each district in my coding scheme. If anything, this coding strategy overrepresents densely populated cities, providing a more rigorous test of the theory of economic reliance. (These data are available upon request from the author.)

22. A similar measure capturing the number of military bases in a district did not produce statistically meaningful results, so the variable was dropped from the models.

23. Committee membership is accessed from *Congressional Directory*, assignments of representatives to committees, 103rd–105th terms (Washington, DC: US Government Printing Office). Defense committees include members of the Armed Services Committee, the Defense Appropriation Subcommittee, and the Select Subcommittee on Technical and Tactical Intelligence. The Select Subcommittee on Technical and Tactical Intelligence is part of the House Permanent Select Committee on Intelligence (HPSCI) and is responsible for making recommendations on military operations, weapons programs, and communications systems, as well as producing an annual intelligence authorization bill (and classified budget schedule) for all elements of the intelligence community. (While the Armed Services Committee was briefly renamed the National Security Committee in 1995, I use these terms interchangeably.)

24. The data are drawn from the Center for Responsive Politics, "Defense Aerospace: Money to Congress, 1992–96" (lagged), http://www.opensecrets.org/industries/summary .php?cycle=2012&ind=D.

25. Independent Bernie Sanders is coded as a Democrat because he regularly caucuses with the Democratic Party.

26. Accessed from Royce Carroll, Jeff Lewis, James Lo, Nolan McCarty, Keith Poole, and Howard Rosenthal, "DW-NOMINATE Scores with Bootstrapped Standard Errors," Legislator Estimates, 103rd–105th Houses, updated February 17, 2013 (http://voteview.com/dwnominate .asp). For discussion of dimensionality in congressional roll-call votes, see Poole and Rosenthal 1991.

27. For example, see Jackson and Kingdon 1992, and Jenkins, Schickler, and Carson 2004. The problems associated with using votes to predict votes are not unique to the application of DW-NOMINATE scores. In fact, all available national security scores measure ideology based on previous voting patterns, producing similar problems in models of congressional voting behavior.

28. There are various difficulties interpreting the coefficients associated with interaction terms. Unlike standard additive models, interactive models examine conditional relationships among the interactive coefficients. Rather than operating as controls (set to a variable's respective mean value), interactive coefficients display the effect of the variable when the other interactive coefficients are set to zero. See Brambor et al. 2006 on the interpretation of interaction terms. See http://gking.harvard.edu/clarify to access CLARIFY software.

29. See Hooks 1993, 50; Hooks and Bloomquist 1992.

30. Appendix 5.3 shows that an increase in economic reliance (*low density*facilities*) corresponds with higher levels of support for defense spending across all three congressional terms ($p < .05$). Although the interactive component, *defense facilities*, yields a negative value, the variable takes on the expected positive direction when the interaction term is removed from the model (condensed model, column 4). All other variables perform consistently when the interaction term is excluded. The results are also consistent when controlling for ideology instead of partisanship. Multicollinearity prevents the use of both party and ideology the same model ($r = .93$).

31. The mean value for *low density*facilities* is more than 25% larger in Republican districts than Democratic districts, indicating greater overall economic reliance among Republican constituencies (see appendix 5.1).

32. Appendix 5.5 displays the effect of economic and political factors on Democratic and Republican support for controversial weapons expenditures, defense cuts, and policies relax-

ing or restricting arms sales, respectively. Voting averages are pooled across the 103rd, 104th, and 105th congressional terms in order to increase the number of cases examined. As stated previously, the models do not include fixed effects because data limitations preclude a longer time series. However, the variables under study perform similarly across the relevant years. This stability over time minimizes the need for a control for the time period.

33. Center for Defense Information 1992.

34. Cited in Aldrich and Rohde 2000, 15.

35. Fiscal 1994 Defense Authorization, H.R. 2401, Lloyd Amendment to reduce the amount authorized for overseas operations and maintenance costs by $580 million and reallocate those funds for the operation of military facilities inside the United States, 103rd Cong. (1993) (Roll Call Vote no. 419, Passed 424-0, September 9, 1993). (The amendment was excluded from the analysis because it reallocated funding rather than adjusting the defense overall budget.)

36. George H. W. Bush, Address before a Joint Session of Congress on the State of the Union, January 28, 1992, American Presidency Project (http://www.presidency.ucsb.edu/ws/index.php?pid=20544).

37. Quoted in Song 2012.

CHAPTER 6

1. On his website, Representative Flake expressed his commitment to cutting federal spending levels, reducing waste, and eliminating pork projects, while emphasizing the need for tax relief. He promoted these issues by mounting a campaign to reform legislative earmarks (Flake 2005). Although he sat on the Appropriations Subcommittee on Military Construction and Veterans Affairs during the 109th Congress, he did not belong to a defense committee with jurisdiction over weapons programs.

2. For example, see Lindsay 1991; Markusen et al., 1991, 40; Mayer 1991; Ray 1980, 1981b; Rundquist 1973, 1978.

3. Markusen et al. 1991; Mayer 1991; but also see Rundquist and Carsey 2002 and Bertelli and Grose 2009 for evidence of partisan and ideological influences in defense contracting. "Prime defense contracts" refer to the military procurements awarded by federal agencies. Principal assignments (referred to here as "subcontracts") occur when prime contractors or defense industry management award the primary construction of contracted weapons systems to another location or company. (I use the terms "prime" and "primary" interchangeably.)

4. Contract benefits distributed after the prime contracting stage are either assigned to a company's own facilities and subsidiaries (located in-house or at another plant) or subcontracted out to another company. I apply the term "subcontracting" loosely, referring to both scenarios.

5. Kenneth Mayer (1990) and Barry Rundquist (1978) have speculated at length that defense subcontracts may be distributed for political purposes. As Mayer (1990, 218) notes, "Scholars and procurement analysts have long suspected that prime contractors distribute subcontracts . . . so as to maximize the geographic spread of acquisition programs."

6. Fiorina 1987; Shepsle and Weingast 1994; Weingast and Marshall 1988.

7. Adler and Lapinski 1997; Arnold 1979; Rohde and Shepsle 1973; Shepsle and Weingast 1994; Weingast and Marshall 1988.

8. For example, see Adler and Lapinski 1997; also see Arnold 1979; Goss 1972; Rohde and Shepsle 1973. (Goss's 1972 study estimates private defense employment, but the figures are based on prime contract allocations.)

9. Adler and Lapinski 1997, 901.

10. Hall 1987, 1996.

11. Adler and Lapinski 1997; Carsey and Rundquist 1997.

12. See Lindsay 1991; Mayer 1991; Ray 1980, 1981b; Rundquist 1973, 1978.

13. Bertelli and Grose 2009; Bickers and Stein 2000; Carsey and Rundquist 1999; Rundquist and Carsey 2002.

14. For example, see Berry, Burden, and Howell 2010; Bertelli and Grose 2009; Garrett and Sobel 2003; Kriner and Reeves 2012; Mayer 1990, 216–18.

15. Many scholars have acknowledged this limitation. For example, see Lindsay 1990, 278–79; Markusen et al. 1991, 14; Mayer 1990; Rundquist 1978; also see USGAO, "Defense Spending: Trends and Geographical Distribution of Prime Contract Awards and Compensation," report for Committee on Appropriations, House of Representatives, GAO-NSIAD-98-195, August 1998, US Government Accountability Office, Washington, DC.

16. Government Accountability Office (GAO) Report, "Defense Acquisitions: Additional Guidance Needed to Improve Visibility Into the Structure and Management of Major Weapon System Subcontracts," GAO-11-61R, October 28, 2010 (accessed at http://www.gao.gov/assets/100/97156.pdf).

17. According to Defense Federal Procurement and Acquisition Policy guidelines, a contractor may select a subcontractor on a noncompetitive basis (one that does not offer the lowest price) as long as s/he has "adequately substantiated the selection as offering the greatest value to the government" (Office of Secretary of Defense, US Department of Defense, Defense Federal Acquisition Regulation Supplement, "Subcontracting Policies and Procedures: Consent to Subcontract" [Subpart 244.2-02], effective August 17, 1998, Office of Under Secretary of Defense for Acquisition, Technology, and Logistics, Washington, DC, accessed at http://www.acq.osd.mil/dpap/dars/dfarspgi/current/index.html.).

18. According to the Center for Public Integrity, no-bid contracts account for 40% of defense obligations from 1998 to 2004, averaging $150 billion per year. Also see Kovacic 1990, 110.

19. Mayer 1991, 9.

20. Markusen et al. 1991; Rundquist and Carsey 2002.

21. Defense committees with jurisdiction over weapons programs include the Defense Appropriations Subcommittee, the Armed Services Committee, and the Select Subcommittee on Technical and Tactical Intelligence.

22. According to OMB Watch (http://www.fedspending.org), the Department of Defense distributed an average of $194 billion per year from FY2000 to FY2005. Lockheed Martin, the Boeing Company, Raytheon, Northrop Grumman, General Dynamics, and Science Applications International accrued $73.4 billion per year, on average, or approximately 38.8%.

23. The models include defense contracts allocated to all fifty states, excluding foreign nations, and nonstate entities (e.g., Washington, DC; Puerto Rico; and American Samoa).Federal Procurement Data System, http://www.fpds.gov.

24. See US Department of Defense Statistical and Information Analysis Division (SIAD), "100 Companies Receiving the Largest Dollar Volume of Prime Contract Awards," US Department of Defense, Washington, DC (accessed at http://siadapp.dmdc.osd.mil/procurement/historical_reports/statistics/procstat.html); and Washington Technology, "Top 100 Contractors," 2006 (accessed at http://washingtontechnology.com/toplists/top-100-lists/2006.aspx). SAIC, ranked numbers 10 and 3, respectively, is the top recipient of intelligence-related contract dollars. (While evidence suggests that SAIC exploits contracting decisions by hiring top federal officials [see Barlett and Steele 2007], approximately 78% of SAIC's defense contracting dollars resulted from full and open processes in the 2000–2005 fiscal years. By contrast, only

46% of overall defense contract dollars resulted from full and open competition in FY2000–2005 [including contracts with only one bid]. See OMB Watch (at www.fedspending.org) for detailed figures.)

25. US Bureau of Census, *Congressional District Atlas: 106th–109th Congresses* (Washington, DC: US Government Printing Office). The map layers were extracted from nationalatlas.gov (http://nationalatlas.gov/mld/cgd109p.html). While hand coding helped narrow the number of potentially relevant districts, the method does not entirely obviate the problem of multiple districts spread across city limits. When I could not determine which specific district a subcontract falls within, I divided the number of subcontracts by the number of congressional districts in the home city. For example, if there was one subcontract in Oakland, California then the two districts that overlap with Oakland were coded as having 0.50 subcontracts (1 subcontract/ 2 districts). The coding methods account for 98% of the principal places of performance listed in the relevant years based on data extracted from fpds.gov (4468/4581). The remaining 2% are excluded on account of difficulties pairing cities, towns, and unincorporated areas with corresponding congressional districts. (These data are available upon request from the author.)

26. Sources accessed include: SEC EDGAR Database Archives (accessed at http://www .sec.gov/edgar.shtml); Vault Companies, Lockheed Martin, Boeing Co., Raytheon, Northrop Grumman, General Dynamics, Science Applications International Co. (accessed at http:// www.vault.com/wps/portal/na/companies); Washington Technology, "Top 100 Government IT Contractors" (accessed at http://washingtontechnology.com/toplists/top-100-lists/2007 .aspx); "The Aerospace Industry: The Dirty Dozen, Corporate Profiles and PDF Fact Sheets," World Policy Institute, research compiled by Frida Berrigan (accessed at http://www.reaching criticalwill.org/resources/publications-and-research/research-projects/6202-dirty-dozen -corporate-partners-in-mass-destruction); Google Maps (http://maps.google.com).

27. Given the absence of comprehensive annual data on weapons industries, the analysis employs a snapshot of defense facility locations based on the most current records available at the time of the data collection (in 2006). Although the use of static measure of district-wide defense facilities over a multi-year period is not ideal, the defense industry structure itself contributes to the validity to the measure. Defense employment levels result from large investments in physical infrastructure and past DoD decisions, contributing to industry stability over short increments of time. (These data are available upon request from the author.)

28. While defense facilities vary in size and employment, reporting requirements for 10K reports at the SEC allowed me to distinguish "major facilities" based on area per square mile. This variable did not add any explanatory power to the analysis and was dropped from the models.

29. Markusen et al. 1991.

30. In Census Bureau terms, West North Central consists of Iowa, Kansas, Minnesota, Missouri, North Dakota, and South Dakota. East North Central comprises the Rustbelt, or Illinois, Indiana, Michigan, Ohio, and Wisconsin. All other states are included in the Gunbelt region, consistent with Markusen et al.'s (1991, 12) classification.

31. Disproportionately economic reliant areas span across regions and partisan affiliation. See appendix 6.2 for a list of the most economically reliant districts in the 109th Congress (2005–6).

32. I use negative binomial regression instead of Poisson regression to account for overdispersion in the models (LR test of alpha = 0: $c^2 = 720, p < .001$).

33. King, Tomz, and Wittenberg 2000; http://gking.harvard.edu/clarify.

34. Unlike the analysis presented in chapter 5, which emphasizes the effect of a larger defense-sector presence within a more rural setting on legislators' support for weapons spending,

expected, nonpolitical defense distributions should flow to locations with a large number of defense facilities. Therefore, it is critical to isolate the conditional effects of population density. To do so, the logit model employs *population density*facilities* and places the emphasis on the interactive component, *defense facilities*, which captures the effect of defense facilities when population density is equal to zero. For more substantive interpretation (since population density is never equal to zero in any populated area), the figures display the predicted probabilities of observing defense committee membership as district population density increases, given a small, medium, and large defense-sector presence.

CHAPTER 7

1. After a brief standoff, Congress passed a compromise resolution that deferred the cutoff of funds for forty-five days. See below for further elaboration.

2. Howell and Pevehouse 2007; Kriner 2010; Levinson and Pildes 2006.

3. Kriner 2010.

4. For example, see Ackerman 2010; Adams 2011; Farrier 2010; Koh 1988, 1990; Mann and Ornstein 2006; Silverstein 1997.

5. For instance, see Howell and Pevehouse 2007; Kriner 2010 (on partisan incentives); Bernstein and Anthony 1974; Fleisher 1985; Friedberg 2000; Lindsay 1990, 1991; Ray 1981a (on ideological influences); Ackerman 2010; Farrier 2010; Koh 1988, 1990; Silverstein 1997 (on legislative deference to the executive branch).

6. Aldrich and Rohde 2000; Theriault 2008 (on increasing party polarization); also see Mayhew 1974 (on electoral connection and credit-claiming).

7. Yandle 1983, 1999. (I thank Mark A. Smith for providing this reference.)

8. Of course, there are also congressional defense hawks who do not represent economically reliant constituencies. Clearly, economic dependence is not the only factor that contributes to the formation and durability of political ideologies.

9. For example, the case studies do not include the 1991 Gulf War, the Afghanistan War of 2001, or covert actions.

10. The log transformation of *low density* is employed to correct for nonlinear properties.

11. I applied both the first and second dimensions of the NOMINATE scores for two of the models in the 1990s. The first dimension is commonly interpreted as a standard liberal/conservative division dating back to the New Deal. The second dimension is typically viewed as the North/South divide on civil rights issues.

12. Following Grose and Oppenheimer (2007), I constructed the variable by accessing a list of military fatalities in Operation Iraqi Freedom from a Department of Defense personnel report. The report includes the hometown of each US soldier killed in Iraq (https://www.dmdc.osd.mil/dcas/pages/report_oif_namesalp.xhtml). To compile the number of military deaths per district, I used the online *Congressional Directory* and congressional district atlases to pair cities with congressional districts. If a city's boundaries included multiple districts, then I counted each death as belonging to all possible congressional districts. (Employing Grose and Oppenheimer's (2007) methodology and the coding system applied in the previous chapter, I also divided the number of Iraq War deaths in a city by the number of congressional districts in the home city. For example, if there was one death in Birmingham, Alabama then the two districts that overlap with Birmingham were coded as having 0.50 deaths (1 death/2 districts). This measure did not produce statistically meaningful results, so I dropped it from the models.)

13. See King, Tomz, and Wittenberg 2000.

14. From the late 1940s through the 1960s, congressional deference to executive control over the national security agenda was routine. Congressional interest arose only when embarrassing incidents occurred, such as when the Soviet Union shot down a U2 spy plane in 1960 or after the Bay of Pigs, when a CIA-sponsored invasion of Cuba by anti-Castro Cuban exiles failed.

15. The bill passed with three votes opposed in the Senate and one opposed in the House. See Department of Defense Appropriations 1968 totaling $70.3 Billion, H.R. 10738, 90th Cong. (1967) (House Vote no. 74, approved 408-1, and Senate Vote no. 185, approved 74-3). (All statutes and bills are drawn from "Roll Call Votes Database, 1789–2011," accessed at http://www .govtrack.us/. Also see Congressional Research Service Report for Congress, "U.S. Armed Forces Abroad: Selected Congressional Roll Call Votes since 1982," prepared by Lisa Mages, January 27, 2006, Congressional Research Service, Washington, DC.)

16. Department of Defense Appropriations 1968 totaling $70.3 Billion, H.R. 10738, Morse Amendment providing for a cut of 10% in the defense appropriations budget with the provision that the Secretary of Defense may Make adjustments and transfers, 90th Cong. (1967) (Senate Vote no. 169, Rejected 5-85),

17. Quoted in Adams 2011, citing "The Congress: It Is Edgy Toward Johnson," *New York Times*, August 6, 1967, 142, ProQuest Historical Newspapers, *New York Times* (1851–2007).

18. Former Senator and Vice President Hubert Humphrey (D-MN) aptly described Johnson's stealth in circumventing the legislature: "Now Johnson used to rob the Senate, but when he wanted to take something from you he'd invite you to lunch. He'd put his arm around you and talk to you while he picked your pocket" (quoted in Fry 2006, 154).

19. Ibid.

20. A series of amendments offered by George McGovern (D-SD) and Mark Hatfield (R-OR) would have cut off military appropriations to enforce a complete withdrawal of US forces from the region. However, these amendments were ultimately rejected. An amendment to a foreign military sales act offered by Frank Church (D-ID) and John Cooper (R-KY) would have restricted funding for military operations in Cambodia. After a seven-week filibuster and six months of debate, the amendment passed the Senate on June 30, 1970, but ultimately died in the House after only an hour of debate. A revised version of the amendment stalled until after Nixon had already withdrawn US ground troops and legislators omitted the key provision aimed at limiting air strikes—a concession necessary to secure passage in the House in December 1970.

21. Military Draft, H.R. 6531, Mansfield Substitute Amendment declaring U.S. policy to terminate at the earliest practicable date all U.S. military operations in Indochina, and providing for withdrawal of all such forces therefrom not later than 9 months after date of enactment, 92nd Cong. (1971) (Senate Vote no. 100, Approved 57-42). By contrast, also see Defense Appropriations for FY 1972, H.R. 11731, 92nd Cong. (1971) (Approved 42-8).

22. Quoted in Adams 2011, citing Nick Thimmesch. "Fight Is Gone from Fulbright," *Los Angeles Times*, February 15, 1971, C6, ProQuest Historical Newspapers *Los Angeles Times* (1881–1987).

23. According to a 1973 Gallup poll, 57% of Americans expressed disapproval of the bombing, compared to 28% that approved of the air strikes (cited in Goldstein 2007, 158).

24. 119 Cong. Rec. 15317–23 (1973).

25. 119 Cong. Rec. H21778 (1973).

26. Goldstein 2007, 165.

27. 119 Cong. Rec. S17130 (1973) (statement of Sen. Thomas Eagleton).

28. Quoted in Goldstein 2007, 184.

29. 119 Cong. Rec. S22285 (1973) (statement of Sen. Mark Hatfield); 119 Cong. Rec. S22303 (1973) (statement of Sen. Rupert Vance Hartke); 119 Cong. Rec. S22310 (1973) (statement of Sen. Thomas McIntyre).

30. 119 Cong. Rec. S22306–07 (also quoted in Goldstein 2007, 167–68).

31. All of the participants in the 1993 bombing of the World Trade Center had either served in Afghanistan in the 1980s, when the United States armed and trained the Afghan mujahideen, or were linked to a fundraising base for the Afghan jihad that also served as al Qaeda's principal US headquarters. Osama bin Laden, a participant in the Afghan jihad who rose to prominence after the Soviet defeat, later led the same networks in the attacks of September 11, 2001 (see Bergen and Reynolds 2005).

32. The act permits the president to submit three types of reports—when US armed forces are introduced "into hostilities" or imminent hostilities; into foreign territories, airspace, or waters designed for combat; or in numbers that substantially enlarge a combat unit. The law's sixty-day clock for removing troops from combat runs only from the date that a report is submitted regarding moving troops in "hostilities," and not when one of the other two types of reports are filed (Public Law 93-148, 87 Stat. 555, § 4(a) & 5(b)).

33. See Law Library of Congress, War Powers, accessed at http://www.loc.gov/law/help/war-powers.html (last updated January 2, 2009). Also see Congressional Research Service Report for Congress, "The War Powers after 30 Years," prepared by Richard Grimmett, March 11, 2004 (http://www.fas.org/man/crs/RL32267.html), and "War Powers Resolution: Presidential Compliance," prepared by Richard Grimmett, November 15, 2004 (http://www.fas.org/man/crs/IB81050.pdf).

34. Koh 1988, 1990.

35. Lebanon Emergency Assistance Act of 1983, Public Law 98-43, 97 Stat. 214 (1983).

36. Statement on Signing the Lebanon Emergency Assistance Act of 1983, June 27, 1983, American Presidency Project (http://www.presidency.ucsb.edu/ws/index.php?pid = 41523 #axzz1QuuNaLG3).

37. Multinational Force in Lebanon Resolution, Public Law 98-119, 97 Stat. 805 (1983).

38. Kriner 2010, 195

39. A joint resolution declaring that the requirements of section 4(a)(1) of the War Powers Resolution became operative on October 25, 1983, when United States Armed Forces were introduced into Grenada, H.J. Res 402, 98th Cong. (1983) (House Vote no. 407, Approved 403-23).

40. Expressing the sense of Congress concerning Operation Just Cause in Panama, H. Con. Res 262, 101st Cong. (1990) (House Vote no. 12, Approved 389-26).

41. Resolution Authorizing the Use of United States Armed Forces in Somalia, S.J. Res 45, 103rd Cong. (1993) (House Vote no. 183, Approved 243-179, Approved in Senate by voice vote). (The House version of the resolution would have terminated the War Powers authorization one year from enactment or following UN withdrawal from the region.)

42. "Address on Somalia," Presidential Speech Archive, Miller Center at the University of Virginia, October 7, 1993, accessed at www.millercenter.org/president/clinton/essays/biography/5.

43. Ackerman and Hathaway 2011, 490; Fisher 2004, 179; Howell and Pevehouse 2007, 16; Kriner 2010, 23–25.

44. Department of Defense Appropriations for FY1994, H.R. 3116, Byrd Amendment to provide funding for the Armed Forces in Somalia through March 31, 1994, unless the President requests and Congress authorizes an extension of that date, 103rd Cong. (1993) (Senate Vote no. 314, Approved 76-23 on October 21, 1993).

45. See Adams (2011) for a more detailed account. Also see "U.N. Intervention in Somalia," C-SPAN Video Archive, October 7, 1993, accessed at http://www.c-spanvideo.org/program/51502-1 (cited in Adams 2011).

46. On November 9, the House passed a nonbinding resolution urging the president to withdraw by January 31, 1994 (Directing the President pursuant to section 5(c) of the War Powers Resolution to remove United States Armed Forces from Somalia by January 31, 1994, H. Con. Res. 170, 103rd Cong. (1993) (passed by voice vote)). However, under pressure from the White House and House Speaker Tom Foley (D-WA), Congress reversed its position. An hour later, the House voted 226–201 in support of a nonbinding resolution affirming the president's original March 31 withdrawal date with Democrats largely in favor and Republicans united in opposition. H. Con. Res. 170, Hamilton Substitute Amendment directing the President to remove U.S. Armed Forces from Somalia by March 31, 1994, 103rd Cong. (1993) (House Vote no. 556, Approved 226-201. 223 Democrats and 2 Republicans supported the measure, while 30 Democrats and 170 Republicans voted in opposition).

47. For example, see H. Con. Res 290/ S. Res. 259, 103rd Cong. (1994) (House Vote no. 424, Approved 353-45, Senate Vote no. 301, Approved 94-5), § 5 (calling for "an orderly withdrawal as soon as possible"). Also see Limited Authorization of United States–led Force in Haiti Resolution, H.J. Res. 416, Dellums Substitute Amendment, 103rd Cong. (1994) (House Vote no. 498, Approved 258-167).

48. For example, Congress rejected Department of Defense Appropriation Act, 1994, H.R. 3116, Helms Amendment to limit the use of funds for conducting operations in Haiti, 103rd Cong. (1993) (Senate Vote no. 321, Rejected 19-81, October 21, 1993) and Foreign Operations, Export Financing Appropriations Act, 1995, H.R. 4426, Gregg Amendment to reflect the sense of the Senate regarding military operations in Haiti, 103rd Cong. (1994) (Senate Vote no. 172, Rejected 34–65). The only measure that Congress agreed on prior the complete withdrawal of US troops in April 1996 required the president to submit regular reports to Congress regarding the scope and duration of the mission while reaffirming the "sense of Congress" for "a prompt and orderly withdrawal as soon as possible" (A Joint Resolution Regarding U.S. Policy Toward Haiti, P.L.103-423, 108 Stat. 4358 (1994)).

49. To prohibit the use of funds appropriated to the Department of Defense from being used for the deployment on the ground of United States Armed Forces in the Republic of Bosnia and Herzegovina, H.R. 2606, 104th Cong. (1995) (House Vote no. 214, Approved 243-171, Senate Vote no. 601, Rejected 22-77); To prohibit Federal funds from being used for the deployment on the ground of United States Armed Forces in the Republic of Bosnia and Herzegovina as part of any peacekeeping operation, H.R. 2770, 104th Cong. (1994) (House Vote no. 856, Rejected 210–218). On the Senate measure see, for example, To Remove the United States Arms Embargo of the Government of Bosnia and Herzegovina, S. 2042, § 3c(3) prohibiting combat forces in Bosnia and Herzegovina, 104th Cong. (1994) (Approved in Senate by voice vote on May 12, 1994). (Although the House and Senate had both passed measures calling for US humanitarian support in the Bosnia region, each chamber explicitly refrained from authorizing the use of force.)

50. Concerning the Deployment of United States Armed Forces in Bosnia and Herzegovina, S.J. Res. 44, 104th Cong. (1995) (Senate Vote no. 603, Approved 69-30); Relating to the deployment of Armed Forces in and around the territory of the Republic of Bosnia and Herzegovina, H. Res. 302, 104th Cong. (1995) (House Vote no. 857, Approved 287-141).

51. For example, see National Defense Authorization Act for FY1998, H.R. 1119, Hilleary Substitute Amendment prohibiting the obligation of funds for ground troops in Bosnia after

December 31, 1997, 105th Cong. (1997) (House Vote no. 233, Rejected 196-231); Public Law 105-56, 111 Stat. 1203 (1997), § 8132 prohibiting funding for military operations in Bosnia after June 30, 1998, subject to line-item veto on October 21, 1997; Directing the President pursuant to section 5(c) of the War Powers Resolution to remove United States Armed Forces from the Republic of Bosnia and Herzegovina, H. Con. Res. 227, 105th Cong. (1998) (House Vote no. 58, Rejected 193-225).

52. Department of Defense Appropriations Act, 1998, H.R. 2266, 105th Cong. (1997), became Public Law 105-56, 111 Stat. 1203 § 8132 (1997).

53. National Defense Authorization Act for FY1998, S. 936, §1083(b)(1-6), 105th Cong. (1997).

54. National Defense Authorization Act for Fiscal Year 1999, S. 2057, §1072(b)(2), 105th Cong. (1998).

55. *Campbell v Clinton*, 52 F. supp. 2d 34 (D.D.C. 1999)

56. 1999 Emergency Supplemental Appropriations Act, P.L. 106-31, 113 Stat. 57 (1999).

57. The four models include: a 1993 amendment requiring immediate withdrawal from Somalia (model 1); a 1994 amendment deleting $1.2 billion in emergency funds that would replace money already spent on peacekeeping operations in Iraq, Somalia, Bosnia, and Haiti (model 2); the 1994 amendment among Republican members only (model 3); and a 1999 amendment to retain funding for operations in Kosovo and eliminate any spending deadline (model 4).

58. Republicans with more defense dependent constituencies are also no more likely to support these military operations than other Republicans.

59. Emergency Supplemental Appropriations Act for FY1994, H.R. 3759, Frank Amendment to delete $1.2 billion appropriated for DoD humanitarian and peacekeeping assistance in Haiti, Somalia, Bosnia, and the Iraq "no-fly" zone, 103rd Cong. (1994) (House Vote no. 8, Rejected 158–260). Russ Feingold (D-WI) offered a similar amendment in the Senate, which failed by a vote of 19–76 (Senate Roll Call no. 40, February 10, 1994).

60. For example, the Senate passed the Department of Defense Appropriations Act, 1994, H.R. 3116, Mitchell Amendment expressing the sense that no funds should be used to deploy additional US ground troops in Bosnia (Senate Vote no. 320, Approved 99–1). However, House failed to follow suit.

61. 140 Cong. Rec. H233 (1994) (quoting Rep. Barney Frank).

62. 140 Cong. Rec. H233 (1994) (Representative Frank went on to point out, "For instance, this says that they need $478 million additional because they sent a boat to Haiti and brought it back. They did not even spend the night. I do not think they should get $478 million per diem if they did not even spend the night there").

63. 140 Cong. Rec. H233 (1994).

64. Since both parties split their votes on this measure, I also ran a model isolating Democratic voting patterns. However, local defense dependence does reach statistically meaningful levels.

65. Consistent with the full model, Republicans belonging to defense committees voted to retain the supplemental defense funding at greater rates than other Republicans, all else equal ($p < .05$, model 3). The interactive component, *low density*, also takes on a negative coefficient in model 3, indicating that Republicans from more rural areas with no defense facilities are less likely to support the supplemental DoD funds than their colleagues ($p < .05$, one-tailed test model 3). (The negative value associated with the other interactive component, *defense facilities*, lacks substantive meaning.)

66. For example, President Clinton relied on the reprogramming of DoD funds and supplemental spending requests to carry out military operations in Bosnia (see National Defense Authorization Act for Fiscal Year 1999, S. 2057, § 1065(2)-(3), 105th Cong. (1998)).

67. 150 Cong. Rec. S311–S312 (2004) (statement of Sen. Ben Nelson).

68. Only six Republicans in the House and one in Senate opposed the president's request for an authorization for use of force. Authorization for Use of Military Force Against Iraq Resolution 2002, H.J. Res. 114, 107th Cong (2002), became Public Law 107-243, 116 Stat. 1498 (2002).

69. The table exhibits five models, including overall legislative support for the Authorization for Use of Military Force (AUMF) in Iraq that passed the House on October 11, 2002 (model 1); Democratic members' support for the AUMF of 2002 (model 2); a restricted model of Democrat members' support for the AUMF without the interaction term (model 3); opposition to Rep. Jim McGovern's (D-MA) bill requiring a troop withdrawal within 90 days and subsequent funding restrictions that the House rejected on May 10, 2007 (model 4); and Democratic members' opposition to the McGovern bill (model 5).

70. Low density exhibits a statistically meaningful, negative value after removing the interaction term from the model (model 3). The interactive component, *low density*, also takes on a negative coefficient in model 2, indicating that Democrats from more rural areas with no defense facilities were less likely to support the AUMF than their partisan colleagues ($p < .05$, one-tailed test, model 2). (The second interactive component, *defense facilities*, takes on a negative coefficient when low density is equal to zero. However, the finding lacks substantive meaning. The effect of defense facilities is not statistically meaningful when the interaction term is removed from the model.)

71. US House Committee on Oversight and Government Reform. Iraq Intelligence and Nuclear Evidence. Various Reports, 2003-2007 (Washington, DC: US House of Representatives); accessed at http://oversight-archive.waxman.house.gov/investigations.asp?ID=204. (Reports and investigations led by Rep. Henry Waxman include, for example, "What Intelligence Officials Knew about Forged Evidence in Iraq" and "The Bush Administration's Use of Forged Iraq Nuclear Evidence.")

72. Grose and Oppenheimer 2007; Kriner and Shen 2007.

73. See US Congress, Senate Democratic Policy Committee, *Oversight Hearing on Iraq Contracting Processes*, Hearing before the Democratic Policy Committee, 108th Cong., 2d sess., February 13, 2004 (http://www.dpc.senate.gov/hearings/hearing12/transcript.pdf); US Congress, House Committee on Oversight and Government Reform: Subcommittee on National Security and Foreign Affairs. "US Mismanaged Iraqi Funds," June 21, 2005.

74. Supplemental Appropriations Act, 2008, H.R. 2642, 110th Cong. (2007-8), became Public Law 110-252, 122 Stat. 2329 (2008). Also see Report for Congress, "FY2008 Supplemental Appropriations for Global War on Terror Military Operations, International Affairs and Other Purposes," RL34278, prepared by Stephen Daggett et al., December 19, 2007, Congressional Research Service, Washington, DC.

75. President Truman requested 98% of the costs of the Korean War through the regular defense appropriations by the second year of war, while President Johnson used the normal appropriations process to requests funds for Vietnam by year 3 (see de Rugy 2008).

76. While war costs were factored back into the budget in the 2010 fiscal year, President Obama continued to use supplemental funding requests to account for various contingencies in war planning.

77. According to the White House Office of Management and Budget (OMB), Congress approved $513 billion in the Defense Department's base budget authority in FY2009, in addition to $145 billion in war funding for a total of approximately $659 billion in discretionary budget authority (Office of Management and Budget, Budget of the US Government, FY2011, p. 58).

78. Disapproving of the decision of the President . . . to deploy more than 20,000 additional United States combat troops to Iraq, H. Con. Res. 63, 110th Cong. (2007) (House vote no. 99, Approved 246-182).

79. Christina Bellantoni, "Top Democrats Rebuff Calls to Cut Off War Funds," *Washington Times*, December 6, 2006, A03.

80. To Provide for the Redeployment of United States Armed Forces and Defense Contractors in Iraq, H.R. 2237, 110th Cong. (2007) (House Vote no. 330, Rejected 171-255).

81. Grose and Oppenheimer 2007, 549.

82. Stiglitz and Bilmes 2008. For three full years after President Obama took office, the chaos, insurgent violence, and political instability in Iraq continued to confound an exit strategy. With the uninterrupted congressional appropriation of war funds, Obama continued to prosecute the Iraq War, despite intermittent protests from his Democratic cohort in Congress. On October 21, 2011, the president announced a full US withdrawal from Iraq on his own terms.

83. In addition to reduced levels of confidence in the logit coefficients in tables 7.1 and 7.2, the findings also suggest that Democrats representing urban districts were *more* likely to support the 2002 AUMF than their rural counterparts, all else being equal (table 7.2, model 3, $p < .05$).

84. More than five defense facilities yields high standard errors and statistically insignificant outcomes in models predicting Democratic members' opposition to the 2007 withdrawal initiative, perhaps because of the relatively small number of observations (n = 59 prowar votes).

CHAPTER 8

1. Quoted in DeConde, Burns, and Logevall 2002, 215–16.
2. Ibid.
3. Quoted in Glennon 1991, 84.
4. *CQ Weekly Report*, January 12, 1991, 71.
5. See Fisher 2004; Glennon 1991.
6. See Adler and George 1996; Ackerman 2010; Ackerman and Hathaway 2011; Ely 1993; Fisher 2004; Koh 1990; Schlesinger 2004 [1973]; Silverstein 1997; Sofaer 1976.
7. Hamilton, "Federalist No. 70" and "Federalist No. 71."
8. Madison, "Federalist No. 51."
9. For example, see Black 1980; Koh 1988, 1990; Yoo 1999, 2005.
10. Quoted in Frisch 2007.
11. Tocqueville 2000 [1835], 123.
12. Black, quoted in Koh 1988, 1292. A more nuanced argument emphasizing structural factors suggests that constitutional war powers should be reassessed based on inter-branch struggles for interpretative authority, as opposed to inconclusive legal text (see Zeisberg forthcoming 2013).
13. Lee 2008; Whittington and Carpenter 2003.
14. For a list of declassified directives, see Digital National Security Directives Archive (accessed at http://nsarchive.chadwyck.com/home.do); Federation of American Scientists, Presidential Directives and Executive Orders (accessed at http://www.fas.org/irp/offdocs/direct.htm). Also see Gordon 2007, 361.

15. Gordon 2007, 359; also see USGAO, "National Security: The Use of Presidential Directives to Make and Implement US Policy," report to the chairman, Legislation and National Security Subcommittee, Committee on Government Operations, House of Representatives, NSIAD-92-72, January 1992, US Government Accountability Office, Washington, DC.

16. Moe and Wilson 1994, 25.

17. Still, presidents have secured reductions in some aspects of US weapons development. President Barack Obama and Defense Secretary Robert Gates achieved unprecedented success in capping the number of purchases for the F-22 stealth fighter jet at 147 planes and eliminating a controversial second engine for the less expensive fighter jet purchased in its place. (However, President Obama's subsequent attempt to retire several naval platforms failed to overcome congressional opposition, despite a fiscal crisis and pending budget "sequestration.")

18. Gansler 1980, 26.

19. Oleszek 2007, 45.

20. See Higgs 2007.

21. Quoted in DeConde, Burns, and Logevall 2002, 216.

22. Whittington and Carpenter 2003, 505.

23. Schlesinger 2004 [1973], 47.

24. Todd Harrison, "Analysis of the FY2012 Defense Budget," Center for Strategic and Budgetary Assessments, July 15, 2011.

25. The broad cloak of secrecy shielding CIA activity has allowed administrations to downgrade or ignore the series of events that led to the attacks of September 11, 2001: the CIA-sponsored overthrow of democratically elected Iranian prime minister Mohammad Mossadegh in 1953 and US support for the repressive shah of Iran, followed by the overthrow of the shah in 1979 and rise of the fundamentalist Ayatollah Khomeini; the US alliance with Saddam Hussein in the 1980s to counter Iranian influence in the region; CIA support for jihadists in Soviet-occupied Afghanistan during the same decade; and the US military occupation of the Persian Gulf after the first Gulf War in the 1990s.

26. On December 22, 1974, journalist Seymour Hersh (1974) broke a front-page report on illegal domestic spying conducted by the CIA.

27. In 1984 P.L. 98-473 barred all military and covert assistance to the Contras by the CIA, DoD "or any other agency or entity involved in US intelligence activities . . . for the purpose or which would have the effect of supporting, directly or indirectly, military or paramilitary operations in Nicaragua" (Continuing Appropriations Resolutions for FY1985, 98 Stat 1837, Sect. 8066). For comprehensive documentation of the Iran-Contra events, see the National Security Archive, "The Iran-Contra Affair 20 Years Later," Electronic Briefing Book No. 210, posted November 24, 2006 (accessed at http://www.gwu.edu/~nsarchiv/NSAEBB/NSAEBB210/index .htm). Also see Fisher (1989) for a detailed account of President Reagan's efforts to circumvent Congress's explicit withholding of funds by seeking money from private parties and friendly foreign governments to finance the Nicaraguan Contras.

28. US Executive Office, Intelligence Oversight Board, "Report on the Guatemala Review," June 29, 1996, available at the George Washington University National Security Archive, http:// www.gwu.edu/~nsarchiv/NSAEBB/NSAEBB27/04-01.htm (posted June 29, 2006).

29. On June 28, 1978, President Carter issued Executive Order 12065, which designated an official basis for classifying information. The Information Security Oversight Office (ISOO) later formed to oversee security classifications. ISOO is a component of the National Archives and Records Administration (NARA) and receives program guidance from the NSC. The organization maintains public records of the level and designation of all executive classification

activity within each fiscal year beginning in FY1979 (see NARA, ISOO Reports, http://www
.archives.gov/isoo/reports/). While the reports do not indicate the size of the classified documents, they do provide a preliminary estimate of the volume of covert communications within
the executive branch.

30. Koh 1990, 123.

31. Hersh 2008, 60–67.

32. Scahill 2011.

33. Rumsfeld 2002, 20.

34. Figures compiled by the author (not displayed here) show systematic declines in civilian
employment throughout agencies providing combat and logistical support as well as contract
and financial management. In contrast, the agencies managing defense legal services and arms
transfers experienced increases in personnel strength over the same time period. The data are
drawn from DoD Statistical Information Analysis Division, Civilian Personnel Statistics, DoD
Employment by Organization and Function, Fiscal Year 1998-2011 (September). Department
of Defense, Washington DC (accessed at http://siadapp.dmdc.osd.mil/personnel/CIVILIAN/
CIVTOP.HTM).

35. Representative Schakowsky, quoted in Scahill 2007, 356.

36. For example, PMSCs employed third-party nationals after Congress capped the number of US contractors authorized in Plan Colombia in 2001 (see Avant 2010, 246–47). The
restructuring of DoD civilian support services and weak oversight mechanisms also created
opportunities for contractors to exploit third world nationals for cheap labor in US war zones,
while pocketing the bulk of their profits (see Stillman 2011).

37. Avant and Sigelman 2010.

References

Ackerman, Bruce. 2010. *The Decline and Fall of the American Republic*. Cambridge, MA: President and Fellows of Harvard College.

Ackerman, Bruce, and Oona Hathaway. 2011. "Limited War and the Constitution: Iraq and the Crisis of Presidential Legality." *Michigan Law Review* 109:447–518.

Adams, Aaron. 2011. "The Backseat Driver Effect: Why Congress Does Not Stop Wars." Unpublished manuscript.

Adams, Gordon. 1981. *Politics of Defense Contracting: The Iron Triangle*. New Brunswick, NJ: Transaction Books.

Adams, Walter, and William James Adams. 1972. "The Military-Industrial Complex: A Market Structure Analysis." *American Economic Review* 62:284.

Adler, David Gray, and Larry N. George, eds. 1996. *The Constitution and the Conduct of American Foreign Policy*. Lawrence: University of Kansas Press.

Adler, E. Scott. "Congressional Data District File." 103rd–105th terms. University of Colorado, Boulder, CO.

Adler, E. Scott, and John S. Lapinski. 1997. "Demand-Side Theory and Congressional Committee Composition: A Constituency Characteristic Approach." *American Journal of Political Science* 41:895–918.

Aldrich, John H., and David W. Rohde. 2000. "The Republican Revolution and the House Appropriations Committee." *Journal of Politics* 62:1–33.

Arnold, R. Douglas. 1979. *Congress and the Bureaucracy*. New Haven, CT: Yale University Press.

———. 1990. *Logic of Congressional Action*. New Haven, CT: Yale University Press.

Arthur, Brian. 1994. *Increasing Returns and Path Dependence in the Economy*. Ann Arbor: University of Michigan Press.

Avant, Deborah. 2010. "War Recruitment Systems and Democracy." In *In War's Wake: International Conflict and the Fate of Liberal Democracy*, ed. Elizabeth Kier and Ronald Krebs, 235–52. New York: Cambridge University Press.

Avant, Deborah, and Lee Sigelman. 2010. "What Does Private Security Mean for Democracy? Lessons from the U.S. in Iraq." *Security Studies* 19:230–65.

Bacevich, Andrew. 2010. *Washington Rules: America's Path to Permanent War*. New York: Metropolitan Books.

Bailey, Michael, and David W. Brady. 1998. "Heterogeneity and Representation: The Senate and Free Trade." *American Journal of Political Science* 42:524–44.

Barlett, Donald L., and James B. Steele. "Washington's $8 Billion Shadow." *Vanity Fair*, March 2007. Accessed at http://www.vanityfair.com/politics/features/2007/03/spyagency200703.

Beale, Calvin. 1996. "Rural Prisons: An Update." *Rural Development Perspectives* 11:25–27.

———. 1993. "Prisons, Populations and Jobs in Nonmetro America." *Rural Development Perspectives* 8:16–19.

Beaver, Daniel R. 1977. "The Problem of American Military Supply, 1890–1920." In *War, Business and American Society: Historical Perspectives on the Military-Industrial Complex*, ed. Benjamin Franklin Cooling, 73–92. Port Washington, NY: Kennikat Press.

Bender, Brian, and John Robinson. 1997. "Shali: More Stealth Bombers Mean Less Combat," *Defense Daily*, August 5.

Bergen, Peter, and Alec Reynolds. 2005. "Blowback Revisited." *Foreign Affairs* 84:6.

Bernstein, Robert A., and William W. Anthony. 1974. "The ABM Issue in the Senate, 1968–70: The Importance of Ideology." *American Political Science Review* 68:1198–1206.

Berry, Christopher R., Barry C. Burden, and William G. Howell. 2010. "The President and the Distribution of Federal Spending." *American Political Science Review* 104:783–99.

Bertelli, Anthony M., and Christian R. Grose. 2009. "Secretaries of Pork? A New Theory of Distributive Public Policy." *Journal of Politics* 71:926–45.

Bickers, Kenneth M., and Robert M. Stein. 2000. "The Congressional Pork Barrel in a Republican Era." *Journal of Politics* 62:1070–86.

Black, Charles. 1980. "The Working Balance of the American Political Department." *Hastings Constitutional Law Quarterly* 1:20.

Brambor, Thomas, William Roberts Clark, and Matt Golder. 2006. "Understanding Interaction Models: Improving Empirical Analyses." *Political Analysis* 14:63–82.

Bryan, Kevin A., Brian D. Minton, and Pierre-Daniel G. Sartre. 2007. "The Evolution of Density in the United States." *Economic Quarterly* 93:341–59.

Burnett, William B., and Frederic M. Scherer. 1990. "The Weapons Industry." In *The Structure of American Industry*, ed. Walter Adams, 289–317. New York: Macmillan.

Campbell, Jason H., and Jeremy Shapiro. 2009. "Brookings Afghanistan Index: Tracking Variables of Reconstruction and Security in Post-9/11 Afghanistan." Brookings Institution, Washington, DC. Accessed at http://www.brookings.edu/foreign-policy/~/media/Files/Programs/FP/afghanistan%20index/index20090526.pdf.

Carlson, Katherine. 1995. "Prisons and Rural Communities: Making the Most and Losing the Least from a Growing Industry." In *Rural Development Strategies*, ed. J. Norman Reid and David Sears, 189–203. Chicago: Nelson Hall Publishers.

Carsey, Thomas M., and Barry Rundquist. 1997. "The Reciprocal Relationship between State Defense Interest and Committee Representation in Congress." Submitted to the Political Methodological Electronic Paper Archive as a Working Paper.

———. 1999. "Parties and Committees in Distributive Politics: Evidence from Defense Spending." *Journal of Politics* 61:1156–69.

Cavanaugh, John. 1999. "Jobs, Jobs, Jobs, and the Defense Industrial Base: What Did *Seawolf* Save?" In *The Changing Dynamics of U.S. Defense Spending*, ed. Leon V. Sigel, 135–52. Westport, CT: Praeger.

Champagne, Anthony, Douglas B. Harris, James W. Riddlesperger Jr., and Garrison Nelson. 2009. *The Austin-Boston Connection: Five Decades of House Democratic Leadership, 1937–1989*. College Station: Texas A&M University Press.

Ciccone, Antonio, and Robert E. Hall. 1996. "Productivity and the Density of Economic Activity." *American Economic Review* 86:54–70.

Cobb, Stephen S. 1976. "Defense Spending and Defense Voting in the House: An Empirical Test of the Military Industrial Complex." *American Journal of Sociology* 82:163–82.

Cooper, Phillip. 2002. *By Order of the President: The Use and Abuse of Executive Direct Action.* Lawrence: University Press of Kansas.

Corwin, Edward. 1957. *The President: Office and Powers.* 4th rev. ed. New York: New York University Press.

Cox, Gary W., and Mathew D. McCubbins. 2005. *Setting the Agenda: Responsible Party Government in the U.S. House of Representatives.* New York: Cambridge University Press.

Cunningham, William Glenn. 1951. *The Aircraft Industry: A Study in Industrial Location*. Los Angeles: L. L. Morrison.

de Rugy, Veronique. 2008. "The Trillion Dollar War." Reason.com, May. Accessed at http://reason.com/archives/2008/04/07/the-trillion-dollar-war.

DeConde, Alexander, Richard Dean Burns, and Frederick Logevall. 2002. *Encyclopedia of American Foreign Policy*, vol. 3, 2nd ed. New York: Scribner.

Dowd, Maureen. 1992. "The 1992 Campaign: Republicans; Immersing Himself in Nitty-Gritty, Bush Barnstorms New Hampshire." *New York Times*, January 16. Accessed at http://query.nytimes.com/gst/fullpage.html?res=9E0CE2D6133DF935A25752C0A96495 8260&sec=&spon=&pagewanted=2.

Downs, Anthony. 1973. *Opening Up the Suburbs*. New Haven, CT: Yale University Press.

Edling, Max M. 2003. *A Revolution in Favor of Government: Origins of the U.S. Constitution and the Making of the American State*. Oxford: Oxford University Press.

Elliot, Jonathan, ed. 1836. *The debates in the Several State Conventions on the Adoption of the Federal Constitution, at Philadelphia, in 1787. 2d ed. Collected and revised from contemporary publications*, Published under the sanction of Congress. 5 vols. Accessed at http://oll.libertyfund.org/index.php?option=com_staticxt&staticfile=show.php?title=1904&Itemid=27.

Ely, John Hart. 1993. *Constitutional Lessons from Vietnam and Its Aftermath*. Princeton, NJ: Princeton University Press.

Farrier, Jasmine. 2010. *Congressional Ambivalence: The Political Burdens of Constitutional Authority*. Lexington: University Press of Kentucky.

Ferrand, Max, ed. 1911. *The Records of the Federal Convention of 1787*. 3 vols. New Haven, CT: Yale University Press. Accessed at http://oll.libertyfund.org/title/1785.

Fiorina, Morris. 1987. "Alternative Rationales for Restrictive Procedures." *Journal of Law, Economics and Organization* 3:337–45.

———. 1989. *Congress: Keystone of the Washington Establishment*. 2nd ed. New Haven, CT: Yale University Press.

Fisher, Louis. 1989. "How Tightly Can Congress Draw the Purse Strings?" *American Journal of International Law* 83:758–66.

———. 2000. *Congressional Abdication on War and Spending*. College Station, TX: Texas A&M University Press.

———. 2004. *Presidential War Power*. 2nd ed. Lawrence: University Press of Kansas.

Fitzpatrick, John C., ed. 1931–44. *The Writings of George Washington from the Original Manuscript Sources, 1745–1799*. Washington Resources at the University of Virginia Library, Electronic Text Center. Retrieved at http://etext.virginia.edu/washington/fitzpatrick/.

Flake, Jeff. 2005. "Keeping Earmarks Out of the Homeland Security Appropriations Bill." Washington, DC, April 20. Accessed at http://flake.house.gov/News/DocumentSingle.aspx?DocumentID=41475.

Fleisher, Richard. 1985. "Economic Benefit, Ideology, and Senate Voting on the B-1 Bomber." *American Politics Quarterly* 13:200–211.

Fordham, Benjamin O. 2007. "The Evolution of Republican and Democratic Positions on Cold War Military Spending: A Historical Puzzle." *Social Science History* 31:603–35.

Freeman, J. Leiper. 1955. *The Political Process: Executive-Bureau-Legislative Committee Relations*. Garden City, NY: Doubleday.

Friedberg, Aaron L. 2000. *In the Shadow of the Garrison State: America's Anti-Statism and Its Cold War Strategy*. Princeton, NJ: Princeton University Press.

Frisch, Morton J., ed. 2007. *The Pacificus-Helvidius Debates of 1793–1794: Toward the Completion of the American Founding, Alexander Hamilton and James Madison.* Indianapolis, IN: Liberty Fund.

Fry, Joseph A. 2006. *Debating Vietnam: Fulbright, Stennis, and Their Senate Hearings.* Oxford: Rowman and Littlefield.

Gansler, Jacques. 1980. *The Defense Industry.* Cambridge, MA: MIT Press.

Garrett, Thomas A., and Russell S. Sobel. 2003. "The Political Economy of FEMA Disaster Payments." *Economic Inquiry* 41:496–509.

Gelpi, Christopher, Peter D. Feaver and Jason Reifler. 2005/6. "Success Matters: Casualty Sensitivity and the War in Iraq." *International Security* 30:7–46.

Gholz, Eugene. 2000. "The Curtiss-Wright Corporation and Cold War–Era Defense Procurement: A Challenge to Military-Industrial Complex Theory." *Journal of Cold War Studies* 2:35–75.

Gholz, Eugene, and Harvey Sapolsky. 1999–2000. "Restructuring the U.S. Defense Industry." *International Security* 24:5–51.

Gimpel, James G., and Scott L. Althaus. 2009. "The Geography of Mass Media Exposure and Political News Consumption." Paper presented at the annual meeting of the American Political Science Association, Toronto, Canada, September 3–6.

Glennon, Michael J. 1991. "The Gulf War and the Constitution." *Foreign Affairs* 70:84–101.

Goldsmith, Raymond. 1946. "The Power of Victory: Munitions Output in World War II." *Military Affairs* 10:69–80.

Goldstein, Joel K. 2007. "Assuming Responsibility: Thomas F. Eagleton, the Senate, and the Bombing of Cambodia." *St. Louis University Press* 52:151–86.

Gordon, Vikki. 2007. "Unilaterally Shaping U.S. National Security Policy: The Role of National Security Directives." *Presidential Studies Quarterly* 37:349–67.

Goss, Carol. 1972. "Military Committee Membership and Defense-Related Benefits in the House of Representatives." *Western Political Quarterly* 25:215–33.

Grose, Christian R., and Bruce I. Oppenheimer. 2007. "The Iraq War, Partisanship, and Candidate Attributes: Variation in Partisan Swing in the 2006 U.S. House Elections." *Legislative Studies Quarterly* 32:531–57.

Hall, Richard L. 1987. "Participation and Purpose in Committee Decision Making." *American Political Science Review* 81:105–28.

———. 1996. *Participation in Congress.* New Haven, CT: Yale University Press.

Harrison, Todd. 2011. "Analysis of the FY2012 Defense Budget." Center for Strategic and Budgetary Assessments, July 15. Accessed at http://www.csbaonline.org/wp-content/uploads/2011/07/2011.07.16-FY-2012-Defense-Budget.pdf.

Hersh, Seymour M. 1974. "Huge CIA Operation Reported in U.S. against Anti-War Forces, Other Dissidents in Nixon Years." *New York Times*, December 22.

———. 2008. "Preparing the Battlefield." *New Yorker*, July 7, 60–67.

Higgs, Robert. 1990. *Arms, Politics, and the Economy: Historical and Contemporary Perspectives.* New York: Holmes and Meier.

———. 2006. *Depression, War, and Cold War: Studies in Political Economy.* Oxford: Oxford University Press.

———. 2007. "The Trillion Dollar Defense Budget Is Already Here." *Independent Institute Newsroom*, March 15. Accessed at http://www.independent.org/newsroom/article.asp?id=1941.

Hooks, Gregory. 1993. "The Weakness of Strong Theories: The U.S. State's Dominance of the World War II Investment Process." *American Sociological Review* 58:37–53.

Hooks, Gregory, and Leonard E. Bloomquist. 1992. "The Legacy of World War II for Regional Growth and Decline: The Cumulative Effects of Wartime Investments on U.S. Manufacturing, 1947–1972." *Social Forces* 71:303–37.

Hooks, Gregory, and Brian McQueen. 2010. "American Exceptionalism Revisited: The Military-Industrial Complex, Racial Tension and the Underdeveloped Welfare State." *American Sociological Review* 75:185–204.

Hormats, Robert D. 2007. *The Price of Liberty: Paying for America's Wars.* New York: Times Books.

Howell, William G. 2003. *Power without Persuasion: The Politics of Direct Presidential Action.* Princeton, NJ: Princeton University Press.

———. 2005. "Unilateral Powers: A Brief Overview." *Presidential Studies Quarterly* 35:417–39.

Howell, William G., and Jon C. Pevehouse. 2007. *While Dangers Gather: Congressional Checks on Presidential War Powers.* Princeton, NJ: Princeton University Press.

Jackson, John E., and John W. Kingdon. 1992. "Ideology, Interest Group Scores and Legislative Votes." *American Journal of Political Science* 36:805–23.

Jacobs, Jane. 1969. *The Economy of Cities.* New York: Random House.

Jefferson, Thomas. 1801. Letter to Wilson Cary Nicholas, June 11. In *Works of Thomas Jefferson*, vol. 9, ed. Paul Leicester Ford (New York: G. P. Putnam's Sons, 1904–5). Accessed at http://oll.libertyfund.org/?option=com_staticxt&staticfile=show.php%3Ftitle=757&chapter=87309&layout=html&Itemid=27.

Jenkins, Jeffery A., Eric Schickler, and Jamie L. Carson. 2004. "Constituency Cleavages and Congressional Parties: Measuring Homogeneity and Polarization, 1857–1913." *Social Science History* 28:537–73.

Karol, David, and Edward Miguel. 2007. "The Electoral Cost of War: Iraq Casualties and the 2004 U.S. Presidential Election." *Journal of Politics* 69:633–48.

Kennedy, David M. 1999. *Freedom from Fear: The American People in Depression and War, 1929–1945.* Oxford: Oxford University Press.

King, Gary, Michael Tomz, and Jason Wittenberg. 2000. "Making the Most Statistical Analyses: Improving Interpretation and Presentation." *American Journal of Political Science* 44:347–61.

Koh, Harold Hongju. 1988. "Why the President (Almost) Always Wins in Foreign Affairs: Lessons of the Iran-Contra Affair." *Yale Law Journal* 97:1255–1342.

———. 1990. *The National Security Constitution: Sharing Power after the Iran-Contra Affair.* New Haven, CT: Yale University Press.

Kohn, Richard. 1975. *Eagle and Sword: The Federalists and the Making of the Military Establishment in America, 1783–1802.* New York: Free Press.

Kotz, Nick. 1988. *Wild Blue Yonder: Money, Politics and the B-1 Bomber.* New York: Pantheon Books.

Kovacic, W. E. 1990. "The Sorcerer's Apprentice: Public Regulation of the Weapons Acquisition Process." In *Arms, Politics, and the Economy*, ed. Higgs, 104–31.

Kriner, Douglas L. 2010. *After the Rubicon: Congress, Presidents and the Politics of Waging War.* Chicago: University of Chicago Press.

Kriner, Douglas L., and Andrew Reeves. 2012. "The Influence of Federal Spending on Presidential Elections." *American Political Science Review* 106:348–66.

Kriner, Douglas L., and Francis X. Shen. 2007. "Iraq Casualties and the 2006 Senate Elections." *Legislative Studies Quarterly* 32:507–29.

———. 2010. *The Casualty Gap: The Causes and Consequences of American Wartime Inequalities*. New York: Oxford University Press.

Kurth, James R. 1972. "The Political Economy of Weapons Procurement: The Follow-on Imperative." *American Economic Review* 62:304–11.

Lasswell, Harold. 1941. "The Garrison State," *American Journal of Sociology* 46:455–68.

Ledbetter, James. 2011. *Unwarranted Influence: Dwight E. Eisenhower and the Military-Industrial Complex*. New Haven, CT: Yale University Press.

Lee, Frances. 2008. "Agreeing to Disagree: Agenda Content and Senate Partisanship, 1981–2004." *Legislative Studies Quarterly* 33:199–222.

———. 2009. *Beyond Ideology: Politics, Principle and Partisanship in the U.S. Senate*. Chicago: University of Chicago Press.

Levinson, Daryl J., and Richard H. Pildes. 2006. "Separation of Parties, Not Powers." *Harvard Law Review* 119:2311–86.

Lewis, David. 2008. *The Politics of Presidential Appointments: Political Control and Bureaucratic Appointments*. Princeton, NJ: Princeton University Press.

Lindsay, James M. 1990. "Congress and the Defense Budget: Parochialism or Policy?" In *Arms, Politics and the Economy*, ed. Higgs, 172–201.

———. 1991. "Testing the Parochial Hypothesis: Congress and the Strategic Defense Initiative." *Journal of Politics* 53:860–76.

Lucas, Robert E., Jr. 2001. "On the Mechanics of Economic Development." In *Landmark Papers in Economic Growth*, ed. Robert Solow, 147–86. Northampton, MA: Edward Elgar Publishing.

Machiavelli, Niccolò. 1998. *The Prince*. Translated by Harvey Mansfield. 2nd ed. Chicago: University of Chicago Press.

Mack, Elizabeth, Tony H. Grubesic, and Erin Kessler. 2007. "Indices of Industrial Diversity and Regional Economic Composition." *Growth and Change* 38:474–509.

Maddow, Rachel. 2012. *Drift: The Unmooring of American Military Power*. New York: Crown.

Madison, James. 1787. "Letter to Thomas Jefferson 1." In *The Writings of James Madison*, ed. Gaillard Hunt, vol. 2 (1783–87). New York: G. P. Putnam's Sons, 1900. Accessed at http://oll.libertyfund.org/title/1934/118614/2395162.

———. 1792. "Universal Peace 1." In *The Writings of James Madison*, ed. Gaillard Hunt, vol. 6 (1790–1806). New York: G. P. Putnam's Sons, 1900. Accessed at http://oll.libertyfund.org/?option=com_staticxt&staticfile=show.php%3Ftitle=1941&chapter=124396&layout=html&Itemid=27.

Mahon, John K., and Romana Danyish. 1972. *Army Lineage Series: Infantry Part I: Regular Army*. Washington, DC: Office of the Chief of Military History.

Maier, Pauline. 2010. *Ratification: The People Debate the Constitution, 1787–1788*. New York: Simon and Schuster.

Mann, Thomas, and Norman Ornstein. 2006. *The Broken Branch: How Congress Is Failing America and How to Get It Back on Track*. Oxford: Oxford University Press.

Markusen, Ann, Peter Hall, Scott Campbell, and Sabina Deitrick. 1991. *The Rise of the Gunbelt: The Military Remapping of Industrial America*. Oxford: Oxford University Press.

Mayer, Kenneth R. 1990. "Patterns of Congressional Influence in Defense Contracting." In *Arms, Politics, and the Economy*, ed. Higgs, 202–35.

———. 1991. *The Political Economy of Defense Contracting*. New Haven, CT: Yale University Press.

Mayhew, David R. 1974. *The Electoral Connection.* New Haven, CT: Yale University Press.

Melman, Seymour. 1974. *The Permanent War Economy: American Capitalism in Decline.* New York: Simon and Schuster.

Mills, C. Wright. 1956. *The Power Elite.* Oxford: Oxford University Press.

Moe, Terry, and William G. Howell. 1999. "The Presidential Power of Unilateral Action." *Journal of Law, Economics and Organization* 15:132–79.

Moe, Terry, and Scott Wilson. 1994. "Presidents and the Politics of Structure." *Law and Contemporary Problems* 57:1–44.

Mueller, John. 1973. *War, Presidents and Public Opinion.* New York: John Wiley and Sons.

———. 2005. "The Iraq Syndrome." *Foreign Affairs* 84:44–45.

O'Hanlon, Michael. 2009. "Brookings Iraq Index: Tracking Variables of Security and Reconstruction in Post-Saddam Iraq." Brookings Institution, Washington, DC. Accessed at http://www.brookings.edu/saban/~/media/Files/Centers/Saban/Iraq%20Index/index20090625.pdf.

Oleszek, Walter J. 2007. "The Congressional Budget Process." In *Congressional Procedures and the Policy Process,* 7th ed., 40–77. Washington, DC: CQ Press.

Olson, Mancur. 1971. *The Logic of Collective Action: Public Goods and the Theory of Groups.* Cambridge, MA: Harvard University Press.

Patillo, Donald M. 1998. *Pushing the Envelope: The American Aircraft Industry.* Ann Arbor: University of Michigan Press.

Pfiffner, James. 2008. *Power Play: The Bush Presidency and the Constitution.* Washington, DC: Brookings Institution Press.

Pierson, Paul. 2000. "Path Dependence, Increasing Returns and the Study of Politics." *American Political Science Review* 94:251–67.

———. 2004. *Politics in Time: History, Institutions and Social Analysis.* Princeton, NJ: Princeton University Press.

Poole, Keith T., and Howard Rosenthal. 1991. "Patterns of Congressional Voting." *American Journal of Political Science* 35:228–78.

Ray, Bruce A. 1980. "Congressional Losers in the U.S. Federal Spending Process." *Legislative Studies Quarterly* 5:359–72.

———. 1981a. "Defense Department Spending and Hawkish Voting in the U.S. House of Representatives." *Western Political Quarterly* 34:439–46.

———. 1981b. "Military Committee Membership in the House of Representatives and the Allocation of Defense Department Outlays." *Western Political Quarterly* 34:222–34.

Richardson, James D., ed. 2004. "A Compilation of Messages and Papers of the Presidents, 1789–1897, Vol. X, Part 2: William McKinley: Messages, Proclamations and Executive Orders Relating to the Spanish-American War." Project Gutenberg EBook. Accessed at http://onlinebooks.library.upenn.edu/webbin/gutbook/lookup?num=13893.

Rohde, David, and Kenneth Shepsle. 1973. "Democratic Committee Assignments in the House of Representatives: Strategic Aspects of a Social Choice Process." *American Political Science Review* 67:889–905.

Rossiter, Clinton, ed. 2003. *The Federalist Papers.* New York: Signet Classics.

Rudalevige, Andrew. 2005. *The New Imperial President: Renewing Presidential Power after Watergate.* Ann Arbor: University of Michigan Press.

Rumerman, Judy. n.d. "The Hughes Company." U.S. Centennial of Flight Commission. Accessed at http://www.centennialofflight.gov/essay/Aerospace/Hughes/Aer044.htm.

Rumsfeld, Donald H. 2002. "Transforming the Military." *Foreign Affairs* 81:20.

Rundquist, Barry. 1973. "Congressional Influence on the Distribution of Prime Military Contracts." PhD dissertation, Stanford University.

———. 1978. "On Testing a Military Industrial Complex Theory." *American Politics Research* 6:29–53.

Rundquist, Barry, and Thomas M. Carsey. 2002. *Congress and Defense Spending: The Distributive Politics of Military Procurement.* Norman: University of Oklahoma Press.

Rundquist, Barry, and David E. Griffith. 1976. "An Uninterrupted Time-Series Test of the Distributive Theory of Military Policy-Making." *Western Political Quarterly* 29:620–26.

Sahr, Robert. 2009. "Inflation Conversion Factor for Dollars 1774 to Estimated 2019." June 4. Accessed at http://oregonstate.edu/cla/polisci/faculty-research/sahr/sahr.htm.

Scahill, Jeremy. 2007. *Blackwater: The Rise of the World's Most Powerful Mercenary Army.* New York: Nation Books.

———. 2011. "JSOC: The Black Ops Force That Took Down Bin Laden." *The Nation*, May 2. Accessed at http://www.thenation.com/blog/160332/jsoc-black-ops-force-took-down-bin-laden#.

Schickler, Eric, and Douglas L. Kriner. 2012. "Investigating the President: The Dynamics of Congressional Committee Probes, 1898–2006." Presented at the annual meeting of the Midwest Political Science Association, Chicago, April 12–15.

Schlesinger, Arthur M., Jr. 2004 [1973]. *The Imperial Presidency.* New York: Houghton Mifflin.

Schulman, Bruce J. 1991. *From Cotton Belt to Sunbelt: Federal Policy, Economic Development and the Transformation of the South, 1938–1980.* New York: Oxford University Press.

Shepsle, Kenneth, and Barry Weingast. 1994. "Positive Theories of Congressional Institutions." *Legislative Studies Quarterly* 19:149–80.

Silverstein, Gordon. 1997. *Imbalance of Powers: Constitutional Interpretation and the Making of American Foreign Policy.* Oxford: Oxford University Press.

Skocpol, Theda. 1992. *Protecting Soldiers and Mothers: The Political Origins of Social Policy in the United States.* Cambridge: Cambridge University Press.

Skowronek, Stephen. 1982. *Building a New American State: The Expansion of National Administrative Capacity, 1877–1920.* Cambridge: Cambridge University Press.

Smith, Elberton. 1959. *The Army and Economic Mobilization.* Washington, DC: Office of the Chief of Military History.

Smith, Merritt Roe. 1977. "Military Arsenals and Industry before World War I." In *War, Business and American Society: Historical Perspectives on the Military-Industrial Complex,* ed. Benjamin Cooling, 24–42. Port Washington, NY: Kennikat Press.

Sofaer, Abraham. 1976. *War, Foreign Affairs, and Constitutional Power: The Origins.* Cambridge: Ballinger.

Song, Kyung M. 2012. "Plan for New Navy Wharf Fires Up Nuke Debate." *Seattle Times,* January 8, Accessed at http://seattletimes.nwsource.com/html/localnews/2017193326_navywharf09m.html.

Stein, Robert M., and Kenneth M. Bickers. 1995. *Perpetuating the Pork Barrel: Policy Subsystems and American Democracy.* New York: Cambridge University Press.

Stiglitz, Joseph E., and Linda J. Bilmes. 2008. *The Three Trillion Dollar War: The True Cost of the Iraq War.* New York: W. W. Norton.

Stillman, Sarah. 2011. "The Invisible Army." *New Yorker*, June 6, 56–65.

Stofft, William A. 1989. *American Military History: Army Historical Series.* Washington: CMH.

Storing, Herbert, ed. 1985. *The Anti-Federalist: Writings by the Opponents of the Constitution.* Abridged ed. Chicago: University of Chicago Press.

Theriault, Sean. 2008. *Party Polarization in Congress.* New York: Cambridge University Press.

Thompson, Mark. 2007. "V-22 Osprey: A Flying Shame." *Time,* September 26. Accessed at http://www.time.com/time/magazine/article/0,9171,1666282,00.html.

Tocqueville, Alexis de. 2000 [1835]. *Democracy in America.* Edited by Harvey Mansfield and Debra Winthrop. Chicago: University of Chicago Press.

Trubowitz, Peter. 1998. *Defining the National Interest: Conflict and Change in American Foreign Policy.* Chicago: University of Chicago Press.

Twight, Charlotte. 1990. "Department of Defense Attempts to Close Military Bases: The Political Economy of Congressional Resistance," In *Arms, Politics, and the Economy,* ed. Higgs, 236–80.

Weingast, Barry R., and William J. Marshall. 1988. "The Industrial Organization of Congress; or, Why Legislatures, Like Firms, Are Not Organized as Markets." *Journal of Political Economy* 96:132–63.

Wheeler, Winslow T. 2004. *The Wastrels of Defense: How Congress Sabotages U.S. Security.* Annapolis, MD: Naval Institute Press.

Whittington, Keith E., and Dan Carpenter. 2003. "Executive Power in American Institutional Development." *Perspectives on Politics* 1:495–513.

Whittle, Richard. 2010. *The Dream Machine: The Untold History of the Notorious V-22 Osprey.* New York: Simon and Schuster.

Wilentz, Sean. 2005. *The Rise of American Democracy: Jefferson to Lincoln.* New York: W. W. Norton.

Wilson, James. 1787. "Pennsylvania Ratifying Convention." In *The Founders' Constitution,* ed. Philip B. Kurland and Ralph Lerner, vol. 1, chap. 7, doc. 7. Chicago: University of Chicago Press. Accessed at http://press-pubs.uchicago.edu/founders/documents/v1ch7s17.html.

Wood, Gordon. 1998. *The Creation of the American Republic, 1776–1787.* Chapel Hill: University of North Carolina Press.

———. 2003. *The American Revolution: A History.* New York: Modern Library.

Wright, Gavin. 1986. *Old South, New South: Revolutions in the Southern Economy since the Civil War.* New York: Basic Books.

Yandle, Bruce. 1983. "Bootlegger and Baptists: The Education of a Regulatory Economist." *Regulation* 7:12–16.

———. 1999. "Bootleggers and Baptists in Retrospect." *Regulation* 22:5–7.

Yoo, John C. 1999. *The Misuse of History in the War Powers Debate,* 70 U. Colorado L. Rev. 1169–1222.

———. 2005. *The Powers of War and Peace: The Constitution and Foreign Affairs after 9/11.* Chicago: University of Chicago Press.

Zeisberg, Mariah. 2013 (forthcoming). *War Powers: The Politics of Constitutional Authority.* Princeton, NJ: Princeton University Press.

Zelizer, Julian E. 2009. "Congress and Resurgence of a Democratic National Security Advantage, 1954–1960." Paper presented at the annual meeting of the American Political Science Association, Toronto, Canada, September 3–6.

Index

Academi, 177
Adams, John, 33–34
Addabbo, Joseph, 76, 77
Adler, Scott, 100, 112
Afghanistan War: al Qaeda in, 214n31;
defense budget and, 168; funding for, 149,
152; Iraq War and, 148; legislative authorization of, 198n30; military technology and,
166; Reagan's Afghanistan policy and, 137,
214n31, 219n25; security contractors in, 84,
205n28; US casualties in, 85–86; US troop
counts as percentage of population and, 83
Aidid, Mohamed, 141
Alliant Techsystems, 99, 132, 207n18
All-Volunteer Force (AVF), 19, 68, 82, 83,
91, 184
al Qaeda, 137, 214n31
Anti-Federalists, 28, 29, 199n12
appendixes not in print, 187
Aristide, Jean-Bertrand, 142
arms sales to foreign nations: congressional
votes on from 1993 to 1998, 192–93; Iran-
Contra scandal and, 173; national security
directives (NSDs) and, 164; overprocure-
ment and, 168; roll-call votes on, 98, 99
Army: Army Rangers and, 176;
early-twentieth-century reorganization
of, 40; federal lending to private companies and, 204n21; professionalization of,
36, 42; War of 1812 and, 35, 36
Articles of Confederation, 27, 28
AT&T, 61–62
Avco, 75
aviation: aircraft industry in military production and, 203n12; federal funding of
facilities expansion and, 204n19; as foundation of military industrial complex, 51

B-1 stealth bomber, 93, 94, 166, 206n9
B-2 stealth bomber, 99, 207n18
Bacevich, Andrew, 199n32
BAE Systems, 64

Bailey, Michael, 94–95
balance of war power: congressional deference to executive, 1940s–1960s, and,
213n14; Congress's black-check policy and,
127; in Constitution, 24, 25, 28, 30; in constitutional ratification debates, 31–33, 127;
in eighteenth and nineteenth centuries, 8,
24–25; expansive interpretation of president's war powers and, 180; facilitation of
peace and, 32; through history, 182–83;
incentives underlying congressional
decision-making and, 11–12; inter-branch
struggles for interpretive authority and,
218n12; James Madison and, 161; partisan
loyalties and, 21; post–World War II weakness in, 162; power of the purse and, 13,
31–32; reasons for shift of to executive
branch, 7; standing army and, 36–37 See
also separation of powers
Balkans conflict, 83–84, 142–43, 176
Bay of Pigs invasion, 170, 213n14
Bell Aircraft Corporation, 52, 54, 73, 75
Bethlehem Steel, 41, 61
bin Laden, Osama, 176, 214n31
Blackwater USA, 177
Boeing: acquisitions and, 60, 205n12; ballistic
missile defense program and, 207n18; controversial weapons systems and, 207n18;
defense allocations and, 109; defense
production sites of, 73–74, 75, 79, 96; dollar value of contracts of, 210n22; as leading
defense corporation, 61–64; plant closings
and, 58; in study methodology, 99, 115, 132;
technology procurement and, 78; World
War II–era expansion and, 52, 57–58
Boland Amendments, 173
Bosnia conflict (1995–2004): defense budget
and, 168; economic reliance on defense
spending and support for, 216n57; executive independence and, 8, 162; funding
for, 146, 156; interbranch conflict over,
140, 142, 147, 215n49, 215n51, 216nn59–60

membership and defense dependency of district and, 112, 123, 165–66; committee membership and defense votes, 1993–98, and, 188–93; committee membership and economic reliance on defense, 1999–2005, and, 194–95; committees in defense budget decisions and, 111, 112–13; committees with jurisdiction over weapons programs and, 210n21; defense budget process and, 111–12; defense facility siting decisions and, 18–19, 74–75; distribution of defense contracts and, 109–11; districts reliant on defense facilities and, 11, 17–18, 19, 22; early-twentieth-century actions in Latin America and, 41; executive circumvention of legislative oversight by, 22, 171; influence of over procurement, 40; institutional weakness of, 128; intelligence apparatus and, 171–72; legislative atrophy and, 180; members' limited authority in, 13; military privatization and, 176–78; mobilization and demobilization and, 170; nineteenth-century executive deference to 34–35, 37; oversight by as Maginot line, 178; party leadership in, 198n17; political costs of presidential military action and, 128; political incentives in post–World War II defense production and, 67; political self-preservation in, 13; power of defense committees and, 74–75; preference intensities in, 113, 120; preservation of questionable weapons systems by, 93–94; versus president on military engagement, 21; protests of unpaid soldiers and, 199n8; as reactive to executive actions, 42; reductions in nuclear weapons and, 107; refusal of to reduce defense spending, 184; relinquishment of control to executive by, 180–81, 185; short-term interests of representatives and, x; Spanish-American War (1898) and, 39; support for local versus national defense in, 77; Texas annexation and, 37; treaty approval and, 31; voters' interest in lower military spending and, 9, 25; War of 1812 and, 35–36; war versus diplomacy under George Washington and, 24–25;

worldview versus constituency view for, 206n8. *See also* congressional authorization of war; congressional power of the purse

congressional authorization of war: Afghanistan War and, 198n30; after war appears inevitable, 182; Andrew Jackson's deference to, 202n58; bombing of Cambodia and, 136; Clinton-era conflicts and, 83, 127–28, 142; emergency funding without, 140–41; Iraq War and, 148–49, 150–51, 198n30, 217nn68–69; Korean War and, 7, 59; versus legislation to stop military actions, 137, 143; as matter of mere expediency post–World War II, 20, 165; Mexican War (1846–48) and, 37; as necessary until World War II, 179; open-ended actions and unpopular wars and, 129–30; Persian Gulf War and, 161–62, 198n30; unilateral presidential action versus, 7; Vietnam War and, 133, 135, 198n30; War of 1812 and, 35; War Powers Resolution (1973) and, 138–39; World War I and, 41

congressional power of the purse: blank-check mentality and, 6–7, 8, 20–22, 127, 152; colonial origins of, 31; in Constitution, 28, 199n14; in constitutional ratification debates, 200nn15–17; constitutional ratification debates over, 12–13, 31–33; demobilization after conflicts and, 26; in early US, 33–34; ease of moving troops and, 37; emergency funding without war authorization and, 140–41; high baseline of spending and, 11; in House versus Senate, 201n33; insufficiency of amid perpetual military mobilization, 134, 135–37; Iraq troop surge and, 128; late-nineteenth-century peacetime navy buildup and, 38; legislators' refusal to limit military operations and, 128–29, 133, 159–60; Libya air strikes and, 128; limits on, 30, 200n26, 201n37; local dependence on defense spending and, 129; pre–World War II exercise of, 22–23; restraint on executive and, 42, 127; Vietnam War and, 134–37; War of 1812 and, 36 conscription: Civil War and, 38; draft deferments and, 82; elimination of the draft and, 83, 86–87; military service and citizenship and, 82; public support for wars and, 84; selective versus universal, 87; Vietnam War protests and, 134; War of 1812 and, 36; World War I and, 41

Consolidated (defense company), 53–54

Consolidated-Vultee, 60, 61, 73

Constitution: army clauses of, 28–32, 199n14; balance of war power in, 24, 25, 28, 30, 182; divided military authority in, 4; failure of structural safeguards in, 181–84, 185; fear of standing armies and, 28, 29, 179; historical sources for, 12; institutional safeguards against tyranny in, 29–30; legislative authorization of war in, 24, 25, 26; time limit on military appropriations in, 30

Continental Army (eighteenth-century), 26–28

Continental Congress, First and Second, 26–27

Continental Motors, 52

Contract with America (1994), 97

Cooper, John, 213n20

corporations. See private corporations in defense industry

Costello, Jerry, 118

cost-plus incentives, 59–60, 121, 204n29

costs of war. See public costs of military spending and war

covert military action, 22, 137, 166, 171–73, 175–76

Cuba, 39–41, 202n67, 202n69, 213n14

Cunningham, Randy ("Duke"), 146–47

Curtiss-Wright Corporation, 52–54, 60, 61, 73–74, 76

DADT ("don't ask don't tell"). See gays in the military

D'Amato, Al, 76

declaration of war. See congressional authorization of war

defense budget: Alexander Hamilton on, 200n15; allocation of FY1966 defense contracts and dollars and, 15–16, 71–72, 73–74; allocation of FY2006 defense contracts and dollars and, 16–17, 71, 73; authorizations, obligations, and outlays in, 169–70; black budget and, 172; Civil War spending and, 202n63; after Cold War, 71, 77, 93, 107, 168; Cold War and, 71; congressional votes on cuts to, from 1993 to 1998, 192–93; constitutional time limits on, 30; for contracting in 2010, 197n1; in Contract with America (1994), 97; cyclical trends in, 71; deficit spending and, 14, 48, 170, 182, 184; degree of enemy investment and, 6; disproportionately expensive weapons systems and, 18; efforts to reduce, 166, 197n8; failed efforts to reduce, 184; federal borrowing and, 88, 90–92; Federalists on limits on, 29, 200nn16–17; under George W. Bush, 152, 218n77; graphs of from 1789 to 2010, 9, 10; House defense committees and, 74–75; inefficient spending and, 6; iron triangle and, 18, 111; Keynesian economics and, 71; Korean War and, 15, 170; Lloyd Amendment (1994) and, 209n35; local versus national considerations in, 77; under Lyndon Johnson, 134, 213nn15–16; national debt and, 170; no-bid contracts as proportion of, 210n18, 210n24; party affiliation and, 76–77; paying down war debts and, 87–88; peacekeeping operations and, 146–47; as percentage of GDP and, 90; perpetual military buildup and, 206n11; persistently large size of, 3–4, 14, 15–16; postwar reductions in, 8–9, 11, 36, 170, 173, 202n56; post–World War II baseline of funding and, 165, 167, 170; process of passing, 111; public resentment of, 25; reasons for growth in, ix, 4–5, 42–43; during Reconstruction, 202n65; roll-call votes on, 98, 99; after September 11, 2001, terrorist attacks, 184; sequestration and, 3–4, 219n17; versus State Department budget, 7, 197n6; beyond strategic requirements, 124; supplemental funding and, 91, 140–41, 143, 149, 152, 154–58, 169, 216–17nn65–66, 217n76; time limits on appropriations and, 30, 200n26, 201n37; in US versus other countries, 198n21; after Vietnam War, 65,

Iraq War (*continued*)

for, 87; repeated tours of duty in, 87; run-up to, 148–49; security contractors in, 84, 177; troop surge in, 21, 128, 170, 173; uniformed personnel versus defense contractors in, 205n28; US alliance with Saddam Hussein and, 219n25; US casualties in, 85–86, 87; US troop counts as percentage of population and, 83; value of stakes in, 87; withdrawal of forces from, 150–51. *See also* Persian Gulf War

Iredell, James, 30–31

iron triangle, 18, 66, 111

Italy, 172

ITT, 64

Jackson, Andrew, 37, 164, 202n58

Japan, 165

Jefferson, Thomas, 33–35, 201n44, 201n46

Johnson, Lyndon: defense budget under, 134, 167, 213nn15–16; defense production sites under, 74; Dominican Republic and, 41; political style of, 213n18; Vietnam War and, 15, 134, 167, 217n75

Joint Special Operations Command (JSOC), 176

Julius Caesar, 181

Kennedy, David M., 49–50

Kennedy, John F., 74, 137, 164

Keynesian economics, 65, 71

Khomeini (Ayatollah), 219n25

Koh, Harold, 175

Korean War: defense budget and, 170; draft deferments during, 82; executive independence and, 165; existing forces and weapons and, 183; funding for, 217n75; military expenditures as percentage of GDP and, 90; national debt and, 88; plant reopenings and, 58; as police action, 7; private-sector jobs and, 15; procurement obligations and, 170; as undeclared, 7, 59, 83; US casualties in, 85–86; US troop counts as percentage of population and, 83; value of stakes in, 87

Kosovo War (1999): defense budget and, 168; economic reliance on defense spend-

ing and support for, 144–45, 148, 216n57; executive independence and, 8, 162; interbranch conflict over, 140, 142–43; lack of congressional approval and, 127–28; security contractors in, 83, 176

Kriner, Doug, 87

Kucinich, Dennis, 152

Kuwait, 161

L-3 Communications, 64, 65

Laird, Melvin, 136

Laos, bombing of, 127, 135–37, 212n1, 213n20, 213n23

Lapinski, John, 112

Lasswell, Harold, 197n8

Lebanon conflict (1982–84), 85–86, 139–40

Lebanon Emergency Assistance Act (1983), 139

Legal Tender Act (1862), 38

liberty, Federalists' structural view of, 32

Libya conflict (2011), 20, 128, 169

Lincoln, Abraham, 38, 84, 86

Little, George, 34

Litton (defense company), 62–64

local defense facilities: author's database and, 19, 68–71; B-1 stealth bomber and, 94; closure of, 15; locations of in study methodology and, 99–100; map of FY1966 defense contracts and, 16; map of FY2006 defense contracts and, 17; obsolete weapons systems and, 93; population density and economic diversity and, 69–71, 72–73; proliferation of during World War II, 23; as proportion of local economy, 68, 78–79; research limitations regarding, 94; support for war and, 154–58; variability of spending on, 67–68. *See also* economic reliance on defense spending; geography of military production

Locke, John, 12

Lockheed Aircraft: acquisitions and, 60; defense production sites of, 54, 73, 75; as leading defense corporation, 61–63; merger and, 60; World War II–era expansion and, 52, 56–57

Lockheed Martin: ballistic missile defense program and, 207n18; controversial weapons systems and, 207n18; defense allocations and, 109; dollar value of contracts of, 210n22; as leading defense corporation, 63–64; merger and, 60; in study methodology, 99, 115, 132; technology procurement and, 78

LTV (defense company), 62

Machiavelli, Niccolò, 12, 81

Mack, Elizabeth, 70

Madison, James: on congressional power of the purse, 200n16; on creditor state, 199n9; diplomacy versus military action under, 33–34; on limits on defense funding, 29, 200n17, 201n37; on perpetual war as enemy of liberty, 3; precautions against permanent military establishment and, 4; on public costs of war, 81–82; separation of powers and, 12–13, 127, 161, 181–82; War of 1812 and, 35–36

Maginot line, 178

Mahon, George, 75

Maine (battleship), 39

Mansfield, Mike, 135

Markusen, Ann, 76

Marshall, John, 34

Martin Corporation, 53, 54, 60, 61–62, 74

Martin Marietta, 63

Mason, George, 32

Mayer, Kenneth, 209n5

McCain, John, 204n29

McDermott, Jim, 96, 107

McDonnell (defense company), 54, 62

McDonnell Douglas, 60, 62–63, 75

McGovern, George, 213n20

McGovern, Jim, 132, 152, 217n69

McKeon, Howard "Buck," 109–10

McKinley, William, 39, 202n69, 203n71

Meehan Amendment, 144–45

methodology. *See* research methodology

Mexican War (1846–48), 8, 36–37, 83, 85

Mexico, twentieth-century intervention in, 41

Michel, Robert, 162

military establishment: aviation as foundation of, 51; beneficiaries of, 199n32; defense employment levels and, 198n19; difficulty for Congress to end hostilities and, 159–60; difficulty of changing course in, 48; dispersal of subcontracts and, 6, 197n2; executive independence and, 162–63; founders' precautions and, 4, 28, 29; Franklin Roosevelt's economic policies and, 14–15; as hostile to liberty, 3; as limited before World War II, 33; market characteristics of, 18; origins of military-industrial machine and, 59–65; overlapping political and economic interests and, 162; path-dependent process in, 48; permanent crisis and, 206n11; permanent war economy and, 3–4, 20–21; perpetuation of, 106–7; policies to promote industry stability and, 49, 50; postwar reductions in size of army and, 36; from private to government ownership of plants and, 58; privatization agenda in, 176; shifted costs of, 11, 163, 180, 185; socialized risks and private profit in, 50, 59; US hegemony and, 162–63. *See also* economic reliance on defense spending; geography of military production; private corporations in defense industry

Military Professional Resources Incorporated, 176

militias, state, 29, 35, 37, 38, 200nn22–23

Mitchell Amendment, 216n60

Moe, Terry, 164–65, 197n13

Monroe Doctrine, 40

Montesquieu, 12

Montgomery, Sonny, 75

Morris, Gouverneur, 31

Morse, Wayne, 134, 213n16

Mossadegh, Mohammad, 219n25

Moynihan, Patrick, 76, 170–71

Murtha, John, 152

Nash-Kelvinator, 52

National Archives and Records Administration, 219n29

national debt, 27, 88–90, 170, 199n9, 206nn35–36

National Resources Planning Board, 53

National Security Act (1947), 171

National Security Agency, 171–73

National Security Council, 175, 219n29
national security directives (NSDs), 164
Native Americans, 36, 37
NATO, 207n16
Navy: early-twentieth-century expansion of, 40; in early US, 34; federal lending to private companies and, 204n21; Great White Fleet and, 40; interference with shipping and, 34, 201n44; late-nineteenth-century peacetime investment in, 38; Navy SEALS and, 176; pre–World War II buildup of, 33; protection of America property abroad and, 37; Spanish-American War (1898) and, 39–40; War of 1812 and, 35; World War I buildup of, 41
Neutrality Proclamation (1793). See Proclamation of Neutrality (1793)
Nicaragua, 37–38, 41, 173, 219n27
Nixon, Richard: All-Volunteer Force (1973) and, 83; bombing of Cambodia and Laos and, 127, 135, 136–37, 212n1, 213n20; defense budget under, 11, 168; national security directives (NSDs) and, 164; resignation of, 168; Vietnam War and, 134, 167–68; War Powers Resolution (1973) and, 138; Watergate and, 127, 135
Noriega, Manuel, 140
North American (defense company), 53–54, 57, 60, 61–62, 73
North American–Rockwell, 62
Northrop (defense company), 57
Northrop Grumman: ballistic missile defense program and, 207n18; controversial weapons systems and, 207n18; defense allocations and, 109; dollar value of contracts of, 210n22; expansion of, 205n12; headquarters of, 79; as leading defense corporation, 63–64; merger and, 60; in study methodology, 99, 115, 132; technology procurement and, 78
NSDs (national security directives). See national security directives (NSDs)
nuclear weapons, 107
Nunn, Sam, 162

Obama, Barack: defense budget and, 168–69; drones and, 169, 176; Iraq troop withdrawal and, 154; Iraq War and, 218n82; legal advisor to, 175; Libya air strikes under, 20, 128; supplemental war funding and, 217n76; weapons production limitations under, 107, 219n17
O'Neill, Tip, 77
Oppenheimer, Bruce I., 212n12
Ordnance Department, 36

Packard Motor, 52
Palestine Liberation Organization (PLO), 139
Panama and Panama Canal, 39–40, 85–86, 140, 203n75
party affiliation: 1980s realignment on defense issues and, 97; defense committee membership, 1999–2005, and, 194; defense subcontract locations and, 195; economic reliance on defense spending, 104–8; House members' defense votes, 1993–98, and, 188–93; ideological shifts and, 96–97; increasing partisanship after 1995 and, 97; interbranch conflict over military action and, 132; Iraq War and, 148–49, 152–58; opposition to presidents' military actions and, 143, 159; in study methodology, 100, 117; support for minor military operations and, 143–46, 147–48; support for weapons expenditures and, 103–4, 208n32
path dependence, 48
peacekeeping, US troops in, 146
Pentagon: annual operating budget of, 152; "black" activities and budget of, 172, 175; contracting decisions and, 111, 114; military privatization and, 176; obsolete weapons systems and, 98–99; shrinkage of civil defense agencies, 176, 220n34; transfer authority and, 135–36. See also Department of Defense
Persian Gulf War, 83, 85–86, 161–62, 198n30, 219n25
Piasecki Helicopter, 73, 205n12
Pinckney, Charles, 31, 201n30
Plan Colombia, 220n36
Plant Site Board, 53
PMSCs. See security contractors

political support for defense spending: campaign contributions and, 147; economic homogeneity of supplier communities and, 6, 94–95; geographical distribution of defense plants and, 6, 109–11; Iraq War and, 154–58; minor military operations and, 143–46, 147–49; modeling patterns of, 97–102; overlapping political and economic interests and, 180–81, 184–85; party affiliation and, 208n32; research limitations and, 94; unusual political alliances and, 130; US military hegemony and, 130–31

Polk, James, 36–38, 42, 182

Poole, Keith T., 132

population: decline of after plant closures, 57; density of and industrial diversity, 69–71, 72–73, 99; density of and Iraq War support, 154–57, 217n70; density of and support for minor military operations, 156; density of in areas receiving post–Cold War allocations, 77–78; density of in political targeting of subcontracts, 121–23; density of in study methodology, 100, 116, 132, 150–51, 205n7, 205n9, 208n30, 211n34, 216n65, 217n70, 218n83; economic reliance on defense spending and, 122–23, 144–45; growth of and economic vitality, 204n4; growth of near defense plants, 54–57, 58, 66, 69; low density of as advantageous to defense production and, 78, 79–80; military, in research methodology, 100

Pratt and Whitney, 60

presidency. *See* executive branch

private corporations in defense industry: 10-K reports of, 99, 207n19, 211n28; access to data on, 6, 94, 98–99, 112, 115–16, 206n7, 211n27; automobile companies and, 48–49, 52–53, 203n12; aviation companies and, 203n12; broad distribution of benefits by, 114; contract decisions and, 109–11, 113–19, 121–23; contract obligations and, 169–70; cost-plus incentives and, 59–60, 121, 204n29; excess capacity and, 65; federally subsidized private investments and, 204n21; geographical

dispersal of contracts and, 6, 11, 15–19, 197n2; government incentives for, 50; government ownership of formerly private plants and, 58; guaranteed profit and, 53; industry stability and, 65; international arms exports and, 168; jobs during Korean War and, 15; leading recipients of contracts and, 60–64; market concentration and, 65; mergers and acquisitions and, 60, 65; military privatization and, 171–78; noncompetitive contract awarding and, 204n30, 210n18, 210n24; political aims of subcontracting and, 121–23, 209n5; prime contractors versus subcontractors and, 113, 114, 121, 209n3; production-site decisions and, 111, 123; rent-seeking by, 18; security contractors and, 19, 22; socialized risks and private profit in, 50, 65–66; subcontracting discretion and, 113–14. *See also* security contractors

Proclamation of Neutrality (1793), 24–25

procurement: allocation of FY1966 defense contracts and dollars and, 15–16, 71–72, 73–74; allocation of FY2006 defense contracts and dollars and, 16–17, 71, 73; author's database and, 68–71; bidding before World War II and, 59; civilian control over contract decisions and, 40; Civil War–era investments and, 38; classification activity and, 174–75; congressional influence over, 40; contract obligations and, 169–70; federal guidelines for, 210n17; Federal Procurement Data System and, 115, 210n23; geographical extension of production and, 48; geographical spread without increased budget for, 80; House defense committees and, 74–75; incentives originating in World War II and, 59; insensitivity to cost in, 59–60; national debt and, 170; navy expansion and, 40; from nonmilitary companies, 52–53; Ordnance Department and, 36; policies to promote industry stability and, 49, 50; political and administrative criteria in, 60; post–Cold War technological shift in, 78; prime contracts and, 209n3; profit versus cost control and, 48, 49; standardization procurement (*continued*)

of, 37; in study methodology, 115–16; War Industries Board and, 41–42; War of 1812 and, 35–36; weapons outlays from 1951 to 2011 and, 166–71; World War I and, 41–42; World War II aviation and, 51

Project for a New American Century, 176

Pryor, David, 106

PSYOPS, 176

public costs of military spending and war: broken window fallacy and, 91–92; as check on policymakers, 81, 82; constitutional framers' fear of standing armies and, 29, 32–33; Constitution's recognition of, 25, 28; cost-plus arrangements and, 59–60; decline in after World War II, 82; deficit spending and, 19, 82; diminished need for public sacrifice and, 67; diminished perception of, 20; economic sacrifices and, 87–91; elimination of draft and, 19; executive independence on war and, 162–63; externalization of, 81–91; groups bearing costs and, 20–21, 23; through history, 182–83; to nonvoting populations, 181, 185; security contractors and, 83–84, 177–78; sophisticated military technologies and, 184; voters' restraint of lawmakers and, 182, 184; wage and price controls and, 90; during World War II, 90. *See also* defense budget

raising armed forces: All-Volunteer Force (1973) and, 83, 184; Civil War and, 38; congressional power of the purse and, 32; in Constitution, 29; declining importance of, 166; expansible army and, 36, 182; fear of standing armies and, 29, 200nn19–23; forces retained from previous conflicts and, 37; in Great Britain versus US, 31; Iraq War and, 87; public support for wars and, 84; security contractors and, 83–84, 177–78, 184; Spanish-American War (1898) and, 203n71; timing of deployment and, 36–37, 42; US troop counts as percentage of population and, 82–83. *See also* conscription

Randolph, Edmund, 31, 201n33

Ray, Bruce, 93

Rayburn, Sam, 74–75

Raytheon: ballistic missile defense program and, 207n18; defense allocations and, 109; dollar value of contracts of, 210n22; emergence of as defense contractor, 60; headquarters of, 79; as leading defense corporation, 62–64; in study methodology, 99, 115, 132; technology procurement and, 78

RCA Corporation, 62

Reagan, Ronald: Afghanistan and, 137; defense buildup under, 80, 88, 168; foreign policy of, 77; interbranch conflict over military actions under, 132, 139–40; Iran-Contra scandal and, 173, 219n27; national debt and, 88; national security directives (NSDs) and, 164; signing statements and, 139; War Powers Resolution (1973) and, 139

rent-seeking, by defense contractors, 18

Republican Party: 1980s party realignment on defense issues and, 97; emergency supplemental funding and, 216n65; influence of economic reliance on defense spending on, 104–6, 108, 208n31, 216n58; as pro-defense, 97, 105, 118. *See also* party affiliation

Republic Aviation, 54, 61–62

research methodology: case studies and quantitative analyses in, 133; classified information and, 173; congressional opposition to presidents' military actions in, 133; congressional support for defense spending and, 97–102; congressional weapons spending and, 102–4; control variables and, 100–101, 116, 132, 133; dependent variables and, 98–99, 115–16, 132; distribution of defense contract benefits from 1999 to 2005 and, 114–15, 117–18; economic reliance on defense spending and, 114–19, 131–33; empirical limitations and, 101–2, 116, 133; explanatory variables and, 99–100, 116; gays in the military and, 131; interpretation of coefficients and, 208n28; modeling patterns and, 101–2, 118–19, 131–33; number

128, 142–43; ineffectiveness of, 138–39, 140; provisions of, 214n32; Reagan-era conflicts and, 139–40, 214n39; Somalia conflict (1992–96) and, 214n41, 215n46; Vietnam War and, 138–39

Washington, George: Articles of Confederation and, 28; desire for effective executive power and, 30; diplomacy versus military action under, 33–34; neutrality proclamation by, 164; on overgrown military establishments, 3; Proclamation of Neutrality (1793) by, 24–25; Revolutionary War and, 26–27, 199n6

weapons production: ballistic missile defense program and, 207n18; Civil War–era boom in, 38; controversial expenditures and, 93, 98–99, 107, 192–93, 207n18, 219n17; cyclical trends in, 167; domestic versus overseas, 43; failure to eliminate product lines and, 7, 166, 197n5; fortifications in early US and, 202n51; Ordnance Department and, 36; presidents' efforts to reduce, 197n8; private business leadership in, 41–42; roll-call votes on, 98–99; supply buildup and, 166; US production as percent of global total and, 203n1; weapons testing in early US and, 202n51; World War I and, 41–42; World War II and, 47–48. *See also* geography of military production; private corporations in defense industry

Westinghouse, 62–64

Wilentz, Sean, 35

Wilson, James, 24, 31, 201n33

Wilson, Scott, 164–65, 197n13

Wilson, Woodrow, 41, 43, 182–83, 201n33

wiretapping. *See* surveillance activity

Wolfowitz, Paul, 176

Wood, Leonard, 40

World Trade Center bombing (1993), 214n31

World War I: congressional declaration of war in, 41; defense budget and, 9; economic conditions during, 14; reduction of military spending after, 42; US casualties in, 85; US troop counts as percentage of population and, 83

World War II: economic conditions during, 14, 49–50, 51; explosive military production during, 47–48; full-scale war economy after, 67, 183; geographical spread of defense facilities and, 23, 51–52; improvement of US economy and, 47; Keynesian economics during, 65; Lend-Lease in, 47; military expenditures as percentage of GDP and, 90; military mobilization for, 14–20; national debt and, 88–90; plant closings after, 58; procurement practices originating in, 59; public costs of, 90; US casualties in, 84–86; US troop counts as percentage of population and, 83

Wright Aeronautical, 57

Xe, 177

Yandle, Bruce, 130

Yugoslavia, former. *See* Balkans conflict; Kosovo War (1999)

CHICAGO STUDIES IN AMERICAN POLITICS

Edited by Benjamin I. Page, Susan Herbst, Lawrence R. Jacobs, and Adam J. Berinsky

SERIES TITLES, CONTINUED FROM FRONTMATTER:

The Submerged State: How Invisible Government Policies Undermine American Democracy
    by Suzanne Mettler

Disciplining the Poor: Neoliberal Paternalism and the Persistent Power of Race
    by Joe Soss, Richard C. Fording, and Sanford F. Schram

Why Parties? A Second Look
    by John H. Aldrich

News That Matters: Television and American Opinion, Updated Edition
    by Shanto Iyengar and Donald R. Kinder

Selling Fear: Counterterrorism, the Media, and Public Opinion
    by Brigitte L. Nacos, Yaeli Bloch-Elkon, and Robert Y. Shapiro

Obama's Race: The 2008 Election and the Dream of a Post-Racial America
    by Michael Tesler and David O. Sears

Filibustering: A Political History of Obstruction in the House and Senate
    by Gregory Koger

In Time of War: Understanding American Public Opinion from World War II to Iraq
    by Adam J. Berinsky

Us against Them: Ethnocentric Foundations of American Opinion
    by Donald R. Kinder and Cindy D. Kam

The Partisan Sort: How Liberals Became Democrats and Conservatives Became Republicans
    by Matthew Levendusky

Democracy at Risk: How Terrorist Threats Affect the Public
    by Jennifer L. Merolla and Elizabeth J. Zechmeister

Agendas and Instability in American Politics, Second Edition
    by Frank R. Baumgartner and Bryan D. Jones

The Private Abuse of the Public Interest
    by Lawrence D. Brown and Lawrence R. Jacobs

The Party Decides: Presidential Nominations before and after Reform
    by Marty Cohen, David Karol, Hans Noel, and John Zaller

Same Sex, Different Politics: Success and Failure in the Struggles over Gay Rights
    by Gary Mucciaroni